D0845388

German Workers in Industrial Chicago, 1850–1910

German Workers in Industrial Chicago, 1850–1910: A Comparative Perspective

Hartmut Keil and John B. Jentz, Editors

Northern Illinois University Press · DeKalb, Illinois · 1983

Library of Congress Cataloging in Publication Data
Main entry under title:

German workers in industrial Chicago, 1850–1910.

Based on papers given at a 1981 conference in Chicago organized by the Chicago Project based at the America Institute of the University of Munich.
Includes bibliographical references and index.
1. German Americans—Employment—Illinois—Chicago—History—Addresses, essays, lectures. 2. Chicago (Ill.)—Emigration and immigration—History—Addresses, essays, lectures. 3. Labor and laboring classes—Illinois—Chicago—History—Addresses, essays, lectures. 4. German Americans—Employment—History—Addresses, essays, lectures. I. Keil, Hartmut, 1942– . II. Jentz, John B., 1944– . III. Chicago Project (Universität München)
HD8081.G4G47 1983 331.6′2′43077311 83-11397
ISBN 0-87580-089-0

Published by the Northern Illinois University Press,
DeKalb, Illinois 60115
Manufactured in the United States of America

Design by Joan Westerdale

Contents

Acknowledgments vii

Introduction 1
Hartmut Keil and John B. Jentz

1. German Immigrant Workers and Their Place in American Urban Society

Chicago's German Working Class in 1900 19
Hartmut Keil

Occupational Patterns of German-Americans in Nineteenth-Century Cities 37
Nora Faires

Industrialization, Class, and Competing Cultural Systems: Detroit Workers, 1875–1900 52
Richard J. Oestreicher

2. Industrialization and the Transformation of Work

Skilled Workers and Industrialization: Chicago's German Cabinetmakers and Machinists, 1880–1900 73
John B. Jentz

Ethnicity in the Formation of the Chicago Carpenters Union: 1855–1890 86
Thomas J. Suhrbur

Immigrant Workers in Early Mass Production Industry: Work Rationalization and Job Control Conflicts in Chicago's Packinghouses, 1900–1904 104
James R. Barrett

3. Neighborhood and Everyday Life

Chicago's German North Side, 1880–1900: The Structure of a Gilded Age Ethnic Neighborhood 127
Christiane Harzig

"For Whom Are All the Good Things in Life?" German-American Housewives Discuss Their Budgets 145
Dorothee Schneider

4. Politics and Culture

Free Soil, Free Labor, and *Freimänner:* German Chicago in the Civil War Era 163
Bruce Carlan Levine

Class Conflict, Municipal Politics, and Governmental Reform in Gilded Age Chicago, 1871–1875 183
Richard Schneirov

German Radicals in Industrial America: The Lehr- und Wehr-Verein in Gilded Age Chicago 206
Christine Heiss

German Socialists and the Roots of American Working-Class Radicalism 224
Paul Buhle

German Working-Class Culture in Chicago: Continuity and Change in the Decade from 1900 to 1910 236
Klaus Ensslen and Heinz Ickstadt

Acknowledgments

THIS volume grew out of the work of the Chicago Project based at the America Institute of the University of Munich in the Federal Republic of Germany. The Project organized the conference in Chicago in the fall of 1981 at which earlier versions of the essays published here were originally presented. We wish to thank all the scholars who contributed to the conference and especially those appearing in this book, since their essays help put the Chicago Project's research into a larger perspective, while making important contributions in their own right.

Funded by the Volkswagen Foundation for a period of four years, the Chicago Project has been researching the social history of German immigrant workers in Chicago from 1850 to the First World War. Led by Hartmut Keil as project director and by John Jentz, it has cooperated closely with the John F. Kennedy Institute for North American Studies at the Free University of Berlin and with the Newberry Library in Chicago. Affiliated with it have been Klaus Ensslen, a staff member of the America Institute in Munich, and a research team in Berlin led by Heinz Ickstadt and Christiane Harzig. Five essays in this book—those by Hartmut Keil; John B. Jentz; Christiane Harzig; Christine Heiss; and Klaus Ensslen and Heinz Ickstadt—present some of the results of the Project's research. (Christine Heiss's essay was condensed from her M.A. thesis, which she wrote in conjunction with the Project.) In one way or another, these five essays also draw upon the valuable work of our research assistants: Michael Bührer, Dagmar Ebert, Theo Fuss, Martin Geyer, Christine Heiss, Silvia Huth,

Sissi Pitzer-Täubrich, Ruth Seifert, Jan Stefanek, and Norbert Streich.

More people and institutions have contributed to the Chicago Project and the 1981 conference. Support from our American advisers has been especially valuable. Herbert Gutman, on a visit to Munich in the summer of 1977, inspired the Project and generously helped us from the initial planning stage. David Brody, Kathleen Neils Conzen, and David Montgomery regularly participated in discussions and exchange on the Project's progress and difficulties. Without the generous four-year grant by the Volkswagen Foundation, it would, of course, never have seen the light of day. F. G. Friedmann, then director of the America Institute, was a great aid in getting the Project launched; and the Project has continued to enjoy the support of the Institute.

The Chicago conference was also made possible by the financial support of the Volkswagen Foundation and by a substantial contribution from the Goethe Institute of Chicago. The Newberry Library provided meeting space, and Jan Reiff of its Family and Community History Center did an excellent job arranging all the organizational details. We would also like to thank the Chicago Historical Society for hosting part of the conference. We hope that this book adequately reflects the open and fruitful exchange of ideas that took place at the conference in Chicago.

Introduction

Hartmut Keil and John B. Jentz

WHY do we need a book about German immigrant workers? Weren't the Germans mostly farmers and store owners? Or brewers and saloonkeepers? Or doctors and musicians? And didn't the melting pot work wonderfully for them, at least? Such stereotypes have obscured the real character of German immigration to America and diverted attention from the critically important role of Germans in the development of the modern American working class. America's largest immigrant group in the nineteenth century, the Germans arrived in greatest numbers at the height of the country's industrial revolution and were increasingly pulled into the factories and workshops of America's burgeoning cities. And yet, despite their pervasive impact on labor in the United States, German industrial workers have received little attention from scholars. The recently published twenty-year cumulative index of *Labor History*, the standard scholarly journal in its field, did not even include a heading for Germans.[1]

But if a book is needed on German workers, why concentrate on Chicago? Why not Milwaukee, America's prototypical German city? For one thing, Chicago also had a large German population, numerically larger, in fact, than Milwaukee's in the last three decades of the nineteenth century. But more important, Chicago's advanced industrial economy was of greater national significance and had a much more ethnically mixed working class, one more comparable to the work forces of the other industrial centers like Detroit, Cleveland, Pittsburgh, Philadelphia, and New York City. Chicago's German workers were part of the more typical develop-

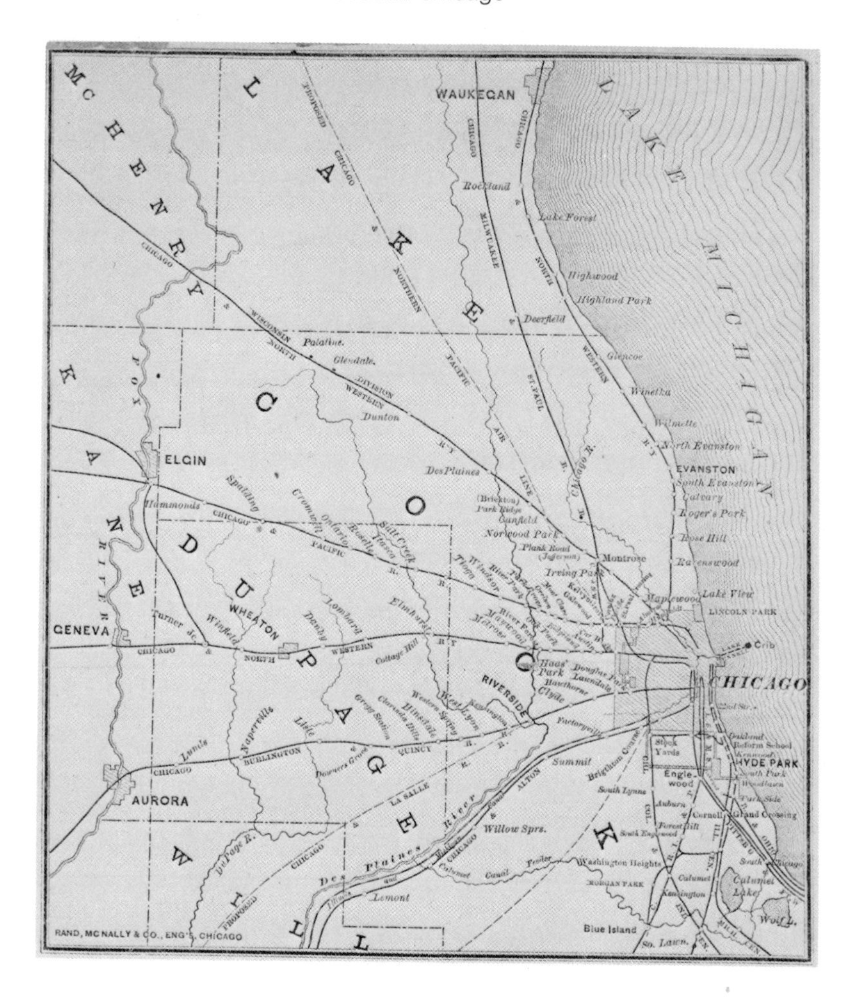

This map from the early 1870s shows the network of railroad lines converging on Chicago, making the city the transportation hub and immigration center of the Midwest. From a real estate promotion map, Rand, McNally and Company. Reproduced with permission of the Chicago Historical Society (ICHi-13513).

ment of America's industrial working class, with its occupational diversity by national group; transition from the old to the new immigration; and ethnic, political, and union conflicts. It was in Chicago, after all, one of the most unionized cities in the country, where some of the fundamental issues in the American labor movement were fought out. Chicago is therefore not a parochial example, and its development invites comparisons such as those made in this volume with other American cities with similar work forces.

Comparisons must rely on the work of others, and any scholarly enterprise as a whole utilizes concepts, methodologies, and findings in its own discipline as well as in related fields. This is especially the case in the study of German-American workers. Since so little previous work directly about them is available, the relevant material must be assembled from various branches of the history discipline and from fields like sociology. A review of this scholarly literature will provide a perspective on the essays in this book as well as substantiate the need for work on the subject.

THERE is, of course, a considerable body of historical literature on German immigration and Germans as an ethnic group. It includes some significant works on Chicago's Germans written in the late nineteenth and early twentieth centuries. Striving to document the contributions of Germans to Chicago and America at large, these filio-pietistic authors concentrated on the German intellectual and political leadership and generally on the successful few who, as prototypes of the self-made man, could serve as examples for the rest of the group. Such books obviously say little about the lives of German workers, but they do provide a wealth of detail about the successful German manufacturers who employed so many of their countrymen. Scholarly works written after World War I, which were often influenced by the Chicago School of Sociology, made more systematic efforts to understand America's ethnic groups and the integration of German immigrants into American society.[2]

Yet the genuine flood of books on America's immigrant groups had to await the revival of interest in ethnic and local history that came in the 1960s and 1970s. Every American ethnic group, no matter how small, now has its historian. Although not so much as other groups, Chicago's Germans have also profited from this revival. Thus their overall contribution to the city, the fate of their culture during World War I, their political life, and their ethnic institutions have recently been explored. Since the major focus of these analyses, however, is the changing character of Chicago's Germans as an ethnic group, such studies do not deal directly with German workers, that is, with where they worked, how their work changed, what distinctive traditions they had, and how their integration into American society may have differed from that of the middle- and upper-class Germans who supported Chicago's more famous German cultural institutions.[3]

Some light is shed on such questions by the new urban history that emerged in the 1960s, when scholars began to apply quantitative analytical techniques borrowed from the social sciences to the study of local communities. In this way they hoped to find new and more substantially grounded answers to major historical issues like the nature of puritanism and the degree of upward mobility in the United States. In a pathbreaking work published in 1964, Stephan Thernstrom investigated the workers in the New England manufacturing city of Newburyport, Massachusetts. Other scholars following him investigated cities and towns with significant German populations. The questions asked and the period studied by these scholars, however, limit the usefulness of their findings for a student of the German-American working class. Interested in upward mobility within the local status hierarchy, these scholars had little to say about the history of the crafts which gave the Germans their relatively high position among American workers. In addition, they did not analyze the cultural traditions of German workers as expressed, for instance, in the German language press. And they usually stopped their analysis in 1880 at the height of the American industrial revolution—and of German immigration—because the manuscript federal census on which they relied so much for evidence was legally open only until then. Despite such limitations, these social mobility studies made significant contributions to American urban and labor history, in part because their findings began to transcend their underlying questions and conceptual framework. After assuming at first a rather static occupational hierarchy in America's nineteenth-century cities, they became more sophisticated in describing its evolving character, as well as the changes within individual occupations. They also found more transient physical movement by workers from job to job and city to city than upward mobility.[4]

By the 1970s the practitioners of the new urban history had begun to address more systematically the nature of urbanization, the evolution of urban social structures, the character of the urban economy, and the process of decision making in particular communities. The most ambitious of these enterprises has been the Philadelphia Social History Project, some of whose research is directly relevant to understanding the residential patterns of German workers and the sectors of the economy in which they worked. Of urban histories by individual scholars, the most important to students of German workers is *Immigrant Milwaukee, 1836–1860*, by Kathleen Neils Conzen. While addressing issues of assimilation and social evolution within the whole Milwaukee German community, Conzen made quantitative evaluations of the place of Germans in the city's occupational hierarchy. She also used the German language press to discuss the nature and development of German-American culture, and she specifically addressed the character of the German crafts. Other works on Buffalo, Pittsburgh, Poughkeepsie, Jersey City, Allegheny City, St. Louis, Boston, Detroit, and New York City also address the place of Germans in the social structures of these cities during the nineteenth century, offering useful points of comparison for students of the German working class in Chicago.[5]

Like the new urban history, the new political history of the 1960s and 1970s also used social scientific techniques, primarily to analyze political behavior as expressed in elections and legislative votes. It succeeded remarkably in reformulating the contours of American political history around the idea of successive party systems and in analyzing the ethnic and cultural commitments which did so much to determine the party affiliations of American voters. Studies by Richard Jensen, Paul Kleppner, Frederick Luebke, and John Allswang have especially provided new insights into the voting behavior of ethnic groups in the Midwest and Chicago and into the position of these groups within the larger electoral system. And yet these studies do not address the political behavior and traditions of German workers in their own right, especially when they acted in minority parties. Large numbers of German immigrant workers could not legally vote, thought the major parties were not worth voting for if they could, and did not belong to the religious groups which are so often used to explain voting behavior. Nevertheless, these men acted politically in demonstrations, through unions, and in efforts to maintain cultural traditions like those of their crafts, which had political significance and a long heritage. Looking at the politics of such German workers can therefore help fill one of the gaps in the new political history, recently described by Allan G. Bogue. He noted that the ethnocultural political analysts "have made inadequate use of the foreign-language and religious press and have given scant consideration to the presence of large numbers of voters unaffiliated with any church."[6] All German workers, of course, did not attend the socialistically inclined Aurora Turnverein or read the *Chicagoer Arbeiter-Zeitung*, but enough did to make the study of the political culture promoted by such institutions a useful and necessary task. Undertaking it requires a vision of politics that includes much more than elections and tries to root political culture and action in the historical experience and class position of the people in question.[7]

The same trends in the historical profession which produced the new urban and the new political history of the last two decades have also deeply influenced the writing of labor history, broadening it, in fact, into the social history of the American working class. The old labor history had concentrated on the workers organized in unions or in minority, often radical, political parties. This history still has its virtues, however, especially if one wants to learn about organized German workers. Thus, Hermann Schlüter's books, written in the early twentieth century, are still indispensable sources for students of the German-American working class, even though they concentrate on the labor movement. The works of the new labor history of special relevance to German workers include studies of the transformation of craft production in Newark, the role of German artisans in pre–Civil War politics, the politics and culture of Detroit's workers in the late nineteenth century, and German-American socialist literature. These works are exceptions, however. The main thrust of the new labor history has been in community studies of small to medium-sized manufacturing towns in New England and the mid-Atlantic states during the earlier phase of the industrial revolution in the early to mid-nineteenth century; they deal, therefore, with times and places in which German workers were not commonly prominent. Most of the German immigrants who became American industrial workers arrived between 1850 and 1890 and tended to go to manufacturing cities in the mid-Atlantic and midwestern states. The focus for studying them has therefore to shift to those urban industrial centers and to the second half of the nineteenth century and even beyond.[8]

What are the major issues, as we see them, that are of direct relevance to the study of German workers in Chicago? A comprehensive social-historical study of German workers would have to take into account their demographic character and place in the city, the process of industrialization and how it transformed the work they did, the neighborhoods where they lived and their everyday life there, and the politics and culture rooted in all these facets of their lives. The essays in this book are arranged according to these four large areas of investigation. The following discussion outlines the specific focus and interrelationship of our thematic areas and briefly describes and places each individual essay within the framework of the book.

German immigrant workers and their place in American urban society

WHEN studying any group of immigrants to the United States, it is essential to see what characterized the group that came over, what kind of society it entered at a particular point in time, and what changes it experienced as a result of the interplay of traditions with new social and cultural values. Herbert Gutman has said that immigration was a repetitive process that introduced successive groups of pre-industrial workers into the alien world of American industrial society. Gutman's model can serve as a useful analytical tool for describing the fundamental differences among German immigrants beyond the obvious common characteristic of national origin, a quality that has often mistakenly led historians to treat German immigrants as a relatively homogeneous group.[9]

Since significant German immigration to the United States extended throughout the second half of the nineteenth century, there were notable changes in its German regional origins. Reflecting Germany's uneven economic development and varied cultural heritage, these diverse regions of origin sent emigrants of widely varying experience and backgrounds during different periods. A cabinetmaker from the southwestern kingdom of Württemberg and a farm laborer from an East Elbian Prussian province did not have much in common, in a sense not even the language, as they had difficulty understanding each other's regional dialect. Depending on the time of their arrival, the cabinetmaker coming in the 1850s, during the first big wave of German immigration, might have found advantageous opportunities in Chicago's burgeoning economy to set up his own shop, whereas the farm laborer arriving thirty years later was more likely to find employment as an unskilled hand in the furniture factory now owned and directed by the cabinetmaker's son, who had considerably enlarged the firm in the late 1870s to take advantage of the expanding market. Occupationally, socially, and culturally, the generation of the 1850s and their offspring were often worlds apart from the new arrivals of the 1880s, and the German immigrant worker in the Gilded Age found himself not only competing for jobs with newer immigrant groups, like Italians and Poles, but also striking against German-American entrepreneurs.

Given the cultural and class divisions among Germans and within the city at large, it becomes all the more urgent to describe the place German immigrant workers carved out for themselves in the American working class; one cannot simply view them as part of an ethnic group. In attempting such an evaluation, one must not look too narrowly at the peak periods of German immigration. Although the immediate consequences of the immigration waves of the 1850s and 1880s should not be slighted, the lasting impact of Germans on the emerging American industrial working class has yet to be properly assessed. One way of addressing the broader significance of German workers is to look at the second generation, as does **Hartmut Keil**'s essay on Chicago's German working class in 1900. It describes German workers precisely at a moment when German immigration to the United States had dwindled and when transitions from the first to the second generation foreshadowed the disintegration of closely knit working-class life based on the cultural traditions brought over from Germany. **Nora Faires**'s essay allows one to see the Chicago findings in comparative perspective. Her discussion of studies on the occupational structure of several nineteenth-century American cities identifies the overall place of German immigrants in America's urban industrial economy, and she specifically compares the position of German and Irish workers, pointing out that both the acquired skills and the particularities of a city's economy defined the occupational possibilities of the two respective groups.

Also supplying a comparative view, **Richard Oestreicher** looks at the cultural and political options open to all immigrant workers, including Germans, in Gilded Age America. Studying three strikes in Detroit in the early 1890s, he shows how seemingly disparate responses of workers to different strike situations can be explained by three distinct cultural systems, one ethnic, another radical working-class, and the third middle-class American. Oestreicher's analysis is a warning against seeing a unilinear direction in the process of integration of various ethnic working-class groups into the American labor movement.

Industrialization and the transformation of work

MASSIVE German immigration coincided with the decisive period of industrial transition from craft to factory production. Taking place in the whole country, this process affected some Chicago industries, like meat packing and furniture making, with special force. In addition, certain industries in the city, like iron and steel and agricultural implements, were large-scale and highly mechanized from the beginning. In both cases, however, there occurred the destruction of crafts, the transformation and devaluation of skills, and the emergence of new types of skilled work. Germans and other nationalities of workers were intimately affected by this process, but the Germans more so because they predominated in skilled positions in traditional craft industries.

Apart from these very general observations, it is difficult to describe the transformation of work without reference to specific industries, since developments were uneven in time, intensity, and even direction. In selecting two skilled occupations which experienced quite opposite tendencies, **John Jentz** in his essay encompasses the range of possibilities open to German skilled workers and their sons. Cabinetmakers brought skills acquired in Germany into a Chicago-based furniture industry where these skills were increasingly replaced by machines, even in the modest-sized factories which typified the industry. The attractiveness of the trade for the sons of German workers consequently suffered. They turned instead to such occupations as machinist in growth industries like the metal trades, where new skills usually not provided by the immigrant generation were in high demand. The second generation thus adapted to the new requirements of a changing economy, retaining the image of Germans as highly skilled workers, although the character of the skills was changing.

What was the significance of the transformation of work for the labor movement? There can be no doubt that the craft tradition was its indispensable basis, providing a coherent set of values and a common tradition which could, against great odds, unite the workers in an industry despite ethnic rivalries, job competition, and divergent interests. That these common craft values could help overcome such difficulties is demonstrated by **Thomas Suhrbur**'s account of the consolidation of Chicago's carpenters unions. Faced with an open market, a highly volatile labor force, and the erosion of skill standards, the leadership struggled hard and successfully to inaugurate a system of dues, benefits, and representation that would appeal to all carpenters, regardless of ethnicity and ideology. The carpenters unions eventually succeeded in controlling the city's job market and wage level, while keeping ethnic rivalries at a minimum.

Craft labor and its traditions were, however, being undermined in Chicago's large-scale manufacturing industries like meat packing. Following the defeat of the Knights of Labor and the eight-hour movement in the 1880s, the workers in this industry—where labor had been decisively beaten—required more than a decade to use class solidarity regardless of skill as the basis of labor organization. In a case study of the development of shop-floor organization in the five years prior to a big strike in 1904, **James Barrett** traces these transitions in labor organization in a mass production industry. The transformation of work by the opening of the new century had left no other alternative but to start organization from the shop floor. This new solidarity even included very recent immigrants from southern and eastern Europe, workers commonly believed to be unorganizable. Barrett's essay contains important clues about the cooperation between old and new immigrants, the transition of traditions of organization, and the role of old immigrants in providing leadership in industrial unions.

Neighborhood and everyday life

THROUGHOUT the second half of the nineteenth century, local and often small-scale industries defined the neighborhoods in which people lived, and the neighborhood, with its specific institutions, in turn shaped the world of work. The local residents, for example, often supported strikers with consumer boycotts against employers and provided a labor force of young women for such decentralized industries as clothing and cigar making. It was the neighborhood that defined the world of everyday life and leisure and provided the social setting for institutions like family, household, and voluntary associations. It was here in particular that women, as wives, mothers, consumers, and workers, lived most of their lives. Although it is obvious that all neighborhoods were not the same—not even those within one ethnic group—little is known about the peculiar combination of class and ethnic characteristics of Chicago's diverse German neighborhoods. Several German neighborhoods evolved in the city, but industry, length of settlement, and availability of housing made them distinct. German working-class neighborhoods in particular provided the institutions and activities that underlay the class solidarity based on common ethnic traditions which formed the basis of the early labor movement. The ethnic crafts located in the neighborhoods were the first to be organized, and they continued to remain strongholds of organization when the movement expanded citywide to include other shops and factories. Since rapid succession of immigrant groups in neighborhoods and geographic dispersion to suburban areas were the typical developments in Chicago, as in other American cities, their consequences for the stability and continuity of the labor movement are of major import. How was the character of the American labor movement altered because of the disintegration of ethnically based working-class neighborhoods? Did other institutions take over the former function of neighborhood?

To deal adequately with such issues, specific case studies are needed. **Christiane Harzig** looks at the development of Chicago's Northside German neighborhood between 1880 and 1900 in order to analyze the factors that made for the exceptional stability of that area: the neighborhood remained German for more than seventy years. Blessed with a favorable geographic setting, the Northside was a center of retailing and small-scale manufacturing which provided occupational and demographic stability.

Much of the everyday life of such a neighborhood revolved around shopping for the necessities of life. At this point, we can hardly expect more than glimpses at the way working people managed their small household budgets to make these purchases possible. **Dorothee Schneider** has used exceptional personal documents, letters written mostly by German working-class housewives, which discuss living expenses in the early 1880s. The reported personal experience of wives directly responsible for the budget of German working-class families in New York City squares with the statistical evidence which the Illinois Bureau of Labor collected and analyzed in its 1884 biennial report.

Politics and culture

IT was in politics and culture where the everyday experience of German workers took on collective form, where they expressed their ways of coping with a society whose values were new to them and which they did not necessarily share. How were old world political and cultural forms used in Chicago? What transformed them, and how were they finally adapted to changed circumstances? To even approach an answer to these questions, one must understand the heritage of the crafts, the adaptation of German radicalism, and the transmission of these traditions to second-generation workers.

The evolution of the political culture of Chicago's German working class in the 1850s is the topic of **Bruce Levine**'s essay. Building on the democratic-republican ideals of the 1848 Revolution in Germany, German immigrant craftsmen, confronted with the slavery issue, entered a tenuous coalition with German liberals and moderate Republicans. The craftsmen and their leaders did not stop with criticizing the South, however, but applied democratic-republican values to northern society as well, stressing the need for economic justice as well as individual freedom. The tensions in the antislavery coalition broke open after the Civil War with the formation of independent labor parties. The threat of such independent political action, plus the labor upheavals of the 1870s, led Chicago's business interests to fundamentally reorganize the city's decentralized administrative and political structure, as **Richard Schneirov** shows in his analysis. With a governmental system more responsive to its interests, the business elite set the stage for the upcoming battles of the 1880s. Arising in the turbulent

1870s, the Lehr- und Wehr-Verein, a radical German workers' organization, put older democratic-republican traditions rooted in the artisan crafts to use in Gilded Age Chicago. As **Christine Heiss** shows in her history of that association, these German workers saw armed workers' associations as a necessary means for defending their neighborhoods and their vision of the ideal American republic.

The radical response of German immigrant workers to American urban industrial society cannot simply be understood as the inappropriate application of European traditions of socialism to alien political and cultural circumstances. Their radicalism was, in fact, part of the confrontation of a whole culture with American conditions. In their essays **Paul Buhle** and coauthors **Klaus Ensslen** and **Heinz Ickstadt** provide interior views of this cultural engagement of German workers with America. Buhle rejects the common opinion that the radical efforts of the German working class were temporary aberrations, unconnected and irrelevant to the later direction taken by the American labor movement. Instead, he sees the emergence of the radical movement among German immigrant workers in the 1870s and 1880s as a formative period when institutions and cultural forms were tried out, proving their cross-ethnic appeal and establishing a legacy that lasted into the middle of the twentieth century. Ensslen and Ickstadt focus more closely on Chicago's German working-class movement itself. They concentrate on the decisive phase after 1900, when the old forms of agitation and celebration were still used, but when the working class that was addressed had fundamentally changed. Although German workers were no longer in the center of the Chicago labor movement, German radicals continued to promote supportive working-class cultural activities, and not only for their countrymen. On the other hand, nostalgia accompanied these efforts. The people initiating them had grown older, while second-generation German workers had begun to turn their backs on cultural activities which were still exclusively associated with the German language and which disregarded new cultural forms arising out of the American urban experience.

We hope that this close look at Chicago's German workers will shed new light on old historical questions, like the nature of the American industrial revolution and the assimilation of immigrants. The various groups of foreign-born workers had, of course, their own unique traditions and experiences; but they were also part of a larger social and economic process that made their experiences comparable. Hence the history of Chicago's German workers contributes to understanding the history of America's industrial working class in the Gilded Age and Progressive Era.

Notes

1. *Labor History* 22 (Winter 1981): 57–135.

2. Among the most useful works on German immigration to the United States with specific reference to its sources in Germany are Wolfgang Köllmann and Peter Marschalck, "German Emigration to the United States," trans. Thomas C. Childers, *Perspectives in American History* 7 (1973): 499–554; Mack Walker, *Germany and the Emigration 1816–1885* (Cambridge, Mass.: Harvard University Press, 1964); and Wilhelm Mönckmeier, *Die deutsche überseeische Auswanderung: Ein Beitrag zur deutschen Wanderungsgeschichte* (Jena: Verlag von Gustav Fischer, 1912).

Histories of Chicago Germans by local authors include Eugen Seeger and Eduard Schlaeger, *Chicago. Entwickelung, Zerstörung und Wiederaufbau der Wunderstadt* (Chicago: privately published, 1872); Emil Dietzsch, *Chicago's Deutsche Männer. Erinnerungs-Blätter an Chicago's Fünfzigjähriges Jubiläum. Geschichte der Stadt Chicago mit besonderer Berücksichtigung des Einflusses der Deutsch-Amerikaner auf ihre Entwickelung.* (Chicago: Max Stern, 1885); Rudolph Cronau, *Chicago und sein Deutschthum* (Cleveland: German-American Biographical Publishing, 1901–1902).

Histories of broader scope by and about German-Americans are voluminous; for a thorough review of this literature see Kathleen Neils Conzen, "Die Assimilierung der Deutschen in Amerika: zum Stand der Forschung in den Vereinigten Staaten," in *Die deutschsprachige Auswanderung in die Vereinigten Staaten: Berichte über Forschungsstand und Quellenbestände*, ed. Willi Paul Adams (Berlin: John F. Kennedy Institut, 1980), 33–64.

The best example of the more scholarly work published between the wars is Andrew Jacke Townsend, "The Germans of Chicago," *Deutsch-Amerikanische Geschichtsblätter* 32 (1932), 1–153. In addition, the rich body of scholarship produced by the Chicago School of Sociology itself still provides useful insights and a wealth of data for the study of Chicago's ethnic groups, including the city's German workers, even though it rarely deals with them directly. Also of use are articles too numerous to list published in the *American Journal of Sociology* during its first two decades. In a sense, Bessie L. Pierce worked in this tradition, and her *A History of Chicago*, 3 vols. (New York: Alfred A. Knopf, 1937–1957) remains an indispensable resource for students of Chicago history, as does A. T. Andreas's *History of Chicago*, 3 vols. (Chicago: A. T. Andreas Co., Publishers, 1884–1886).

3. One of the most important products of the ethnic studies revival has been the publication of the *Harvard Encyclopedia of American Ethnic Groups*, ed. Stephan Thernstrom (Cambridge, Mass.: Harvard University Press, 1980). The histories on Chicago Germans as an ethnic group include Rudolph A. Hofmeister's *The Germans of Chicago* (Champaign, Ill.: Stipes Publishing, 1976); he seeks, in traditional fashion, to demonstrate the German contribution to the city. Melvin G. Holli's "The Great War Sinks Chicago's German Kultur," in *Ethnic Chicago*, ed. Melvin G. Holli and Peter D'A. Jones (Grand Rapids, Mich.: William B. Eerdmans Publishing Co., 1981), 260–312; and Leslie V. Tischauser's "The German

Question in Chicago, 1917–18" (paper contributed to the Chicago Project's conference on "Working-Class Immigrants in Industrializing Chicago, 1850–1920" held at the Newberry Library and Chicago Historical Society, October 9–12, 1981) both address the fate of German ethnic culture in the city during World War I. A subject of obvious import, the experience of German-Americans during the Great War is addressed from a broader perspective in Frederick C. Luebke's *Bonds of Loyalty: German Americans and World War I* (DeKalb, Ill.: Northern Illinois University Press, 1974). Tischauser's dissertation, "The Burden of Ethnicity; German-Americans in Chicago, 1914–1941" (Chicago: University of Illinois, 1981) follows the Germans in the city between the world wars, and, employing the perspective of historical sociology, Richard Paul Albares's dissertation, "The Structural Ambivalence of German Ethnicity in Chicago" (University of Chicago, 1981) examines the formation and development of a sense of ethnicity among Chicago Germans in the late nineteenth and twentieth centuries.

4. Stephan Thernstrom's *Poverty and Progress: Social Mobility in a Nineteenth Century City* (Cambridge, Mass.: Harvard University Press, 1964) became a model for numerous other studies of local communities. This flowering of local urban history was well represented in *Nineteenth Century Cities: Essays in the New Urban History*, ed. Stephan Thernstrom and Richard Sennett (New Haven, Conn.: Yale University Press, 1969). A study of mobility with special import for Germans is Howard P. Chudacoff, *Mobile Americans: Residential and Social Mobility in Omaha 1880–1920* (New York: Oxford University Press, 1972). For a review and critique of the literature on social mobility, see James A. Henretta, "The Study of Social Mobility: Ideological Assumptions and Conceptual Biases," *Labor History* 18 (Spring 1977): 165–78. For a general review of the new urban history, with valuable bibliographical footnotes, see Kathleen Neils Conzen, "Community Studies, Urban History, and American Local History," in *The Past Before Us: Contemporary Historical Writing in the United States*, ed. Michael Kammen (Ithaca, N.Y.: Cornell University Press, 1980), 270–91.

5. The work of the Philadelphia Social History Project has recently appeared in a collection of essays, *Philadelphia: Work, Space, Family, and Group Experience in the Nineteenth Century: Essays toward an Interdisciplinary History of the City*, ed. Theodore Hershberg (Oxford: Oxford University Press, 1981). Three essays in this collection are of special relevance to students of the German-American working class: Bruce Laurie and Mark Schmitz, "Manufacture and Productivity: The Making of an Industrial Base, Philadelphia, 1850–1880," pp. 43–92; Bruce Laurie, Theodore Hershberg, and George Alter, "Immigrants and Industry: The Philadelphia Experience, 1850–1880," pp. 92–119; and Alan N. Burstein, "Immigrants and Residential Mobility: The Irish and Germans in Philadelphia, 1850–1880," pp. 174–203. The full title of Kathleen Neils Conzen's book is *Immigrant Milwaukee, 1836–1860: Accommodation and Community in a Frontier City* (Cambridge, Mass.: Harvard University Press, 1976). Two other urban case studies with special relevance to German workers appeared in *Immigrants in Industrial America 1850–1920*, ed. Richard L. Ehrlich (Charlottesville, Va.: University of Virginia Press, 1977); they are Laurence Glasco, "Ethnicity and Occupation in the Mid-Nineteenth Century: Irish, Germans, and Native-born Whites in Buffalo, New York," pp. 151–75, and Clyde Griffen, "The 'Old' Immigration and

Industrialization: A Case Study," pp. 176–204. Griffen's essay deals with Poughkeepsie, New York. For a review of the literature of the new urban history with special reference to the social position of the Germans, see Nora Faires's essay in this volume.

6. Allan G. Bogue, "The New Political History in the 1970s," in *The Past Before Us*, p. 250.

7. The most useful books by the new political historians with relevance to Germans in the Midwest and Chicago are Paul Kleppner, *The Cross of Culture: A Social Analysis of Midwestern Politics 1850–1896* (New York: Free Press, 1970); Richard Jensen, *The Winning of the Midwest: Social and Political Conflict, 1886–1896* (Chicago: University of Chicago Press, 1971); Frederick C. Luebke, *Immigrants and Politics: The Germans of Nebraska 1880-1900* (Lincoln, Neb.: University of Nebraska Press, 1969); and John M. Allswang, *A House for All Peoples: Ethnic Politics in Chicago 1890–1936* (Lexington: University of Kentucky Press, 1971). Allan G. Bogue, "The New Political History in the 1970s," in *The Past Before Us*, reviews the new political history of which these books are a part.

8. Two review essays discuss the new labor history of the 1960s and 1970s: David Brody, "The Old Labor History and the New: In Search of an American Working Class," *Labor History* 20 (Winter 1979): 111–26; David Montgomery, "To Study the People: The American Working Class," *Labor History* 21 (Fall 1980): 485–512. Hermann Schlüter's works include *Die Internationale in Amerika: Ein Beitrag zur Geschichte der Arbeiter-Bewegung in den Vereinigten Staaten* (Chicago: Deutsche Sprachgruppe der Sozialistischen Partei der Vereinigten Staaten, 1918); *Die Anfänge der deutschen Arbeiterbewegung in Amerika* (Stuttgart: J. H. V. Dietz, 1907); and *The Brewing Industry and the Brewery Workers' Movement in America* (Cincinnati: International Union United Brewery Workmen of America, 1910). While trying to take a broader perspective on the development of the whole American working class, Friedrich A. Sorge also emphasized the role of German immigrants. His "Die Arbeiterbewegung in den Vereinigten Staaten," series of articles in *Die Neue Zeit*, 9–13 (1891–1895) have been published as a book and translated into English: *Friedrich A. Sorge's Labor Movement in the United States: A History of the American Working Class from Colonial Times to 1890*, ed. Philip S. Foner and Brewster Chamberlin (Westport, Conn.: Greenwood Press, 1977). Also dealing with organized German workers is John H. Laslett, *Labor and the Left: A Study of Socialist and Radical Influences in the American Labor Movement, 1881–1924* (New York: Basic Books, 1970). The new labor histories particularly relevant to Germans are Susan E. Hirsch, *Roots of the American Working Class: The Industrialization of Crafts in Newark, 1800–1860* (Philadelphia: University of Pennsylvania Press, 1978); Bruce C. Levine, "'In the Spirit of 1848': German-Americans and the Fight Over Slavery's Expansion" (Ph.D. dissertation, University of Rochester, 1980); Richard J. Oestreicher, "Solidarity and Fragmentation: Working People and Class Consciousness in Detroit, 1877–1895" (Ph.D. dissertation, Michigan State University, 1979); Carol Jean Poore, "German-American Socialist Literature in the Late Nineteenth Century" (Ph.D. dissertation, University of Wisconsin, Madison, 1979).

9. Herbert G. Gutman, "Work, Culture, and Society in Industrializing America, 1815–1919," *American Historical Review* 78 (June 1973): 531–88.

German Immigrant Workers and Their Place in American Urban Society

1.

Chicago's German Working Class in 1900

Hartmut Keil

CHICAGO entered the new century an optimistic, vibrant industrial center, confident of continued growth. The city's development had been unparalleled since the late 1870s, its economic expansion not even decisively blocked by the severe depression of the nineties, so that by the turn of the century Chicago was second only to New York in industrial output. Population growth was explosive—almost doubling in the 1890s, as in the decade before, to reach about 1.7 million in 1900. Dramatic shifts in the generational and ethnic composition of Chicago's population lie hidden in these figures. While in 1880 the "new" immigration was hardly discernible, by 1900 it had already made a strong impact, especially within Chicago's working class, which the majority of the newcomers entered. At the same time, older immigrant groups were being superseded by their second-generation sons and daughters who had reached adulthood in significant numbers.

For Germans in the city analysis of the census of 1900 is especially important because it provides insights into the effects of the largest wave of German immigration to the United States—that of the 1880s.[1] Also, totaling more than 400,000 in 1900, first- and second-generation Germans reached their highest absolute number in the city's history, contributing about one-fourth of its population. The second generation, which had already been substantial in 1880 but had not yet reached working age in significant numbers, now made up a large part of the mature and established German population.

Thus, 1900 is a point in time that allows for bringing into focus important changes within Chicago's German working class during the second half of the nineteenth century as well as for hypothesizing about the directions in which it would develop up to World War I. Emphasizing the process of industrialization as it affected Chicago's German working class, this essay will concentrate on the basic issues of population development, occupational change, and geographic distribution.

Population development

WHEN the Chicago school census of 1884 recorded a population of some 616,000 for the city, one-third of whom were first- and second-generation Germans, the *Chicagoer Arbeiter-Zeitung* (the city's German working-class daily) reported the findings under the boastful headline "A German City in America," pointing out that there were only five cities in Germany with a larger German population.[2] Sixteen years later, the proportion of Germans within the total population of Chicago had already turned downward to about one-fourth (see Table 1). However, based exclusively on country of origin and thereby excluding the children of immigrants, published figures tend to exaggerate this trend. According to them, 1860 was the year with the all-time high German percentage, coming as it did after the immigration wave of the 1850s; afterward a steady decline set in, interrupted, but not reversed, by the second wave of German immigration in the 1880s. When the second generation is included, however, there was an increase in the German share of the population up to 1880.[3] By 1900, on the other hand, the impact of the German immigration wave of the 1880s on the composition of Chicago's population, still very much apparent in 1890,[4] was weakening relative to the growing importance of new immigrant groups. But, on the basis of our 1900 sample of German households, we can also make out a group of third-generation Germans living as dependent children in second-generation households and constituting approximately 3 percent of the total population.[5] Thus, from 1860 through 1900, Germans contributed about 30 percent of Chicago's population, although a decline set in during the last decade. This noteworthy stability occurred in the face of the profound changes in the composition of Chicago's population, usually described as the shift from the "old" to the "new" immigration. It is also notable that Germans continued to remain the largest nationality group, even when counting native-born Americans of native-born parentage as one such group.

Table 1. The German population of Chicago, 1850–1900

	1850	1860	1870	1880	1890	1900
Total population of Chicago	**29,963***	**109,206***	**298,977***	**503,185***	**1,099,850***	**1,698,575***
German-born, absolute numbers	4,757†	22,230*	52,316*	75,205*	161,039*	170,738*
Percent of total population	15.9†	20.4†	17.5*	14.9*	14.6*	10.0*
Second generation, percent of total population	3.8†			15.8†		14.2*
Percent first and second generations, combined	19.7†			30.7*,†		24.2*
Third generation, percent of total population						2.8†
Ratio, first: second generation	80.7:19.3			48.5:51.5		41.3:58.7

*Figures taken from the published U.S. Censuses on Population.
†Figures based on the analysis of the total German population in 1850 and of systematic samples of 2,222 German households in 1880 and of 1,532 German households in 1900, taken from the manuscript schedules.

This relative stability hides important changes in age, generation, and regional origin within the German population. The age structure reveals that the German population grew older over the years but to a degree that is astonishingly slow if one has only the first generation in mind. Since significant German immigration continued into the early 1890s, Chicago's German community was constantly being replenished by younger newcomers, who held down the age of the first generation. Thus, of all German households in our 1900 sample, over three-fourths were still headed by first-generation Germans; but more than half of these had come to the United States after 1879.

Table 1 also indicates that, despite the large immigration wave of the 1880s, it was the second generation that increasingly came to predominate in the German population of Chicago. In 1850, only an insignificant number of infants and young children were American-born. By 1880, however, the second generation already outnumbered the immigrant generation; and twenty years later three out of five Chicago Germans were second-generation. The age structure, of course, reflects the generational differences even more drastically: in 1900 more than 70 percent of the first generation was older than thirty, while about the same percentage among the second generation was younger than twenty-one.

While most young people were brought up in households headed by first-generation Germans, they were at the same time being educated in Chicago's public schools and thus came increasingly under the influence of American institutions, social norms, and values. Already, complaints were being voiced within the German community over the youths' lack of competence in the German language, and these would increase as the new century progressed. Since by 1900 German immigration had ebbed, the preservation of German culture and customs depended upon the strength of immigrant families and institutions as socializing agencies to counterbalance the influence of American institutions—a hopeless task, as most German leaders early recognized.

The immigration wave of the 1880s also reflected changes in regional origin and traditions of skill. Initially fed by the southwestern and western regions, German emigration increasingly drew upon the population of the agrarian Northeast, which contributed one-third of Germany's immigrants to the United States in the thirty-year period after 1880.[6] Of first-generation Germans in Chicago in 1900, more than 60 percent had immigrated during the 1880s. Since the 1900 census unfortunately failed to trace regional origin—except by implication for Poles from the German Reich who are known to have come overwhelmingly from the East Elbian provinces—we have to rely on unique 1880 census data supplied by a diligent enumerator who faithfully recorded the regional origin of the residents of a recently settled working-class neighborhood on the Northwest Side. The neighborhood was predominantly settled by immigrants from north and northeast Germany, whereas only 15 percent came from the older regions of emigration. Within this neighborhood only 15 percent of the immigrants from the Northeast were skilled, a reflection of the agrarian structure of the northeastern provinces, whereas the proportion rose dramatically to almost two-thirds in the case of the relatively few representatives of old industrial regions like Silesia and Saxony.[7]

Our 1900 data on the Poles emigrating from the East Elbian provinces supplement these findings. This group comprised some 14 percent of the total emigration from the German Reich to Chicago.[8] Two-thirds had immigrated in the twelve-year period from 1880 to 1892, and fully one-half of those employed were unskilled laborers. This is in conformity with the character of the German emigration from the same provinces and the additional regions of Pomerania and Mecklenburg as found in the special 1880 census data. Thus it would be wrong to attribute to ethnic factors the significant occupational differences one finds when comparing Germans with Poles, when in fact the economic structure of the respective regions of origin was decisive.[9]

These findings raise several crucial issues about the composition of the German population of Chicago. After all, it was the Germans from the older emigration regions, the Rhenish provinces of the Southwest, including a substantial share of what

Table 2. Occupational status of German heads of household, 1850, 1880, and 1900

Occupational status	Total for 1850	Total for 1880	First generation	Second generation	Total for 1900	First generation	Second generation
White-collar	**11.7***	**20.1**	**19.9**	**23.2**	**28.8**	**25.1**	**40.0**
Professionals and high white-collar	2.9	1.9	1.9	2.8	2.9	2.6	3.8
Proprietary and low white-collar	8.8	18.2	18.0	20.4	25.9	22.5	36.2
Working class	**84.1**	**72.2**	**72.2**	**72.6**	**67.7**	**71.6**	**55.7**
Skilled crafts	48.1	37.5	36.5	50.7	41.2	42.7	36.7
Unskilled labor	36.0	34.7	35.7	21.9	26.5	28.9	19.0
Specified	7.4	7.7	7.6	9.2	11.2	11.0	11.7
Unspecified	28.5	19.4	20.2	8.5	11.8	14.2	4.4
Other	0.1	7.6	7.9	4.2	3.5	3.7	2.9
Other	**4.2**	**7.7**	**7.9**	**4.2**	**3.5**	**3.2**	**4.4**
N	1,136	2,030	1,888	142	1,377	1,034	343

*Percentages in boldface sum to 100.0, except for rounding error.
Source: Chicago Project, analysis of total German population of Chicago for 1850; systematic sample of 2,222 German households for 1880; and systematic sample of 1,532 German households for 1900; based on the manuscript schedules of the U.S. Censuses on Population for the respective years.

came to be called "Bavarian Jews," who established Chicago's German community in the 1840s and 1850s. After the Civil War they were quickly outnumbered by the newcomers from the North and Northeast. Although the institutional continuity of the German community was basically preserved, new institutions, many of them regionally oriented, were constantly added, and new neighborhoods in the expanding city were formed along regional as well as class lines. Apart from the common ethnic denominator, therefore, the Germans of Chicago were a heterogeneous population divided by time of immigration, regional origin, religion, traditions and skills, generational differences, and length of settlement.

Germans were also clearly divided by class and occupation. As a rough indicator, occupational status categories were used which help point out general occupational fluctuations and give at least a basic idea of the approximate size of the working class.[10] First, it is notable that even in 1850 the occupational stratification of Chicago's German population was complex and mature (see Table 2). The professions then held an even larger share than in 1880, probably a reflection of the sizable number of intellectuals emigrating after the failure of the revolution in 1848. The major movement into white-collar occupations occurred from 1880 to

1900, when the relative numbers increased by ten percentage points. Since these figures refer only to heads of household, they even underrepresent the trend, because they exclude the many sons and daughters who worked as clerks, stenographers, and salespeople in offices and stores. With respect to the working class, we witness a decline of more than 8 percent between 1880 and 1900. When the first and second generations are compared, however, dramatic tendencies show up. Of second-generation German heads of household in 1900, only slightly more than half were working-class, as compared to more than two-thirds of the first generation. The decline of some 16 percent is a complete reversal of the situation in 1880, when both first and second generations were about the same proportion working-class, although generational changes occurred within the working class from unskilled to skilled occupations.

In sum, then, by 1900 Germans had declined in relative importance within the Chicago working class, and the figures for the second generation point to an increase of this trend after 1900. Although Germans still contributed slightly more than their proportionate share to Chicago's working-class population, other immigrant groups, like the Scandinavians, Bohemians, and Poles, were much more strongly composed of workers. Second-generation Germans who had been educated in Chicago's public schools had acquired the basic skill to speak and write the English language that, in addition to more special training, opened to them other expanding sectors of the economy like trade and commerce. One must not forget, however, that in terms of absolute numbers Germans were still the largest ethnic group in Chicago's working class.

Occupational change

CHICAGO'S German immigrant workers from 1850 to 1900 experienced the decline of artisan crafts, the growth of large factories with a high degree of diversification of work tasks, the establishment of new industries, and the transformation from old to new production processes within existing industries. Although all these processes, often overlapping in time and uneven in the pace of their development, helped define the position of German workers in Chicago's industry in 1900, one should not underrate traditions of work and skill that German immigrants brought with them and partially handed on to their children. Thus, especially for the first generation, it was usually not rational choice in terms of the attractiveness of a job as defined by high pay, job security, and decent conditions at the workplace that explained an immigrant's choice of occupation.

In the fifty-year period after 1850, Germans composed the largest group in the work force of the manufacturing and mechanical sector.[11] This also holds if unskilled laborers, who cannot readily be assigned to any one sector, are added. Within the total German work force, manufacturing and mechanical also emerges as the one sector where Germans were always overrepresented, reflecting the high German share of the industrial working class. During the period under consideration, the importance of this sector for the German working class fluctuated from 33.5 percent in 1850 to 41.4 in 1880; it again dipped below the 40 percent line in 1900. Since we know that a sizable share of unskilled laborers also worked in the manufacturing and mechanical sector, it is safe to estimate that between 45 and 50 percent of the German working class were employed in it. This figure does not include building and construction, which accounted for 12.3 percent of the German workers in 1900. In their order of importance the other significant sectors in that year were transportation (6.6 percent), public services (4.8), domestic services (4.7), and printing and publishing (2.4).

A look at specific industries, however, is more relevant for an assessment of the changing position of German workers between 1850 and 1900. Building and construction was the leading industry, although Germans always constituted a minority, even if a sizable one. This sector remained relatively stable throughout the period. The shoe industry, on the other hand, still in second place in 1850, underwent such a drastic relative decline that by 1900 it ranked in twentieth place among Chicago's industries. When Milwaukee and St. Louis gained decisive leads as centers of the brewing industry after the Great Chicago Fire of 1871, the city's breweries could never recapture the place in the regional market they had held before, although the industry continued to grow after 1880 so that more German workers found employment there in 1900. More numerous are those industries into which German workers increasingly entered up to 1880 but had begun to leave by 1900 because of the succession of other immigrant groups (tobacco, clothing), the decline in the industry's importance (leather and tanning), and the dilution of formerly highly valued skills by the division of work tasks as a consequence of technological innovations (wood, furniture). Only in baking and meat, two traditionally German crafts, did the slow rise continue through 1900. It is notable, however, that the rise from 1880 to 1900 was solely attributable to unskilled laborers, whereas a decline had set in among skilled workers. This tendency reflects a move away from the neighborhood bakery and meat market into large-scale, mechanized bakeries and the slaughtering and meat packing plants. Finally, new and expanding industries meeting the demand for new products (metal, printing and publishing) increasingly attracted German workers. By 1900, then, a significant shift had occurred in Chicago, as German workers had begun to turn away from those industries traditionally viewed as distinctly German and characterized by old artisan skills—shoemaking, coopering, baking, butchering, cigar making, cabinetmaking, upholstering, and wagon making. These represented the very craft traditions that German workers had brought with them well into the 1880s.

In 1850, the German working class in the city was neatly divided into two groups: artisans—masters, journeymen and apprentices—on the one hand, dominating the manufacturing and mechanical sector, as well as building and construction. In the other group were common laborers who did menial work in teaming and private services, as well as in industries like brewing, tanning, iron and steel, building and construction, and as day laborers on farms. Especially skilled workers could reasonably expect to rise before long from journeyman to independent master artisan in a rapidly expanding frontier city still largely egalitarian and abounding with economic opportunities. Such expectations were probably shared by many skilled workers immigrating much later, even in the 1880s, although the chances of fulfilling them in Chicago had become minimal, since the meaning of these skills had already changed considerably in the city's modernized industry. The substantial relative increase of German skilled workers in baking, cigar making, clothing, metal, woodworking, and furniture in 1880 may be taken as an indicator of the skills brought before the immigration wave of the 1880s as well as of these expectations. But it hides the fact that these skilled workers increasingly had to work in factories and sweatshops with no hope of becoming independent, that machines had already made some of these skills obsolete, that workers were therefore paid less as they declined in status, or that new skills were required and rewarded accordingly.

Exemplifying the pace of industrialization and the rapidly increasing diversification and specialization of occupations is the proportion of Germans working in the 100 most common occupational designations in 1850, 1880, and 1900. In 1850, they made up 95.3 percent of all occupations Germans held then; in 1880 the percentage had dropped to 83; in 1900 it was 64.5. By the same measure, new occupations and designations were being added. In this process of diversification, the lines between skilled and unskilled were no longer so neatly drawn. A new intermediary level of semiskilled made its impact but was often still counted as belonging to the ranks of the skilled when using old occupational categories derived from earlier phases of industrialization. Our percentages of skilled for 1900 therefore probably contain a considerable share of those semiskilled workers as well as skilled occupations whose skills had become devalued.

These developments are a warning against viewing individual occupations as static over long periods of time, simply because their verbal designations remained the same, when in fact their relative importance and status were considerably affected by fundamental economic transformations. A few examples must suffice. A special report on employees and wages published by the Bureau of the Census in 1903 placed chairmakers in the "second grade" of skilled employees, contrary to their usual inclusion in the skilled category. The "second grade" in wagon making was composed of "employees who do parts of what years ago might have been considered complete processes, as rim-makers, hub borers, most of the machine hands (who now turn out by attendance on machinery parts that used to be made by hand). . . ."[12] In the clothing industry, especially, large numbers of workers were still traditionally considered to be skilled when in fact very little skill was required; seamstresses, whose job was characterized by low pay, unattractive work conditions, and low status, illustrate this tendency.[13]

For the German working class in 1900, this meant that although it was more skilled (56.7) than at any time before, some of these skills had become devalued and some had rather to be characterized as being semiskills. Important differences show up within the group that have to be accounted for in order to understand the role of German workers in Chicago's labor movement. The comparison between the first and second generations of German workers will help to identify long-range tendencies, for it was the second generation that increasingly turned to those occupations that promised more rewards.

Whereas in 1880 the second generation had moved into the manufacturing and mechanical sector and into printing and publishing, a movement out had set in by 1900 among the same group (see Table 3). In building and construction, this tendency was already well on its way in 1880, and it had accelerated by 1900. In contrast, commerce and trade (used here as representing white-collar jobs but not included in the table) had attracted the second generation to a large degree even by 1880 (15.1 percent), and again this trend had increased by 1900 (18.7 percent). Figures for

Table 3. The distribution of the German working class in the Chicago economy in 1880 and 1900 by first and second generation

Sector of the economy	First generation (1880)	Second generation (1880)	First generation (1900)	Second generation (1900)
Manufacturing and mechanical	**39.0**	**47.0**	**38.7**	**37.0**
Baking	1.7	1.7	2.5	1.0
Meat	3.1	2.3	4.2	1.8
Brewing	0.6	0.5	1.3	0.1
Tobacco	1.7	2.0	1.2	0.6
Leather	4.2	3.6	2.6	0.9
Shoes	2.6	1.3	1.3	0.8
Clothing	7.2	14.6	6.0	12.8
Wood	6.9	5.3	3.6	4.0
Furniture	3.7	5.3	3.4	2.0
Metal	6.7	8.5	12.5	12.4
(Iron and steel)	(3.3)	(2.5)	(4.8)	(2.6)
Building and construction	13.1	8.0	14.2	8.9
Printing and publishing	1.1	4.2	1.9	3.2
Transportation	5.2	3.8	6.7	6.1
Domestic services	6.2	9.3	3.8	5.7
Public services	2.1	2.0	4.0	5.9
Labor unspecified	24.1	8.8	16.9	10.7
Other	9.2	16.9	13.8	22.4
N	2,008	787	1,177	784
%	71.8	28.2	60.0	40.0

Source: Chicago Project, analysis of 2,222 German households for 1880 and of 1,532 German households for 1900.

specific industries show that the growth of baking and meat from 1880 to 1900 is attributable only to German immigrants who, on arriving in the 1880s, took unskilled jobs in already-declining trades. Others like furniture and leather, still attracting second-generation Germans in 1880, were unable to keep up this trend because of the relative decline of these industries by 1900. Those industries where significant increases for the second generation show up in 1880 (tobacco, clothing, furniture, metal) were basically of two different kinds. The metal industry, requiring often highly sophisticated skills and paying good wages, constituted a desirable sector into which second-generation Germans continued to move over the next twenty years. (If figures for heads of household, i.e., persons more likely to have reached their permanent occupational position, are taken as further indicators, the trend becomes stronger.) Industries like tobacco and clothing, on the other hand, were neighborhood-based sweatshop industries which required only low levels of skill. Typically, the sons and daughters of immigrants worked there and helped supplement the family income. The decline of the second generation in the clothing and tobacco industries by 1900, as well as the decline in domestic services from 1880 to 1900, indicates that unmarried daughters of German working-class families, mainly because of their English-language skills, now had other avenues open to them, e.g., working as salesladies in department stores or as clerks and typists in offices. That this new orientation did not necessarily entail better overall conditions and a rise in status is made evident by the 1907 Bureau of the Census evaluation of the advantages and disadvantages of working as a saleswoman. It found that "the work is probably less exhausting and the general conditions more attractive than is apt to be the case in the calling of a factory operative, and from a sanitary standpoint it is perhaps to be preferred, although conditions are often far from being ideal. On the other hand, the long, close confinement and the relatively low wages cause it to contrast unfavorably with a number of other occupations."[14] For daughters of Polish families who had emigrated from the German Reich, however, the sweatshop remained the major occupational niche.

Second-generation Germans, on the other hand, who did remain in the working class, tended to enter highly specialized occupations both in traditionally German trades like woodworking and furniture and in the diversified metal industry, as well as in new industries like the electrical industry, whereas unskilled labor receded in significance. Thus, in 1900 the German working class was spread across the whole spectrum of Chicago's industries. Although Germans were still strong in the traditional crafts, these were clearly declining because second-generation Germans entered more rewarding or physically less demanding occupations. The overall tendency was toward a decline of the working class within Chicago's German population, coupled with substantially higher skill levels.

Geographic distribution

IN accordance with their large share of Chicago's population and their high absolute numbers, Germans in 1900 lived in practically every part of the city, but with significant variations which were the result of early patterns of settlement, the direction of Chicago's growth, and the location of its industries. This essay does not attempt to deal with the questions of land use, real estate development, and transportation as they influenced patterns of settlement, especially in the last third of the nineteenth century.[15] The effort here is basically confined to describing the distribution of the German population and specifically the German working class.

Listing its figures according to school districts and wards, the Chicago school census of 1884 gives a rough indication of the ethnic distribution of Chicago's population in that year.[16] Ethnic groups like the Poles, Bohemians, Norwegians, and Swedes were much more geographically concentrated than the Germans. Even the Irish, next to the Germans the largest ethnic group, showed a greater degree of concentration.[17] For Germans, there were clusterings of settlement on the North Side (wards 15 and 16), on the Northwest Side (Ward 14), on the West Side (wards 6 and 7), and on the South Side (Ward 5).

Looking at the relative ethnic distribution within wards, however, one finds that the Germans predominated in particular wards more than any other ethnic group in its respective part of the city.[18] Figures have to be read with caution, however, because in part at least, they are the result of ward size and boundaries. Ward 14 was largest in size and population, for example, and as a consequence differences are blurred. In this case the school district level brings out significant variations. Thus, districts 12 and 14 had a concentration of 75.8 and 73.2 percent Poles; districts 13, 15, and 19 had 81.4, 78.2, and 85.7 percent Germans; and district 29 was 77.9 percent Norwegian.

Our own figures for the years 1880 and 1900 help place the school census findings in a dynamic perspective (see Table 4). The move of Germans to outlying areas by 1900 had taken on major dimensions. In 1900 only 45.5 percent of the German population still lived in the area comprising the former Chicago city limits of 1880, whereas 54.5 percent lived in areas incorporated since then. These figures must be qualified, however. First, suburban centers with large numbers of Germans—e.g., Lake View, which was only later annexed by Chicago—already existed in 1880 but do not show up because the 1880 figures are limited to the city of Chicago, whereas in 1900 Lake View was of course included. Comparing the figures from 1880 and 1900 therefore exaggerates the trend to outlying areas. Second, in terms of absolute numbers, in 1900 even more Germans lived within the old city limits than in

Table 4. Geographic distribution of white-collar and working-class German households in 1880 and 1900

	North Side			Northwest Side			West Side			South Side			S. Chicago	Total for Chicago	
Occupational status	1880	1900	%	1880	1900	%	1880	1900	%	1880	1900	%	1900	1880	1900
White-collar	21.0	34.1*	44.0†	17.5	31.2*	42.2†	15.8	27.0*	57.4†	17.0	32.5*	38.0†	17.1	18.4	31.0
Working-class	63.8	60.3	34.7	66.5	65.1	28.7	72.1	71.1	61.6	66.5	58.1	38.5	72.8	66.5	63.9
Skilled crafts	40.9	39.4	37.5	30.4	42.0	31.1	33.0	41.3	61.7	30.7	33.0	33.9	34.2	34.4	38.9
Unskilled labor	22.9	20.9	29.3	36.1	23.1	24.2	39.1	29.8	61.5	35.8	25.1	44.6	48.6	32.1	25.0
Other‡	15.2	5.7		16.0	3.8		12.1	1.8		16.5	9.4		—	15.1	5.0
Percent of all Chicago German households§	30.9	25.3		25.7	27.7		24.3	21.5		15.8	22.9		2.3	100.0	99.9

*Totals.
†German households in 1900 located within the city limits of 1880.
‡Households where no or no identifiable occupation was given.
§Percentages for 1880 respondents. The respondents for 1900 do not add up to 100 percent because the Central Business District was not included in the table.
Source: Chicago Project, systematic sample of 2,222 German households for 1880 and 1,532 German households for 1900.

1880. But the different sections were differently affected. Whereas the central business district and the most heavily concentrated areas of German population on the North and Northwest Sides suffered a loss of German population, the southern and western sections gained significantly. These categories are still too gross to analyze the changes of distinct German neighborhoods from 1880 to 1900. Impressionistic evidence on the basis of our 1900 sample again suggests differential developments. Thus, the old North Side German neighborhood, although declining in absolute terms compared to 1880, and although tied to a second belt of German settlement in what is now known as Ravenswood and Lake View, still basically retained its location and its German character. On the other hand, the German neighborhood on the Northwest Side had significantly moved outward along Milwaukee Avenue because of the expansion of the Polish settlement closer to the central business district.

How were Chicago's German workers affected by these trends? In 1880, in all sections of the city, working-class households predominated among the German population. Gradations are evident, though. On the North Side, the percent of working-class

This 1883 advertisement in English and German illustrates some of the better housing available to workers on Chicago's expanding Northwest Side. Reproduced with permission of the Chicago Historical Society (ICHi-06577).

households fell below the citywide average (63.8 as against 66.5), whereas the West Side had the highest proportion (72.1). The comparison of skilled and unskilled occupations throws light on the differences of German working-class households between sections. The North Side had a significantly higher percentage of skilled workers and a correspondingly lower percentage of unskilled workers than all the other sections of the city. This was mainly a function of length of settlement. Since the 1840s the North Side had been the distinctly German part of town, so that artisan traditions were carried over into the 1880s and home industries and specialized skills made an important impact. German skilled workers who lived there were in large numbers employed in building and construction, clothing, machine shops, shoemaking, baking, cigar making, and in furniture and printing and publishing. In contrast, leather and tanning, iron and steel (the Chicago Rolling Mills), furniture and machines were the large-scale industries employing German workers on the Northwest Side, whereas home and neighborhood industries were relatively less important. Equal claims can be made with respect to the lumber and furniture industries on the West Side and slaughtering and meat packing on the South Side. It is thus both the location of industries and the length of settlement that made for occupational differences of German workers in these sections.

In 1900, the Northwest Side, along with the West Side, had become the stronghold of the German working class, but its composition had changed. It was now much more skilled; in fact, now the Northwest Side had the highest proportion of skilled German workers, whereas unskilled laborers had decreased below the citywide average. The change is largely due to the growth and changed impact—not the relocation—of major industries in that section of the city. The baking, clothing, building and construction, brewing, and tobacco industries were now added to the list of industries of major importance for the Northwest Side. Also, it had become the section of the city with the largest German population; and it was younger families who lived there, partly a result of the increased settlement of the Northwest Side in the 1880s by new immigrants from Germany. It was the working class on the North Side, as well as on the Northwest Side, that contributed most to the rapid geographic expansion of these sections. Whereas on the North Side close to two-thirds of German working-class households were located in the outer areas, an even higher 71 percent lived in the outer areas of the Northwest Side. German workers were thus overrepresented in these areas. Unskilled laborers contributed heavily to this trend. In addition, generational differences for all heads of household show that it was the well-established families, with middle-aged fathers in their thirties, forties, and fifties, as well as the second generation, that tended to live further away from the center of the city.

Thus, in 1900, the location of the German working class of Chicago had begun to change. The relatively restricted geographic neighborhoods that had been prevalent in 1880 were dissolving. Mostly within walking distance from the place of work, these had also been the basis of contact and communication among workers in their everyday lives. German workers were now more dispersed over larger areas and had to cover longer distances between their homes and places of work. As a result, the world of work on the one hand and family and home on the other were becoming more distinctly separated; and as time went on, it would probably be more difficult to extend common working-class activities beyond those having directly to do with work relations, like strikes and union meetings. Social gatherings, picnics, celebrations would then no longer be bound into the everyday life of German working-class neighborhoods where they had in times of crisis served as important expressions and mechanisms of solidarity for large parts of the working-class community. As the second generation kept moving to suburbia to a larger extent than the first, working-class traditions that German immigrant workers had brought along and maintained on a neighborhood and community basis would be even further weakened.

In sum, Chicago's German working class in 1900 showed the following major characteristics:

1. It had declined in importance both relative to the German work force and Chicago's working class but had a significantly higher skill level than before.
2. The impact of the immigration wave of the 1880s was still strong. The first generation still contributed 60 percent of all German workers. Therefore, skills and traditions brought from Germany still predominated within the German working class, although the generation of the 1880s was more likely to have come from agrarian regions of Germany than the older immigration.
3. Changes in occupations are recognizable, especially with respect to the second generation. The major move here was into white-collar positions. In the manufacturing and mechanical sector, the second generation moved into highly specialized and well-paid skilled jobs, especially in the metal industry and other new and expanding industries.
4. The increasing impact of the second generation points to the inevitable decline of German culture and traditions as the basis of working-class culture.
5. The geographic dispersion of first- and second-generation Germans into Chicago's outer areas had taken on such dimen-

sions that the old German working-class neighborhoods were declining, no longer defining the daily experience of a majority of the German population.

Clearly, then, by the opening of the twentieth century, Chicago's German workers were well on their way toward discarding traditions and their old cultural identity. Whether they did find a new one in the emerging "American" working class, incorporating various traditions, remains to be seen.

Notes

1. In this paper, *German* is defined as both first- and second-generation Germans from the German states for the census of 1850 and from the German Reich for the censuses of 1880 and 1900. The *second generation* is defined as persons born in the United States whose fathers had been born in Germany. The manuscript schedules of the 1850, 1880, and 1900 U.S. population censuses for the city of Chicago were the major source for this essay. For 1850, the total German population of Chicago—more than 6,000—was analyzed. In 1880, a systematic sample was taken of 2,222 German households, which comprised more than 11,000 individuals. The 1900 sample was 5,591 Chicago households, including 1,532 German-headed households with more than 8,000 individuals. The manuscript schedules of the 1910 census were opened in 1982, unfortunately too late for inclusion and use in the Chicago Project.

2. "Eine deutsche Großstadt in Amerika," *Chicagoer Arbeiter-Zeitung*, August 30, 1884.

3. The year 1850 was exceptional, because significant German immigration had been so recent that no substantial second generation could then exist—it constituted only 3.8 percent of the German population—whereas a big jump very probably occurred in the decade up to 1860—for which year we lack figures on the second generation—as a consequence of the birth of children in German families. The immigration wave of the late 1840s and early 1850s was composed largely of young couples and families, the women being in their childbearing years.

4. In that year, the percentage of Germans in Chicago's foreign-born population was 35.7, but it went down to 29.1 in 1900 (Bureau of the Census, U.S. Eleventh Census [1890], *Population*, pt. 1, pp. 670–73; and Twelfth Census [1900], *Population*, pt. 1, pp. 796–99).

5. The figure was arrived at by counting all children in our 1900 sample born in the United States and living in households headed by a person who was second-generation according to our definition.

6. The exact percentage was 32.9. Then followed southwest Germany with 25.2, northwest Germany with 13.6, west Germany with 12.0, and southeast Germany with 7 percent. Figures were computed from Table V of Wolfgang Köllmann and Peter Marschalck, "German Emigration to the United States," *Perspectives in American History* 7 (1973): 535.

7. Analysis of Census Enumeration District No. 144, Ms. Population Census 1880, National Archives, Washington, D.C. (microfilm).

8. In our original sample, we included all persons who gave the area of the German Reich as their place of origin, separating, however, the "Polish Germans" so that we would be able to make comparative analyses. These "Polish Germans" are left out of our analysis of Germans in this article.

9. If one looks at the occupational structure of Germans regardless of regional origin, the percentage of unskilled, for example, is 31.2, as compared to 44.5 for Poles from the German Reich.

10. Occupational status categories were taken from the Philadelphia Social History Project but adapted to the purposes of the Chicago Project study.

11. The published figures for 1880, 1890, and 1900, which cannot readily be compared with our own categorization of Chicago's economy, list a percentage of 24.5 Germans in the manufacturing and mechanical sector in 1880 (the next largest groups are the Scandinavians and Irish, with 8.4 percent each), 21.8 percent in 1890 (12.6 percent for the next largest group, the Scandinavians), and 28.9 percent in 1900 (12.5 for the Scandinavians) (Bureau of the Census, U.S. Tenth Census [1880], *Population*, vol. 1, 870; Eleventh Census [1890], *Population*, vol. 1, pt. 2, 650–51; Twelfth Census [1900], Special Report, *Occupations at the Twelfth Census* (Washington, D.C.: Government Printing Office, 1904), 516–19.

12. U.S. Twelfth Census (1900), *Special Reports*, Davis R. Dewey, *Employees and Wages* (Washington, D.C.: 1903), pp. 1177 and 1180.

13. Bureau of the Census, *Statistics of Women at Work* (Washington, D.C.: 1907), p. 62. The report pointed out that "the occupation includes many of the women working in sweat shops."

14. Ibid., p. 92.

15. For these aspects, compare the respective literature listed in Frank Jewell, *Annotated Bibliography of Chicago History* (Chicago: Chicago Historical Society, 1979).

16. *School Census of the City of Chicago, Taken May, 1884*. The figures in the textual discussion were computed from the tables on nationalities.

17. The percentage of one nationality group for the three wards with the highest total numbers for that group may be taken as a rough measure. Thus, 84.4 percent of Chicago's Poles lived in wards 5, 6, and 14; 86.8 percent of the Bohemians in wards 6, 7, and 8; 79.8 percent of the Norwegians in wards 10, 11, and 14; 65.9 percent of the Swedes in wards 5, 14, and 17; 46.7 percent of the Irish in wards 5, 7, and 8; but only 40.9 percent of the Germans in wards 14, 15, and 16.

18. Thus, of the population of wards 15 and 16, 70.4 percent and 72.7 percent, respectively, were German. The highest percentages for other nationalities were: Poles—18.9 percent (ward 14), Bohemians—32.1 percent (ward 6), Norwegians—15.5 percent (ward 10), Swedes—34.8 percent (ward 17), Irish—39.6 percent (ward 5).

Occupational Patterns of German-Americans in Nineteenth-Century Cities

Nora Faires

THE Germans stand out in the literature on the place of immigrants in the social structure of nineteenth-century American cities as a group whose position and experience have called for a very notable amount of hedging and explanation. In attempting to penetrate the accumulated layers of qualification about this group, one sees that two themes have come to dominate the scholarly discussion of Germans in the United States: the complexity in the German-American experience and the diversity within the immigrant group. This study seeks to explain the variation in occupational patterns among Germans in a number of American cities in the mid- to late nineteenth century, based on a comparison of previous scholarly works and the author's own research on Pittsburgh and Allegheny City, two contiguous cities in Pennsylvania.

Three works published in the mid-1970s provide substantial reviews of the proliferating material on the occupational structures of ethnic groups and their social position in nineteenth-century American cities—Kathleen Neils Conzen's *Immigrant Milwaukee*; JoEllen Vinyard's *The Irish on the Urban Frontier*; and "Occupation and Ethnicity in Five Nineteenth-Century Cities," the collaborative report by Theodore Hershberg, Michael Katz, Stuart Blumin, Laurence Glasco, and Clyde Griffen.[1]

The authors of the 1974 "five-cities study" of the relationship between ethnicity and occupation in five mid-nineteenth-century North American cities expressed their surprise at the uniformity that prevailed in the ethnic hierarchies of Philadelphia, Pennsylvania; Hamilton, Ontario; and Buffalo, Poughkeepsie, and Kingston, New York, particularly for native-born whites, the Irish, and nonwhites. So similar were the occupational patterns for these three groups that the authors concluded: "In some senses it is thus possible to consider ethnicity and class as synonymous; Irish birth usually brought a low ranking as did non-white birth; native-white birth much more often meant high status." Significantly, the immigrant Germans, along with English and Scottish residents of the cities, somewhat blurred this neat occupational breakdown; the five-cities study concluded that these three groups fit between the higher-ranking native-born whites and lower-ranking Irish and nonwhites.[2] Moving beyond gross occupational categories, the study found that Germans were generally absent from the ranks of commercial and professional work and under-represented in the construction trades, while they dominated baking and the apparel trades, especially as tailors and shoemakers. Yet Germans in the five cities differed considerably in their representation in a number of manual jobs, especially as compared to the remarkable concentration of the Irish in the laborer category across the five cities. In all, the five-cities study revealed impressive uniformity in the case of most ethnic groups, but clearly less congruence in the case of the Germans, who had a "more balanced representation" in the occupational hierarchy, particularly in comparison to the Irish.[3] This collaborative work was an early and influential etching of what Blumin later called the "familiar picture."[4]

Deriving their data from two midwestern cities, both Kathleen Conzen and JoEllen Vinyard analyzed their findings in part by comparing them to studies done on eastern cities, such as those examined in the five-cities project and in a number of earlier works. Conzen's and Vinyard's works differed in the primary focus of interest, which was for Conzen the German immigrants in Milwaukee and for Vinyard the Irish who settled in Detroit. Yet the studies grapple with a common problem: explaining why the immigrants they study display different occupational levels than their counterparts in other cities. Neither adopted a simplistic approach to the question, but each concluded that an East/West (or Midwest) distinction helped to explain this variation.[5]

Vinyard examined data on eighteen cities, drawn from other urban case studies and from census statistics for the 1850 to 1880 period. She concluded that the more recently settled and rapidly growing western cities, which lacked an established and preponderant native-born Protestant population, seem to have offered greater opportunities to the Irish immigrants than did eastern

Table 1. Percentage of Germans and Irish in occupational groups in selected U.S. cities, 1850, 1855, 1860*

	Nonmanual		Skilled		Semiskilled		Unskilled		Other and unknown	
Location of study	German	Irish	German	Irish	German	Irish	German	Irish	German	Irish
Milwaukee, 1850 (Conzen)	18	12	41	17	10	10	26	55	5	6
St. Louis, 1850 (Hodes)	13	18	46	19	—	—	37	56	4	7
Detroit, 1850 (Vinyard)	12	19	46	25	—	—	36	50	6	5
Jersey City, 1860 (Shaw)	24	12	60	28	—	—	13	56	3	4
New York City, 1855 (Ernst)	22	12	58	31	14	34	5	23	1	—
Boston, 1850 (Handlin)	22	6	57	23	8	27	12	47	1	—
Pittsburgh, 1850 (Faires)	10	14	38	24	5†	11†	42	46	4	4
Allegheny City, 1850 (Faires)	9	17	53	40	7†	10†	28	27	2	6

*Conzen's study deals with household heads, Vinyard's with male family heads, Shaw's with all males twenty years old and over, and my own with family heads in both Pittsburgh and Allegheny City.
†Operative.

cities. In particular, the gap between the Germans and the Irish in occupational standing tended to be smaller in western than in eastern cities.[6]

Kathleen Conzen's comparison of the occupations of German and Irish immigrants in six cities concentrated on the pattern at mid-century. Table 1 portrays in part the results of her comparison of three midwestern and three eastern cities. Her study of Milwaukee, Vinyard's analysis of Detroit, and Frederick Anthony Hodes's work on St. Louis represent the midwestern cities; the three eastern cities are represented by Douglas V. Shaw's study of Jersey City and by two early classic works on urban life, Robert Ernst's book on New York City and Oscar Handlin's examination of Boston.[7] The most striking pattern that emerges from the data Conzen compiled is the clear predominance of the Irish in the two categories of semiskilled and unskilled labor; in all six cities the Irish exceed the Germans in these job categories. Conzen concluded that "The main difference lay in the German occupational patterns. In comparison with the entire work force, Germans were less overrepresented in skilled crafts in the midwestern cities where their share of the total work force was greater, and a smaller proportion of the employed Germans were found in nonmanual positions as more appeared in the ranks of the common laborers."[8] Her view of the Germans as more occupationally clustered in the middle and lower rungs in midwestern cities conforms with Vinyard's emphasis on the relatively greater achievements of the Irish in these same cities.

Conzen attributed the differences she observed in German occupational patterns among the six cities partly to "selective migration from ports of entry, differential opportunities dependent upon varying urban economies, and the limitations of employment choices set by the ethnic composition of each city." Immigration to midwestern cities typically required more capital than settlement in eastern port cities; at the same time, the smaller, more local, and less industrialized economies of urban areas like Milwaukee, St. Louis, and Detroit, particularly in the period Conzen examined, had less need of individuals with either very specialized trades or factory experience. These factors, she observed, should have acted to select "less skilled but not penniless" migrants to the midwestern cities. On the other hand, in those cities that had a preponderance of Germans—in Milwaukee, for example, they comprised nearly two-fifths of the population—German immigrants could be expected to be found in unusually large numbers in the lower occupational levels simply because they were disproportionately available to fill these numerous jobs. Significantly, it was mostly in midwestern cities like Cincinnati and Chicago that large populations of Germans settled, especially after 1850. Among the other five cities surveyed by Conzen, the percentage of Germans ranged from slightly more than 1 percent in Boston, that most eastern of cities, to 28 percent in midwestern St. Louis.[9] Considered together, the work of Conzen and Vinyard elaborates upon the emerging synthesis regarding German occupational patterns, which stresses both the occupational diversity among German immigrants and the Germans' generally high occupational status relative to the status of the Irish. Their work suggests that in midwestern cities, with their demographic and economic differences from eastern cities and with their requirement for larger amounts of capital for immigrant settlement than eastern ports, the occupational status of Irish and German immigrants was more similar than in eastern cities.

Both the general synthesis and its eastern/western cities revision receive support from data on German and Irish occupational

Table 2. Percentage of Germans and Irish in occupational groups in selected U.S. cities, 1870, 1880, 1890*

	Nonmanual		Skilled		Semiskilled		Unskilled		Other and unknown	
Location of study	German	Irish	German	Irish	German	Irish	German	Irish	German	Irish
Detroit, 1880 (Vinyard)	21	25	39	28	—	—	36	42	3	6
Chicago, 1880 (Jentz and Keil)	21	n.a.[‡]	37	n.a.	—	n.a.	36	n.a.	5	n.a.
Boston, 1890 (Thernstrom)	27	10	48	25	25[§]	65[§]			—	—
Pittsburgh, 1870 (Faires)	17	13	35	18	11[‖]	13[‖]	27	45	10	9
Allegheny City, 1870 (Faires)	11	18	48	30	9[‖]	13[‖]	19	20	12	18

*Vinyard's study deals with male family heads, Jentz and Keil's with employed males, Thernstrom's with the total population, and my own with family heads in both Pittsburgh and Allegheny City.

†For Pittsburgh and Allegheny City, the "unknown" category includes those listed as "works at" a particular firm or factory; they are presumably manual workers.

‡n.a. = not applicable.

§Low manual.

‖Operative.

patterns in other cities in the decades 1870 to 1890, as Table 2 indicates. Of the Irish in Detroit in 1880, 42 percent were unskilled laborers. This percentage exceeded that of the Germans, but by only 6 percent. Furthermore, as a result of the clustering of Germans in skilled work, the Irish actually surpassed the Germans by 4 percent in their percentage of nonmanual workers. Such figures led Vinyard to her conclusions about Detroit's offering opportunities to Irish immigrants.[10] Examining the occupations of Chicago's Germans in 1880, John Jentz and Hartmut Keil reported figures remarkably close to Vinyard's.[11] In both these growing midwestern cities more than a third of the Germans were unskilled workers, almost two-fifths were craft workers, and slightly more than one-fifth held nonmanual jobs. These data are particularly interesting given the differences between the cities at this time. Chicago's population was more than four times larger than Detroit's, and Chicago's economy, expanding more rapidly, was much more complex. The percentage of German-born in these cities, on the other hand, was virtually the same, about 15 percent.[12] As compared to Chicago or Detroit in 1880, the percentage of Germans working at unskilled positions was much lower in Boston in 1890, according to Stephan Thernstrom's calculations.[13] For the

Irish in Boston, Thernstrom's figures for 1890 echo Handlin's for mid-century. In both 1850 and 1890, then, the small numbers of Germans in Boston had a significantly higher occupational standing than did the Irish. These figures lend credence to the East/West distinction between cities in determining the occupational profiles of German and Irish immigrants, a distinction which implies the importance of such factors as time of settlement, rate of economic growth, type of economy, and variation in the percentage of a city's population comprised by an immigrant group.

WORK on Pittsburgh and Allegheny City by this author elaborates upon this East/West distinction among cities but at the same time points out the limits of this conceptualization. Pittsburgh and Allegheny (as Allegheny City was commonly referred to) had economic and demographic configurations and a regional location which placed them literally and figuratively between East and West. These contiguous cities differed in economic bases and ethnic concentrations, but their populations expanded at the same rate, and they varied little in their time of settlement. Generally, Pittsburgh in the mid- to late nineteenth century was more heavily industrial, while Allegheny was more a commercial and light industrial center. Pittsburgh's economy rested squarely on the manufacture of iron, steel, and glass; Allegheny's relied more on the processing of agricultural goods and wood products and the fabrication of metals. Together, the cities' complementary bases comprised a single, developing economy. Reflecting this unity, the populations of the cities grew at the same pace. Pittsburgh, with a population of more than 21,000 in 1840 and nearly 240,000 in 1890, had roughly twice as many inhabitants as Allegheny throughout the same period. The rapid population growth of both cities rested partially on their rich agricultural hinterland, their proximity to vast natural resources, and an excellent transportation network. Both cities experienced massive waves of immigration, but they differed in the proportion of Irish and Germans they received. In Pittsburgh, the percentage of Irish immigrants in the total population exceeded that of Germans in both 1850 and 1870; in Allegheny, by contrast, the ranks of the Germans surpassed those of the Irish.[14]

The cities' location at the headwaters of the Ohio River positioned them just at the eastern edge of the trans-Appalachian West. But as historical geographer David Ward's calculations indicate, these cities were transitional urban areas between eastern and western cities in demographic, as well as geographic, terms.

According to Ward, in 1870 the mean percentage of Irish and German residents in the nation's fifty largest cities was 15 percent Irish and 12 percent German. With 15 percent of its population Irish and 10 percent German, Pittsburgh came closest to the national average for these groups in large urban areas. Allegheny City, on the other hand, had a higher than average proportion of German residents (14 percent) and a lower than average percentage of Irish inhabitants (8 percent) than did many large cities in 1870. Still, Allegheny lay closer to the intersection of the national means than did a majority of the fifty cities. Ward's figures show that Pittsburgh's percentage of Irish and German residents was similar to that of mid-Atlantic industrial and commercial centers, such as Brooklyn, Philadelphia, Utica, and Syracuse. In contrast, the immigrant population of Allegheny in this year resembled the pattern of midwestern cities, such as Dayton, Detroit, and Louisville. Notably, the cities closest to Pittsburgh and Allegheny in their percentages of Irish and German residents were Utica and Louisville, respectively; the growth of both depended, as did the expansion of Pittsburgh and Allegheny, on interregional trade.[15]

JoEllen Vinyard's comparison of eastern and western cities provides further confirmation of the status of Allegheny and Pittsburgh as cities that fit between these two categories. With a 236 percent rate of population growth between 1850 and 1880, Pittsburgh grew faster than five of the eastern cities and more slowly than seven of the western cities she compared; Allegheny would fall in virtually the same slot. Similarly, Vinyard's data on the economic bases of eighteen cities reveal that Pittsburgh, with its heavy industry, more closely resembles the eastern cities than the western cities with which it is listed, whereas Allegheny's more commercial economy would place it closer to the western cities.[16]

This paper provides a closer look at the German and Irish occupational patterns in Pittsburgh and Allegheny in Tables 1 and 2, based on data in the manuscript population censuses of 1850 and 1870.[17] Although generally similar, Pittsburgh's and Allegheny's occupational structures contained differences rooted in their distinct economies. In less heavily industrial Allegheny, there were more craft and fewer unskilled jobs than in Pittsburgh. In 1850 fewer than one of five Allegheny City family heads had an unskilled job, while one of three Pittsburgh family heads held such a position. In contrast, more than half of Allegheny's family heads made their living through craftwork in 1850, compared to only 38 percent across the river. By 1870 skilled workers in Allegheny City had declined to 38 percent, the same percentage of craft workers as Pittsburgh had had twenty years before. By this time, skilled workers in Pittsburgh had dropped to 18 percent. Although both cities had similar proportions of operatives in 1850, the percentage of these industrial workers rose in Pittsburgh from 10 percent to 12 percent by 1870, while in Allegheny the figure stayed at about 9 percent of the family heads over the twenty-year period. Thus, for both cities in both decades the bulk of the work force fell into one of the three categories of manual labor, but the chances of working at a skilled job were much higher in Allegheny, the less industrial city.

Looking at the ethnic composition of the two work forces, one finds that native-born whites in both cities dominated the highest ranks of the occupational structure and were underrepresented in manual work, especially as unskilled laborers; nevertheless, the preponderance of manual jobs in the cities insured that many native-born whites toiled at skilled, operative, and unskilled work. In contrast, blacks were uniformly concentrated in the ranks of unskilled labor and usually held the least secure, lowest-paying, and most hazardous casual laboring jobs. The occupational profiles for the Germans and Irish in Pittsburgh and Allegheny City were substantially more complex, even though in both cities the vast majority of both Irish and German immigrants were clustered in the ranks of manual workers between 1850 and 1870.

As a result of their larger numbers in Allegheny, German family heads exceeded the number of Irish family heads employed at casual laboring jobs. In 1850 31 percent of all laboring family heads in the city were Irish; 36 percent were German. By 1870 the gap had widened: in this year one-fifth were Irish, while more than two-fifths were German. Yet the relative importance of unskilled labor for the occupational distribution of each immigrant group was very similar in both years. In 1850 over one-quarter of the family heads of both immigrant groups in Allegheny worked at unskilled labor. Twenty years later this figure declined by nine percentage points for the Germans and by seven for the Irish. Reflecting the large overall pool of craft workers in Allegheny, 40 percent of Irish family heads were craft workers in 1850, while their ranks were thinned to 30 percent by 1870. The proportion of German family heads in craftwork also declined as the percentage of craft jobs shrank, but at a slower pace; 53 percent of all German family heads were craft workers in 1850, compared to 48 percent two decades later, a figure exceeding that of the Irish by 20 percent. In positions as operatives, on the other hand, the groups were nearly equal; roughly one in ten German and Irish family heads was an operative over the whole twenty-year period.

In Pittsburgh, the Irish remained heavily clustered in the unskilled ranks between 1850 and 1870. Of all unskilled family heads in 1870, fully half were Irish while, similarly, almost half of all Irish family heads were employed as unskilled laborers. In contrast, 42 percent of German family heads toiled at unskilled jobs in 1850, compared to 27 percent two decades later. As craftwork in Pittsburgh declined, German family heads slightly expanded their share of such work, even though its relative importance in the German occupational distribution declined somewhat. In contrast, Irish skilled workers declined as a proportion of all craft workers; the Irish occupational distribution between 1850 and 1870 did likewise. Thus, over these two decades the percentage of Irish family heads with a craft job went down from roughly one quarter to 18 percent. In contrast, approximately 12 percent of the Irish remained as operatives, while the proportion of Germans who held such positions rose from 5 percent to 11 percent.

Looking at manual workers, then, the familiar picture of German and Irish urban occupational patterns emerges, but in modified form in both cities and in slightly different profile in each. Less numerous than their counterparts across the river, the Irish in Allegheny were significantly less concentrated in the ranks of unskilled workers. Their share as operatives, in contrast, was remarkably similar in both cities, regularly exceeding the German percentage by a small amount. Just as consistently, and by appreciably larger percentages, the Irish trailed the Germans in representation among craft workers. In both the smaller craft sector of Pittsburgh and the larger one in Allegheny, German immigrants surpassed the percentage of Irish artisans by between thirteen and eighteen percentage points. The pattern for Germans was not so clear-cut. In both cities the percentage of Germans with operative jobs increased. But this was substantially more so in Pittsburgh, where more such jobs opened up. In the same way, in both Pittsburgh and Allegheny, the percentage of Germans laboring as unskilled workers decreased from 1850 to 1870, although more so in Pittsburgh, where they had begun with a higher proportion.

The generally higher status of the Germans changes significantly when one looks at nonmanual positions. The percentage of both immigrant groups holding nonmanual positions was low, ranging between 9 percent of Allegheny's Germans in 1850 and 18 percent of the same city's Irish in 1870. Interesting variation occurred within this narrow range. In Pittsburgh, the percentage of Germans in the nonmanual ranks trailed that of the Irish slightly in 1850 but exceeded it by 4 percent in 1870. The percentage of

Irish holding nonmanual positions slightly surpassed that of the Germans in both years in Allegheny City.

These occupational contours suggest that in Allegheny the gap between the typically higher-ranking Germans and lower-ranking Irish was smaller than in Pittsburgh. Indeed, outside the world of manual work, the Allegheny Irish seem to have had an edge on the city's Germans. By contrast, the Germans in Pittsburgh, nearly as clustered in unskilled labor as the Irish in 1850, were substantially less so twenty years later. This pattern can be seen to support the comparative work on eastern and western cities, displayed in Tables 1 and 2. From this view, Pittsburgh was the more eastern city: more industrial, larger, and more heavily Irish. Neighboring Allegheny, then, was more a city of the West: more commercial, smaller, and more heavily German. While the percentage of unskilled German workers in Allegheny City was similar to the percentage for Milwaukee in 1850—and closer to the higher Detroit and St. Louis figures—in 1870 it was half that of Germans in most of the other cities. At the other end of the occupational spectrum, Allegheny Germans showed markedly lower concentrations than did Germans in most of the other cities. The gap was particularly wide in 1870, when Allegheny Germans trailed their compatriots in the two midwestern cities by 10 percent and in Boston by 16 percent. In its generally higher rates of skilled work, however, Allegheny City's German occupational profile resembles that of the eastern cities more than does Pittsburgh's, where the lower proportion of German skilled workers in 1850 conforms to the pattern of the three midwestern cities in 1880. Industrializing earlier than Detroit and Chicago, Pittsburgh by 1850 may already have had less need of German workers predominating in traditional crafts, whereas Chicago and Detroit may have reached this same plateau of industrial development thirty years later. This would explain why Germans in Pittsburgh were densely concentrated in the unskilled ranks in 1850. Settling in this industrializing city at mid-century, a large number of Germans clustered in unskilled work. They did this for a number of reasons. Not only did they have no previous industrial experience, they lacked the capital to establish themselves in craftwork or in small shops and were hampered by their inability to speak English. And the city's economy opened up particular opportunities in the unskilled sector. By 1870 the city's economy had become more mature and balanced, providing more jobs for Germans outside the ranks of unskilled labor, in the fields of trade and commerce, for instance. The Irish filled the gap in unskilled work left by the Germans. Thus, as an established industrial city in 1870, Pittsburgh resembled the eastern cities, with their typically heavy concentration of Irish laborers.

ANALYSIS of immigrant occupations in mid- to late nineteenth-century Pittsburgh and Allegheny City supports several conclusions. First, while the data for Pittsburgh and Allegheny City vary, these cities are, in some respects, closer to each other than to other cities. The overall occupational profiles for both the Irish and the Germans are roughly parallel in Allegheny and Pittsburgh, particularly with respect to the generally low representation of both immigrant groups in the ranks of nonmanual workers. These similarities seem to result from the cities' unity as complementary, contiguous economic centers in a developing region. Second, the German occupational profiles in these cities conformed in some respects to the overall pattern described in other scholarly works; occupationally, the Germans generally fit between the more highly ranking native-born whites and the more low-ranking Irish, and certainly the Germans in these cities were employed in the wide range of occupations characteristic of Germans elsewhere.

However, the Pittsburgh and Allegheny data provide some support for revising the eastern/western cities model. The comparatively greater occupational achievement of Irish immigrants in Allegheny must have put a ceiling on the upward mobility of the Germans. At the same time, Allegheny's expansive artisanal sector was able to absorb the large clusters of German-Americans in the city. Thus, Allegheny's greater concentration of both craft occupations and German inhabitants seems to have made immigrant occupational patterns in the city distinct from Pittsburgh's. The data on Pittsburgh and Allegheny suggest that two components are particularly important in explaining the differences between the occupational patterns of Germans: the proportion an immigrant group comprises of the city's population and the city's occupational structure. Yet these two factors may be related to a third, and more comprehensive, component: the nature and timing of a city's economic development. Geographically and demographically, Pittsburgh and Allegheny occupied a transitional region in the mid- to late nineteenth century; more industrial Pittsburgh and more commercial Allegheny City represented different aspects of the complex process of economic change which swept the United States from East to West during these decades.

Eastern cities were, typically, larger and more industrial and had higher representations of Irish than their midwestern coun-

Nicolaus Schwenck, a journeyman coppersmith, arrived in Chicago in the 1850s and was able to fulfill the artisan dream of establishing his own shop. Immigrants like Schwenck gave Germans their reputation as craft workers. Letterhead from correspondence of Nicolaus Schwenck, 1 December 1869. Courtesy of Franz Christian Schwenck, Langenau, Federal Republic of Germany.

terparts in the last fifty years of the nineteenth century. But such factors as size, economic base, and immigrant composition are better understood when related to the timing and type of economic growth of a city than to regional location per se.[18] Regional factors, such as the greater costs of transportation to western cities or the cultural and demographic character of southern cities, can then be evaluated on their own merits.[19]

A brief look at craftwork illustrates the value of concentrating on the phase of economic growth that a particular city went through. The single most uniform finding regarding German immigrant occupations is the consistent clustering of Germans in the ranks of skilled workers. In the five-cities study, for example, Germans concentrated especially in those trades concerned with clothing, leather, and food.[20] Similarly, in Pittsburgh and Allegheny, Germans were clustered in butchering, baking, and coopering and dominated tailoring and shoemaking, those crafts that have come to be regarded as bastions of German immigrant occupational life.[21] In some cities, these were trades threatened by or actually undergoing serious dilution in skill as a result of the transformation of work and were becoming increasingly peripheral to the major expanding sectors of the economy. Susan Hirsch's study of Newark, for example, demonstrated a concentration of German craft workers in the stagnating industries of shoemaking and trunkmaking.[22] Accordingly, Bruce Laurie, Theodore Hershberg, and George Alter concluded that German immigrants in Philadelphia were "locked into declining crafts."[23] These findings are hard to generalize from, even given a broad pattern of German concentration in particular crafts, since the timing of changes in these trades varied widely both from city to city and for particular skills within these trades. Differences in the nature of urban economies, then, affected the size, shape, and status of the skilled trades; and the total proportion of Germans in the city set firm boundaries on the percentage of the immigrant group that could occupy the skilled ranks.[24]

As this example illustrates, one approach to understanding the occupational experience of German immigrants in American cities is to place the profile of German workers within the context of the evolving economic structure of nineteenth-century America. Explicitly linking the study of these immigrants to the examination of the commercializing and industrializing urban areas to which they came (as well as to the changing countryside in which other German immigrants settled) advances both the analysis of the ethnic group and the process of economic development. In particular, such an approach would offer a means by which to integrate the study of German immigrants in smaller cities with distinctive economic bases with the analysis of the German-American experience in larger, more diverse, urban centers.

Notes

1. Kathleen Neils Conzen, *Immigrant Milwaukee, 1836–1860: Accommodation and Community in a Frontier City* (Cambridge, Mass.: Harvard University Press, 1976); JoEllen Vinyard, *The Irish on the Urban Frontier: Nineteenth Century Detroit, 1850–1880* (New York: Arno Press, 1976); Hershberg et al., "Occupation and Ethnicity in Five Nineteenth-Century Cities: A Collaborative Inquiry," *Historical Methods Newsletter* 7 (1974): 174–216.

2. Hershberg et al., "Occupation and Ethnicity in Five Nineteenth-Century Cities," pp. 199, 202, 211–13 (quoted matter is from p. 202).

3. Ibid., pp. 199–201, 211–13 (quoted matter is from p. 213). When the collaborative study considered property ownership in conjunction with the occupational hierarchy, it found the lines between groups less clear, as both immigrants, including the Germans, and nonwhites consistently outstripped their native-born occupational counterparts in the acquisition of real estate; see p. 204.

4. Stuart M. Blumin, *The Urban Threshold: Growth and Change in a Nineteenth-Century American Community* (Chicago: University of Chicago Press, 1976), 89.

5. Conzen, *Immigrant Milwaukee*, 72; Vinyard, *The Irish on the Urban Frontier*, 312.

6. Vinyard, *The Irish on the Urban Frontier*, 314–17, 324–35. She develops the comparison of cities in pp. 312–39.

7. Conzen, *Immigrant Milwaukee*, 73. Conzen derived her data from the following: Frederick Anthony Hodes, "The Urbanization of St. Louis" (Ph.D. diss., St. Louis University, 1973), pp. 72–73; Vinyard, "The Irish

on the Urban Frontier: Detroit, 1850–1880" (Ph.D. diss., University of Michigan, 1972), p. 49; Douglas V. Shaw, "The Making of an Immigrant City: Ethnic and Cultural Conflict in Jersey City, New Jersey, 1850–1877" (Ph.D. diss., University of Rochester, 1972), p. 21; Robert Ernst, *Immigrant Life in New York City, 1825–1863* (New York: King's Crown Press, 1949), 214–17; and Oscar Handlin, *Boston's Immigrants: A Study in Acculturation* (New York: Atheneum, 1968), 250–52.

In preparing Table 1, I was able to recreate Conzen's calculations for her own study and for Vinyard's and Shaw's; my figures for the data drawn from Hodes, Ernst, and Handlin are approximations I derived from Conzen's Figure 7, "Ethnicity and Occupational Status in Selected Mid-Nineteenth Century Cities" (p. 73). In analyzing the data compiled by Conzen and examining the rest of Tables 1 and 2 in this paper, it is important to keep in mind the thorny problems of both comparability of data and the limits of any occupational scheme that can adequately portray differences between and among jobs. On this latter point, see, for example, Clyde Griffen, "Occupational Mobility in Nineteenth-Century America: Problems and Possibilities," *Journal of Social History* 5 (1972): 310–30; Michael B. Katz, "Occupational Classification in History," *Journal of Interdisciplinary History* 3 (1972): 63–88; and Margo A. Conk, *The United States Census and Labor Force Change: A History of Occupation Statistics, 1870–1940* (Ann Arbor: University of Michigan Press, 1980).

In my study of Pittsburgh and Allegheny City, I attempted to clarify the occupational structure of the cities by omitting the confusing category of "semiskilled" work. My scheme follows that developed by the Social Science Computer Research Institute, University of Pittsburgh, in breaking down the manual occupations into skilled, operative, and unskilled jobs. In general, the skilled occupations are the craft, or artisanal, trades. Operative jobs are largely industrial occupations, involving work in factories or in manufacturing shops; they are normally paid at a wage rate. Unskilled labor comprises casual or day labor and other unspecified jobs entailing heaving, hauling, digging, and similar heavy and low-paying work.

8. Conzen, *Immigrant Milwaukee*, 72.

9. Ibid., 72. See p. 8 for a graphic depiction of the concentration of German settlers in midwestern cities.

10. Vinyard, *The Irish on the Urban Frontier*, 144.

11. John B. Jentz and Hartmut Keil, "From Immigrants to Urban Workers: Chicago's German Poor in the Gilded Age and Progressive Era, 1883–1908," *Vierteljahrschrift für Sozial- und Wirtschaftsgeschichte* 68 (1981): 61–62.

12. Ibid., pp. 57–61; Vinyard, *The Irish on the Urban Frontier*, 130, 319, 328; *Tenth Census of the United States, 1880, Population*, vol. 1 (Washington, D.C.: Government Printing Office), 536, 539.

13. Stephan Thernstrom, *The Other Bostonians: Poverty and Progress in the American Metropolis, 1880–1970* (Cambridge, Mass.: Harvard University Press, 1973), 131.

14. For a detailed discussion of the economic and social development of Pittsburgh and Allegheny City see Nora Faires, "The Evolution of Ethnicity: The German Community in Pittsburgh and Allegheny City, Pennsylvania, 1845–1885" (Ph.D. diss., University of Pittsburgh, 1981), pp. 105–34.

15. David Ward, *Cities and Immigrants: A Geography of Change in*

Nineteenth-Century America (New York: Oxford University Press, 1971), 76–78.

16. Vinyard, *The Irish on the Urban Frontier*, 315–33; see especially pp. 319 and 328.

17. See Faires, "The Evolution of Ethnicity," pp. 185–228, for discussion of the occupational structures of these cities and for detailed information on the occupations of Germans and Irish. The data on Pittsburgh and Allegheny City are for family heads, both female and male.

18. A recent paper by Stanley Nadel analyzes variations in German-American occupational patterns with reference to differences in the size of cities: ("German Americans and the American City in the Nineteenth Century" [Paper delivered at the Annual Meeting of the Organization of American Historians, Philadelphia, Penn., April 1982]).

19. For a discussion of southern cities as sites for German settlement, see Nora Faires and Linda K. Pritchard, "The Germans in Texas, 1840–1890" (Paper delivered at the Annual Meeting of the Southwest Social Science Association, San Antonio, Texas, March 1982).

20. Hershberg et al., "Occupation and Ethnicity in Five Nineteenth-Century Cities," pp. 199–201.

21. Faires, "The Evolution of Ethnicity," pp. 201–2.

22. Susan E. Hirsch, *The Roots of the American Working Class: The Industrialization of Crafts in Newark, 1800-1860* (Philadelphia: University of Pennsylvania Press, 1978), 47–50.

23. Bruce Laurie, Theodore Hershberg, and George Alter, "Immigrants and Industry: The Philadelphia Experience, 1850–1880," in *Immigrants in Industrial America*, ed. Richard Ehrlich (Charlottesville, Va.: University of Virginia Press, 1977), 149.

24. Adopting a comparative urban economic development approach would similarly be valuable in evaluating the role of domestic service as an occupation for German-Americans. On German women as domestic servants, see Laurence Glasco, "Ethnicity and Occupation in the Mid-Nineteenth Century: Irish, Germans and Native-Born Whites in Buffalo, New York," in *Immigrants in Industrial America*, ed. Ehrlich, 151–75; Carol Groneman, "'She Earns as a Child—She Pays as a Man': Women Workers in a Mid-Nineteenth-Century New York Community," in ibid., 33–46; and Nora Faires, "German Women and Assimilation" (Paper delivered at the Third Berkshire Conference on the History of Women, Bryn Mawr, June 1976).

Industrialization, Class, and Competing Cultural Systems: Detroit Workers, 1875–1900

Richard J. Oestreicher

INFLUENCED by E. P. Thompson and other English Marxists, contemporary historians of the American working class have devoted increasing attention to the cultural dimensions of class. Thompson argued in *The Making of the English Working Class* that class can best be understood as "an *historical* phenomenon. . . . not . . . as a 'structure,' nor even as a 'category,' but as something which . . . happens in human relationships. . . . class happens when some men as a result of common experiences (inherited or shared), feel and articulate the identity of their interests as between themselves, and as against other men whose interests are different from . . . theirs."[1]

Taking Thompson's cue, recent American labor historians have tried to uncover the inherited and shared common experiences of American workers as a way of approaching the making of the American working class. But the search for an American working-class culture has *not*, in my opinion, given us a clear explanation of The Making of the American Working Class. At least in part that is because the search has been organized around Edward Thompson's definition of class in ways which are inappropriate to American experiences. Thompson takes great care to point out that class is something which happens in a specific way unique to each particular set of historical circumstances. The events that made the English working class, according to Thompson, were the interaction between the traditions developed by a settled and relatively stable population over many generations and the process of capitalist development during the English industrial revolution. There is no counterpart of stable homogeneous communities and ancient universal traditions among American workers during the late nineteenth and early twentieth centuries, the crucial period for American working class development. If the American working class was made in this period, then the event must have been very different from the English one.

What is necessary, therefore, is to search for what is unique in the history of the American working class, for the ways in which a multicultural working class was not only made but also remade by its cultural experiences. Consider the following series of tentative propositions:

1. That the processes of industrialization, urbanization, and centralization of authority stimulated workers to reflect on the changing nature of their lives, and to respond collectively to those changes in an effort to maintain control over work, community, family, and culture; i.e., capitalist development stimulated the making of the American working class.

2. But that the very same processes of social change which stimulated the making of the American working class were also the sources of simultaneous unmaking of the working class. Industrialization increased the range of job categories and the diversity of on-the-job experiences; urbanization disrupted neighborhoods and communities; economic growth attracted new workers and an ever more diverse ethnocultural mix within the work force.

3. Thus the working class was simultaneously being made and unmade; working-class life was not a progression from tradition to modernity, accompanied by some very bitter but temporary conflict, but a continuing state of tension between tendencies *toward solidarity* and tendencies toward fragmentation—both inherent in modern society.

Elaboration of the implications of these propositions should be, in my opinion, one of the central tasks of American labor historians. By looking at a case study, late nineteenth-century Detroit, I would like to show that consideration of these propositions may be a fruitful direction for further analysis.

Three strikes occurred within two months of each other in Detroit in 1891: a four-day strike of streetcar drivers and conductors in April; a brief walkout of laborers at the Michigan Car Company (a railroad car factory), which began the day the streetcar strike was settled; and a month-long citywide strike of stonecutters, which began June 1. The first ended in total victory, the other two in defeat. The key to the streetcarmen's success was the overwhelming and active support of the rest of the city's workers. The events of the streetcar strike suggest the existence of a widespread working-class culture of solidarity. Yet the other two strikes, which followed the streetcar strike by only hours in the first case and weeks in the second, failed precisely because of the breakdown of solidarity. Workers split along ethnic (and to some degree craft) lines. Even more puzzling than the apparently sharp differences in the level of working-class solidarity in the three events are indications that some of the same individuals who refused to support their striking fellow workers in the last two strikes had supported the streetcarmen.

In April 1891 the former leaders of the lapsed Knights of Labor streetcar workers assembly reorganized as the Street Railway Employees Mutual Benefit Association. Within a week fifteen of its organizers had been fired. Reluctantly, the Association declared a strike.[2] The prospects did not seem promising. The Association's 200 members were less than one-third of the 750-man workforce, and only 150 had shown up at the crucial pre-strike meeting. When union members marched over to the car barns after their strike meeting to urge the early morning shift to support them, several veteran drivers crossed picket lines to take out their cars.[3]

Detroit was a worker city. More than half the work force was blue-collar.[4] While union membership had declined by more than one-third since late 1886, local unions had more than 8,000 members.[5] More importantly, much larger numbers of workers had absorbed parts of the unions' informal moral code of solidarity. Memories of the 1886 mass strikes for a shorter workday were still fresh in workers' minds. Six thousand had struck during early May of 1886. Union and Knights of Labor membership swelled to 13,000 that summer; and when the Trades Council and the Knights' District Assembly joined forces to organize a mass demonstration on the first Monday in September (although no governmental body had recognized Labor Day as a legal holiday), the entire city shut down in what approached a de facto general strike.[6] Five years later the Knights were decimated; and many of the worker clubs, cooperatives, and newspapers that had nurtured a workers' subculture of opposition in 1886 were gone as well.[7] But the previous year more than 2,000 carpenters had struck for the eight-hour day with the same rituals of mass picketing and mass marches that had emerged in 1886.[8] Detroit workers had experienced mass strikes, understood what scabs were, recognized that worker power depended on mass action.

And the streetcar company was in a particularly vulnerable position. While its work force was relatively small, thousands and thousands of workers rode in its cars every day. Poor service had antagonized much of the public, middle-class as well as working-class. Equally important, with miles of track spread around the city and more than fifty cars operating at any one time, even with fifty police placed on special service to the Company, there was no way the cars could be protected if other workers joined the streetcarmen's efforts to stop the cars. They did so by the thousands. Large crowds blocked cars at key intersections, most people boycotted the streetcars, deliverymen deliberately drove their wagons onto the tracks, and scab drivers were repeatedly dragged off slow-moving cars and severely beaten.[9]

By the morning of the third day not only had traffic on the streetcar lines been completely stopped but hundreds of workers were leaving their own factories in sympathy strikes, parading through city streets in military rank, and joining crowds which by now were systematically erecting barricades to block the cars and ripping up streetcar tracks. At 8:30 A.M. 200 stoveworkers gathered at the city limits and marched downtown behind an American flag to show their solidarity with the streetcarmen, where they were joined by another parade of 500 Detroit Stove Works workers marching, this time under a red flag. Ironworkers leaving one factory after the afternoon shift spent two hours ripping up two blocks of tracks in front of their shop. When the mayor, who had repeatedly tangled with streetcar company officials over poor service, refused to call in state militia to break the strike, the company capitulated, reinstating the men it had fired and recognizing the union as exclusive bargaining agent for all its employees.[10]

The victory of the streetcarmen suggests the existence of a widespread and deeply felt working-class culture of solidarity. The streetcar workers won not because of their own resources but because thousands of other workers supported them. Other factors contributed to the victory as well. Many political leaders and downtown businessmen endorsed the strike because they were disgusted with streetcar service. Several store owners contributed to the strike fund, and the mayor urged the streetcar company to negotiate. But while a general antagonism to the streetcar company may have added to public sympathy for the strikers, the form of protest was distinctively working-class; and middle-class critics of the car company would probably not have been aroused by the miserable working conditions of streetcar workers if the workers themselves had not taken action.[11] Most important, support was both extensive and intense. Sympathetic workers were willing not only to contribute to the strike fund, to accept the inconvenience of a boycott, but also to strike themselves, to battle police, and to risk arrest on the streetcarmen's behalf. Such support cut across occupational and ethnic boundaries. A list of twenty-four people arrested for strike activities included a butcher, a shoemaker, a bricklayer, a tailor, five metalworkers, three clerks, a messenger boy, a porter, and the editor of a radical German newspaper. The arrest list contained several Irish, Scottish, and German names, as well as one Italian and a Pole; and only one of those on the list was actually a streetcar worker.[12]

But this picture of class solidarity fades quickly as we look at the other two strikes. At the Michigan Car Works, a complex of railroad car construction shops employing over 2,000 workers, news of the streetcarmen's victory provoked a shorter hours strike on Saturday, April 25.[13] The instigators of the walkout were probably motivated by the memory of May Day shorter hours strikes in 1886 and 1890. In May 1886 the Michigan Car Works had been the keystone of the shorter hours movement. Rumors of another round of May Day strikes had been circulating for several weeks before the streetcar strike. With the spectacle of sympathy strikes for the streetcar workers all over the city and May Day approaching in a week, it is not surprising that some car workers could hope to provoke widespread walkouts as they had done in 1886.

But this time the scenario was quite different. Carshop molders and machinists refused to join the strike on Saturday, and they were harbingers of what was to follow. When the carshop workers marched to the Detroit Spring Works, a subsidiary of the carshop, the workers there ignored them. On Monday a crowd of 1,000 gathered at the carshop gates to urge continuation of the strike, but an estimated 300 workers entered the factory. The largely Polish and German crowd battled police, but the workers' appeals for solidarity did not sway English-speaking molders, who complained to reporters that they wanted to go to work but were intimidated by the violence.[14] The strike limped on for several days, but all efforts to broaden it failed. The Spring Works employees ignored strikers' daily chants of "scab." A Tuesday demonstration at the Detroit Stove Works led to further battles with police but no addition to the strikers' ranks. At the May Day meeting of the Trades Council the following evening, even the socialist contingent admitted that the strike was lost. The company fired 300 car workers as it resumed normal operations.[15]

While the carshop workers might have lost nonetheless, the contrast between the response to their appeals for solidarity and to those of the streetcar workers was remarkable. Striking Polish and German carshop laborers had expected to reap the benefits of the enthusiastic solidarity that had propelled the streetcar workers to victory. Yet the same metal trades who had been disproportionately represented in the arrest lists and sympathy strikes the week before proved most resistent to their appeals. The machine shop and the foundry had been the last to shut down, and they were the first to resume operations. By Thursday, April 30, more than 400 workers had re-entered the Michigan Car Works foundry, while only 80 others had resumed work in the rest of the complex. We do not have a breakdown of the composition of the Car Works' work force, but newspaper accounts suggest division both by skill—highly paid metal trades versus largely unskilled yard laborers—and ethnicity—unskilled laborers were primarily Poles and Germans, while the foundry workers were described as English-speaking. Names of those speaking at strike meetings and arrested at plant gate battles confirm these images; all but 2 of 26 such names were German or Polish.[16]

The stonecutters' strike in June revealed equally contradictory examples of solidarity and fragmentation. Stonecutters struck citywide on June 1, demanding an increase in the union wage scale. When contractors imported thirty-seven Italian stonecutters from New York during the third week of the strike, union members met the Italians at the station, explaining the situation. The Italians agreed to join the strikers; "No, no ve no Scab," explained one of them in broken English in an *Evening News* report (June 16, 1891). Yet two weeks later the stonecutters had fractured along ethnic lines into four hostile groups. One group had split off from the Stonecutters Union to form a dual Progressive Union which returned to work on the employers' terms. A few days later twenty German stonecutters also returned to work and formed yet another stonecutter's union. The remaining regular union members, mainly English and Scottish trade union veterans, pledged to continue the struggle; but they too were demoralized when the union president, a young doctor who had worked his way through medical school as a stonecutter, broke ranks and returned to work. Each group blamed the others for the collapse, agreeing only on their mutual hostility to the Italians. The Italians had left town in mid-June, hoping to find work at "the Soo" (Soo Locks at Sault Ste. Marie); but when they arrived there, the largely French Canadian work force refused to work with them. They straggled back to Detroit in early July only to find that with the strike over local employers no longer wanted them, and local stonecutters supported the employers' decision despite the Italians' gesture of solidarity only weeks before. "Italians don't count," declared one local worker, "they are not stonecutters at all. One good man can do as much as half a dozen of them." Another justified the employers' decision by claiming that "the Italians cannot cut the stone used here."[17]

These divisive conflicts among the stonecutters and carshop workers were not isolated incidents. Reading through Detroit daily newspapers in the months surrounding these strikes, I found a long list of incidents suggesting intraclass hostilities and rivalries among ethnic groups, among occupations, and between skilled and unskilled within occupations. Working-class Polish Catholics were bitterly divided between followers of rebel Polish priest Father Dominic Kolasinski, who had been expelled from his parish by Bishop Caspar Borgess, and those who supported the new Polish parish recognized by the bishop. The Kolasinski question led to repeated barroom brawls in Polish neighborhoods. The anti-Kolasinski faction was itself divided over the priest assigned to their church. Father Kazimierz Rochowski, despite his Polish name, was accused of being a German Pole who could not speak proper Polish. Rochowski was supported by a small faction of German Poles, but most of his congregation petitioned the bishop to remove him and threatened to boycott pew rentals, the parish's main source of income, until their request was granted. Widely distributed anti-Rochowski circulars declared, "So long as the world exists a Pole will not become the brother of a German." The Rochowski affair had wider repercussions as Polish street laborers complained that Irish co-workers threatened them with violence for making trouble with Bishop Foley.[18]

Several unions reported serious internal conflicts over ethnicity and religion. The Street Railway Employees Association nearly split in two in January 1892 when eighty Protestants, members of the nativist and anti-Catholic Patriotic Sons of America, met as a separate faction to nominate an anti-Catholic slate in upcoming union elections. Bricklayers did split. A local independent union of 205 bricklayers which required U.S. citizenship as a condition of membership refused to join the 100-member local of the International Union because the International's policy of admitting foreigners took work away from them. The Tailors' Union debated whether its official documents should be printed in English only or in English and German. The English-speaking branch of the Socialist Labor party complained that the party's difficulties were all the fault of the Germans, but socialism was finally spreading "in spite of" the Germans.[19]

Serious intraclass conflict was not confined to such ethnic and religious hostilities. Several trades were torn by bitter rivalries between various subcraft groups. Shoecutters, for example, split off from the Boot and Shoeworkers Union in October 1891. Machine molders and regular ironmolders had a running feud, accusing each other of scabbing. Carpenters were divided between the Brotherhood and the Amalgamated Association; and despite the decline of the Knights of Labor, both the ironmolders and the shoeworkers reported continued discord with the Knights.[20]

The streetcar strike had demonstrated a widespread and deep commitment to the values of a culture of solidarity, values embraced by the Polish and German carshop workers and the Italian stonecutters. Yet it is clear that such values were far from universally honored by Detroit workers. Detroit workers in the early 1890s displayed high levels of both class solidarity and intraclass fragmentation.

This coexistence seems to fly in the face of many notions about class solidarity. Why would workers who respond positively enough to a class appeal to risk their own well-being and safety in behalf of other workers also display such high levels of antagonism to each other? Perhaps it is simply a matter of different individuals. It may be that if one disaggregated such categories as *streetcarmen* or *the metal trades*, he would find that the nativists who threatened the welfare of the Street Railway Union had not been active during the strike or that the ironmolders who battled police and built barricades across the streetcar tracks were not the same individuals who ignored the carshop laborers' appeals for solidarity. Lacking more than fragmentary data about individual behavior during these events, it is impossible to say for sure. But while I would suspect that such reasoning is not entirely inappropriate, I doubt that it is a sufficient explanation. The patterns of available evidence suggest in too many ways that the phenomena of solidarity and fragmentation coexisted, not only temporally but also in the behavior of many individuals. It was, for example, at the Detroit Stove Works, where striking carshop laborers futilely clashed with police as they appealed to the stoveworkers to join their shorter hours strike, that the wave of sympathy strikes for the streetcarmen had begun the week before.

The contradiction is real. To explain it, one must begin to develop a conceptual apparatus that provides some insight into how and why workers made decisions. What are the sources, at an individual level, of what one calls *solidarity* and *fragmentation*? What is it about the way people lived that would lead workers to practice class solidarity sometimes and to fight with fellow workers at other times? To answer those questions, one must know something of the multiple networks of association in which these workers functioned as they attempted to solve their basic problems.

Workers did not face problems as isolated individuals. People

Thomas Nast's cartoon illustrates the conflict between two systems of values appealing to the allegiance of workers in the Gilded Age. From *Harper's Weekly*, 20 May 1871.

draw their very understanding of what is problematic from relationships with other people. But Detroit's workers did not live in a society where most workers shared common values and traditions. Workers came from many different ethnic and cultural backgrounds. Their experiences as workers gave them some common ground, but when workers met across a gulf of widely diverging cultures, such common ground occupied only a narrow range of often very recent experience. Many workers also had much in common with co-religionists, fellow countrymen, lodge brothers, or political associates, and often such shared traits rested on a far older and more emotional heritage. Thus, in contrast to the English workers that Edward Thompson described, for whom tradition, culture, and class combined in a single cultural system, Detroit workers functioned simultaneously in multiple and often competing cultural systems.

By *cultural system*, I mean a mutually reinforcing set of values, informal personal associations, and formal institutions. Late nineteenth-century Detroit workers participated, often simultaneously, in three different kinds of such systems: native middle-class, multiclass ethnic, and a working-class subculture of opposition. The apparent contradictions in working-class behavior—such inconsistencies as the 1891 strike events—can be explained by examining how participation in these cultural systems offered workers alternative approaches to solving their problems while often making conflicting demands on them in return.

Participation in the native middle-class culture can mean both identification with the middle-class values of upward mobility and actual participation in middle-class associational life. As many critics of mobility studies have pointed out, it is necessary to be cautious in attributing significance to mobility. But workers like the machinist who told a State Bureau of Labor Statistics investigator in 1885 that anyone who had "full determination" and "let liquor alone" could get "fair renumeration" or "a small business for himself" or the papermaker who declared that "in most cases it is the employee's fault that he does not get along better" certainly had accepted a middle-class world view.[21]

Outside the workplace some workers functioned as part of the native middle-class cultural system, not only as aspirants but as full members. Native, British, and Canadian skilled workers lived in mixed lower middle-class neighborhoods intermingled with white-collar workers and small businesspeople. They belonged to middle-class churches, fraternal societies, and social clubs, occasionally even serving as officers in them.[22] Such participants in the associational life of the middle-class cultural system were certainly a minority of Detroit's workers, maybe even of the native Protestant workers; but the group included most prominent native-born, English-born, and Canadian-born union officials.[23]

Such trade unionists provided an extremely influential link between the cultural system of the native middle class and a separate working-class subculture of opposition.[24]

Taking shape as a separate and autonomous cultural system in the late 1870s and early 1880s, the working-class subculture of opposition defined itself in negative terms by opposition to great wealth, glaring social inequities, and unsatisfactory working conditions and positively by a commitment to cooperation, mutual trust, and mutual support among workers. It remained a subculture because it was not able to maintain a fully developed range of institutional counterparts to the other cultural systems. It was a goal or ideal for dissatisfied members of other cultural systems who in practice spent much of their lives outside the subculture. Beginning with informal patterns of comradeship and cooperation, Detroit labor organizers struggled throughout the late nineteenth century to formalize a moral code of solidarity in union work rules, to inculcate this code among the non-unionized working population, and to nurture it by creating an interlocking network of autonomous supporting institutions. At their peak in 1886, these workers' institutions had the makings of a counterculture: workers' social and athletic clubs, singing societies, dramatic companies, meeting halls, clubrooms, labor papers, producer and consumer cooperatives, an Independent Labor party, and a workers' militia.[25]

But this separate institutional structure proved to be very fragile. Other than trade unions, few of its institutions survived the demise of the Knights of Labor in the late 1880s. The collapse of much of its institutional structure affected the capacity of the subculture to continue to spread its moral code to the rapidly increasing numbers of newcomers or even to maintain the loyalty of its adherents in the face of more fully developed competing cultural systems.[26]

Labor activists found themselves competing not only against the native middle-class cultural system for workers' attention and allegiance but also against ethnic cultural systems with a far more varied associational life. Detroit's German community, for example, included a complete set of autonomous German-speaking associations paralleling virtually every kind of institution that existed elsewhere in Detroit: from factories, churches, newspapers, athletic clubs, theaters, political, and ward organizations to their own trade union federation and separate lodges of the Odd Fellows and Knights of Pythias. Other ethnic systems like the Polish and Irish had a similar range. Smaller ethnic communities like the Italians did not have the full complement of alternative institutions, but they nevertheless had their own fraternal lodges, mutual insurance societies, and restaurants.[27]

Such ethnic cultural systems were far from homogeneous. Detroit's Deutschtum, for example, included separate organizations for German Catholics, Protestants, Jews, and free thinkers, for natives of various provinces, for radicals and for conservatives. But these various parts of the community combined to form a stable, autonomous, and self-sufficient cultural system. Even the bitterest antagonists took the meaning of their conflicts from their common membership in the same cultural system. Radical working-class Freidenkers and upstanding Catholic burgers could understand their mutual outrage for each other while neither could deal effectively with their religious or ideological equivalents in other ethnic communities.

The working-class subculture of opposition had to be created in a way that competing ethnic cultural systems did not. Ethnic cultural systems rested on generations-old national traditions and national consciousness. Even if, as some scholars have argued, many immigrants had a weak sense of national consciousness until they confronted antagonism and discrimination in this country, such national consciousness was certainly latent and easily developed out of emotional commitments to language, religion, and daily cultural practices.[28] While the working-class subculture of opposition was also rooted to some degree in pre-modern work habits and social traditions, many of those traditions were imbedded in ethnic cultures. But in a multiethnic city, an effective class culture had to transcend ethnic loyalties; a working-class culture could not be too closely identified with any particular ethnic group if ethnic antagonisms were not to be aroused; loyalty to fellow workers had to be a higher value than loyalty to fellow countrymen or workers could be divided along ethnic lines.

Sometimes ethnic and class loyalties did not necessarily conflict. The various ethnic cultural systems all had some overtones of class as well as ethnic consciousness. Of the major immigrant groups, only the Canadians and the British were less than three-quarters working-class in 1890.[29] Ethnic and class consciousness might reinforce each other as well when immigrant workers fought native employers. The gang of Polish street laborers who arrived at the city's public works office armed with stones to confront a sewer contractor who had not paid them acted both as workers and as Poles.[30] For immigrant radicals, ethnic consciousness might also serve as a barrier to the assimilation of the propertied values of the native middle class. Most active socialists in late nineteenth-century Detroit, for example, were Germans. As they contested leadership of the German cultural community with German businessmen, they retained their German identities and interest in German affairs. So long as they maintained this "German-ness," they were also more likely to maintain the socialist faith than were their non-German comrades.[31]

Yet the abundant evidence of ethnic antagonism demonstrates that even when colored by class experiences, ethnic consciousness interfered with cooperation among workers of different ethnic groups. The same German radicals, for example, who opposed the German brewery owners who sponsored a cross-class German Day celebration, were habitually at odds with English-speaking working-class radicals.

Even more important, ethnic cultural systems represented barriers to class solidarity in another, probably more far-reaching, sense. They provided alternative avenues for organization, cooperation, and action to help solve workers' problems. The strength, range, dynamism, and persistence of the complex institutional lives of multiple cultural systems indicates how many people sought wider networks of association. But each cultural system offered a different strategy for dealing with problems. The ideal of native middle-class culture was individual social mobility, but even in achieving an individualist goal, people recognize the need for support. Participation in middle-class cultural, political, and religious organizations was in itself both an indication of successful mobility and a path to it. One of the most effective avenues of upward mobility for labor activists, for example, was the political system. While ethnic organization might also be directed toward upward mobility, it assumed a different strategy for achieving it: mutual support and cooperation within the ethnic community. And to the extent that ethnic organization was motivated by cultural resistance to middle-class assimilationist pressures, it also represented a form of resistance to the middle-class concept of mobility. Finally, the working-class subculture of opposition implicitly challenged the whole notion of individual mobility, assuming instead common action directed toward mutual defense and mutual improvement of the position of workers as a whole.

These alternatives, however, were not mutually exclusive. Many individuals functioned in two or even in all three cultural systems at the same time. These coexisting and overlapping memberships in competing cultural systems explain the original paradox of this paper: the apparently contradictory behavior of the city's workers during the 1891 strikes. If my characterization of multiple and coexisting cultural systems is accurate, the explanation should be clear: workers approached concrete situations with multiple loyalties and an awareness of the possibility of several courses of action. The daily realities of workers' lives involved many sources of antagonism which produced a latent reservoir of hostility to employers, to symbols of authority, to the social inequities of society. This submerged undercurrent of dissatisfaction could periodically reveal itself when such impressive displays of class solidarity as the streetcar strike or the 1886 shorter hour strikes tapped a much wider base of support than the small minority of organized workers. But the same experiences that created such class anger also taught workers the realities of the power relationships in society and the dangers of rash action. Covert forms of resistance such as the stint, the informal agreement to limit output to a specified level, usually involved relatively little risk. Strikes were far more severe tests of courage and the willingness to make sacrifices.

In contrast, personal mobility and ethnic solidarity did not demand the same risks. Often, instead of antagonistically confronting the middle or upper classes, these strategies involved mobilizing some members of those classes on one's own behalf. If such avenues had been closed, then perhaps class solidarity would have been the only feasible strategy for workers to pursue; but the evidence of working-class participation in, and even occasional leadership of, the organizations of the other cultural systems demonstrates that that was not the case. Moreover, the economic basis of class solidarity was often very weak. Detroit's economy was extremely diversified, with a variety of industries, a wide range of sizes and types of firms (even within industries), and many different management practices. The prospects and situations of different types of workers varied dramatically. Makers of hand-rolled cigars faced a 15 percent decline in daily wages in Detroit in the 1880s, while steam fitters' wages rose by 40 percent. Cordwaining was a dying craft; electricians had an exciting new occupation. The actual experiences, grievances, and security of various categories of workers varied widely.[32]

It is not surprising, then, that workers usually tried to avoid strikes. Some grievances could be solved in other ways; even when that was not true, the risks of action might outweigh the possible benefits. But when opportunities to express underlying anger presented themselves, particularly if the situation suggested that the risks of doing so were not excessive, many people eagerly seized the chance.

The streetcar strike was exactly such a situation. With more than fifty streetcars dispersed throughout the city and dozens of separate crowds at various crossings, intersections, and carbarns, the opportunities for action were numerous and widespread while the chances of arrest were relatively small. Equally important, the obvious displeasure of some business and political leaders with the streetcar company may have seemed like a license to act. Those arrested did not face harsh penalties; judges dropped many charges and typically fined the remainder only $5 (no jail sentence).[33] As the displays of solidarity escalated from crowd action to sympathy strikes, the risks also escalated somewhat; but by then it was clear that support for the strike was overwhelming. The streetcar workers were endorsed by several prominent business and political figures, and the mayor's actions clearly suggested his desire for at least a compromise settlement. The sympathy strikes were usually quick affairs, lasting a few hours. Given the atmosphere in the city, no employer risked more serious conflict by discharging such sympathy strikers.

In contrast, the workers at the carshops and stove factories faced a much more difficult decision when some of their fellow workers raised the shorter hours cry. In both industries workers had fought management for more than a decade over a variety of in-plant issues, generally with little success. The shorter hours strike of 1886 had been totally defeated. The managers of these factories had consistently taken punitive actions against strikers and union activists—as the Michigan Car Company did again to those who struck in 1891. The quick strikes in sympathy with the streetcar workers had been ignored by the companies, but many workers must have recognized that mass shorter hours strikes would involve an extended struggle with a poor chance of victory. Under such circumstances, English-speaking skilled workers, even those who had just supported the streetcar workers, must have found it tempting to respond to a crowd of unskilled Germans and Poles not as fellow workers worthy of the obligations of the code of solidarity but as hot-headed foreigners who did not understand the principles of American workmen. If workers could analyze the situation according to the symbols of their ethnic cultural systems rather than those of the subculture of opposition, the dilemma of choosing between moral violations or a losing strike could be avoided.

The stonecutters similarly fell back on ethnic identity to retreat from the difficulties of earlier class action. The stonecutters' multiethnic work force had begun their strike with an impressive display of the power of the code of solidarity. They shut down all the major building sites in the city that had employed stonecutters; and when the Italian strikebreakers were brought in, they too, honored the code. Class solidarity had demonstrated its power. But the stonecutters faced a well-organized group of building contractors who maintained a united front, refusing to bargain or negotiate. As the strike entered its sixth week, many stonecutters began to doubt whether it made sense to continue for the extra quarter a day they had demanded from their employers. If they went back to work at the old wage, they would lose nothing but the wages they had already lost by striking. Why add to the damage by continuing the strike? It was in response to these arguments that stonecutters divided along ethnic lines. For the British trade union veterans, such an ending had symbolic consequences that outweighed monetary considerations—the overriding issue for them was the employers' refusal to recognize the union by engaging in negotiations. Such refusal violated traditions of artisan rights, as well as the traditional Rights of Englishmen, a national, as well as a class, tradition. The stonecutters of other nationalities, without the same tradition, were not persuaded. When the British workers insisted on continuing the strike, the other stonecutters abandoned class organization; and their ethnic systems provided an escape route: go to the employers as national groups, blame the British for the trouble, and humbly ask for the old jobs back.[34]

Thus, the 1891 strikes demonstrate that workers functioned simultaneously in competing cultural systems which offered alternative strategies for solving the problems they faced. These cultural systems rested on both the ideas and traditions workers brought with them to the industrial city and the patterns of industrial and urban development. Following Detroit workers from the late nineteenth into the early twentieth century, one finds that as such factors as technology, work methods, residential patterns, hiring practices, and political organization changed, cultural systems also changed, but the competition between alternative cultural systems continued.

Competing cultural systems influenced workers in most late nineteenth-century American cities; and, as in Detroit, the social changes of the early twentieth century did not erase the contradiction. Even the most consistent advocates of class solidarity in the twentieth century have recognized the existence of such competing loyalties within their constituencies. Despite assimilationist biases in the leadership of both organizations, both the Socialist and Communist parties, for example, allowed for the organization of autonomous foreign language federations within the parties. Twentieth-century American working-class life has been characterized by multiple, and often separate, cultural histories.

The implications of this for a theory of class relevant to the history of the American working class are far-reaching. If the American working class has been made out of a series of class fragments, and if it has lacked a single universal working-class culture, then class formation and development have proceeded as much in spite of traditions as because of them. Yet there has been a working class. The definition of class, then, must emphasize questions of power relationships and common interests, not cultural traditions which have often been too diverse to form a common ground.

Notes

1. E. P. Thompson, *The Making of the English Working Class* (New York: Random House, Vintage Edition, 1963), 9.
2. Detroit *Evening News*, April 3, 1891; April 17, 18, 20, and 21, 1891.
3. Ibid., April 17, 20, 21, 1891.
4. *Eleventh Census*, 1890, vol. 1, pt. 2, 664.
5. *Labor Day Review*, 1892, Joseph Labadie Collection, University of Michigan, Ann Arbor; *Detroit Sunday News*, July 26, 1891. The *News* estimated union membership at 10,000, but the total of membership statistics cited in the *Labor Day Review* is under 8,000. Some small unions were not included in the *Review*.
6. These events are described in my dissertation, "Solidarity and Fragmentation: Working People and Class Consciousness in Detroit, 1877–1895" (Michigan State University, 1979), chap. 6, "1886: May to September."
7. Ibid., chaps. 7–8.
8. *Evening News*, April 18, 20; May 3, 13, 15, 20, 25, 29; and June 7, 14, 19, 21, 23, 24, 1890.
9. Ibid., April 22, 1891.
10. Ibid., April 23, 24, 25, 27, 1891.
11. Melvin Holli, *Reform in Detroit* (New York: Oxford University Press, 1969), 38–41, emphasizes the poor service and middle-class, as well as working-class, support for the strike.
12. *Evening News*, April 22, 23, 24, 1891.
13. Ibid., April 25, 26, 1891.
14. Ibid., April 27, 1891.
15. Ibid., April 28, 29, 30; May 1; and June 12, 1891.
16. Ibid., April 27, 28, 29, 30, 1891.
17. Ibid., June 16, 21; and July 1, 2, 5, 6, 8, 1891.
18. Ibid., December 13, 1890; July 20, 1891; February 17, 1892; June 13, 15, 17, 18, 20, 21, 24, 26; and July 13, 19, 1891.
19. Ibid., January 10, 1892; January 31, 1892; October 25, 1891; and November 27, 1891.
20. Ibid., October 9, 1891; May 10, 1891; May 17, 20, 1891; June 7, 1891; and September 6, 20, 1891.
21. *Michigan State Bureau of Labor Statistics Annual Report*, 1886, especially pp. 158, 160. Workers interviewed for this report were located primarily, but not exclusively, in Wayne County. The location of any particular informant cannot be determined from the *Report*. For a thorough discussion of the problem of underlying assumptions in mobility studies see James A. Henretta, "The Study of Social Mobility: Ideological As-

sumptions and Conceptual Bias," *Labor History* 18 (Spring 1977): 165–78. For data on social mobility in Detroit see JoEllen Vinyard, *The Irish on the Urban Frontier: Nineteenth Century Detroit, 1850–1880* (New York: Arno Press, 1976).

22. For residency patterns see Olivier Zunz, "The Organization of the American City in the Late Nineteenth Century: Ethnic Structure and Spatial Arrangement in Detroit," *Journal of Urban History* 3 (August 1977): pp. 453–57, 461–64; and Zunz, "The Changing Face of Inequality," ms. in preparation. For working-class participation in middle-class cultural and fraternal organizations see the *Evening News*, October 31, 1890; January 10, 1892; and January 18, 1891; and city directories.

23. An article on local labor leaders in the *Detroit Sunday News* on September 6, 1891, for example, included the names of seventeen labor leaders currently employed in political patronage jobs.

24. David Montgomery, *Beyond Equality* (New York: Random House, Vintage Edition, 1972) presents a similar argument for labor leaders of the 1860s and 1870s.

25. Oestreicher, "Solidarity and Fragmentation," chap. 5.

26. Ibid., chaps. 7–8.

27. *Evening News*, October 5, December 21, 1890; February 1, April 26, May 2, 1891; *Irish World and American Industrial Vindicator*, St. Patrick's Day Supplement, 1877; July 15, 1882; Vinyard, *The Irish on the Urban Frontier*; and Holli, *Reform in Detroit*, especially pp. 9–16.

28. Oscar Handlin, *Boston's Immigrants: A Study in Acculturation* (New York: Atheneum, 1975), for example.

29. *Eleventh Census*, 1890, vol. 1, pt. 2, 664–65.

30. *Evening News*, January 2, 1891.

31. Oestreicher, "Solidarity and Fragmentation," chap. 4; *Evening News*, October 5, 6, 12, 1890; and February 1, 1891.

32. *Michigan State Bureau of Labor Statistics Report*, 1884 (Lansing: 1884), pp. 84–87; "Men Who Make Your Cigars," clipping in "Detroit Labor Leaders" File, Labadie Collection; *Labor Day Review*, 1892; Oestreicher, "Solidarity and Fragmentation," chaps. 1–2.

33. *Evening News*, April 24, 1891.

34. Ibid., June 21, 1891; and July 1, 2, 6, 8, 1891.

Industrialization and the Transformation of Work

2.

Skilled Workers and Industrialization: Chicago's German Cabinetmakers and Machinists, 1880–1900

John B. Jentz

TWO images of industrialization have predominated in the writing of American labor history—the concentration of production into monopolistic firms operating huge factories, as in meatpacking and steel, and the proliferation of sweatshops where small bosses tyrannized over a comparative few workers operating rather simple machines, as in the manufacture of clothing and cigars. Within both types of industry, historians have seen the subdivision of tasks formerly performed wholly by skilled artisans, the application of machines to production, and the employment of large numbers of unskilled workers. It is commonly assumed that these processes worked their way through all branches of manufacturing during the industrial revolution, though at different speeds. The new labor history of the 1960s and 1970s has described in detail how industrialization broke down both handicraft production and the social world of the artisan, while also imposing a new set of ethical values that made workers more amenable to the routinized tasks of the mechanized factory.[1]

Yet neither the old nor the new labor history has adequately described the changes in industries like furniture making and the metal trades, both of which were still organized in numerous, often medium-sized plants during the Gilded Age and the Progressive Era. In 1900 Chicago had more than 100 furniture factories averaging about seventy workers per firm and almost 450 machine shops and foundries averaging almost fifty workers each.[2] Of course, the averages hide the existence of several large plants; but, nevertheless, these industries had a different structure than meat-packing, for example, in which twenty-eight firms in 1900 averaged almost 900 workers each. Significantly, both Chicago's furniture industry and metal trades expanded considerably in the last two decades of the nineteenth century—the metal trades explosively—while keeping the relatively modest scale of their firms. It was precisely in industries like these where so many of the renowned German craftsmen worked: in 1900 more than 20 percent of Chicago's skilled Germans in manufacturing were in the metal and furniture industries.[3]

Industrialization nonetheless affected these two industries differently. Employing large numbers of traditional craft workers, the furniture industry underwent the kind of mechanization, division of labor, and diminution of artisanal skills which are familiar to students of nineteenth-century industrialization. In contrast, the metal trades created a new world of skilled work distinctive to the industrial era. For metalworkers, industrialization did not simply mean the destruction of handicraft production. It also required the learning of new skills, including the tending of highly sophisticated modern machines. These new industrial skills in the metal trades were attractive to German workers, and particularly to their children, a fact documented by Hartmut Keil in this volume.[4] The tendency of the immigrants' children to move into the metal trades conforms with a finding of Bruce Laurie, Theodore Hershberg, and George Alter that by 1880 the second-generation German workers in Philadelphia were starting to move away from the crafts of their fathers into the more dynamic and expansive producer goods industries, although these scholars did not analyze the individual industries in detail.[5] A close look at the German workers in Chicago's furniture and metal industries will help to illuminate this occupational shift. This analysis of both the creation of new industrial skills and industries with medium-sized plants will also enrich the concept of industrialization.

Cabinetmakers and the furniture industry

IN the second half of the nineteenth century, Chicago possessed attractive advantages for the manufacture of furniture, and they were aggressively exploited by local entrepreneurs. As the largest wholesale lumber market in the world, Chicago offered ready access to raw materials, while its constantly increasing and largely immigrant work force provided an attractive labor pool of both skilled and unskilled workers. In turn, the explosive population growth of the city created a dynamic local retail market for furniture. In 1880, when furniture ranked fifth among Chicago's industries, the Chicago furniture manufacturers were experiencing an unprecedented boom that increased their work force by more than five times over that of 1870 and which also helped them make a product second only in value to that of New York City's furniture makers. It is small wonder that in 1880 Chicago's furniture industry was mechanized to a relatively high degree: more than half its furniture plants had steam power, for example, compared to only 12 percent of furniture establishments in the older manufacturing center of Philadelphia. This mechanization also promoted industrial concentration: in the same year 15 percent of the local firms, all with more than fifty workers, employed almost half of the industry's work force.[6]

Despite these advances, however, the full effects of mechanization in Chicago's furniture industry had not yet been felt. Skilled workers were still prominent in the production process, even in the larger plants. A special report on wages in the 1880 census used four of the bigger Chicago furniture firms as examples. Of these, one had no "labor-saving machinery," another used "little improved machinery," the third employed "several machines," and the fourth had "introduced" machinery.[7] This last firm employed foremen, cabinetmakers, turners, carvers, varnishers, finishers, engineers, machine hands, packers, and laborers. Of these, only the laborers and packers were unskilled; the rest were either skilled or semiskilled. The special status of the cabinetmakers was exemplified by their being the only workers in the plant required to use part of their wages to buy tools. During a chairmakers' strike at Bruschke and Company in 1880, thirty-six chairmakers returned to the job—but only to get their tools, after which they left again. Such skilled furniture workers were not simply a tiny elite within the furniture factories: during this same strike, seventy-five chairmakers walked out of Zangerle and Company, almost half of the manufacturer's work force.[8] Thus in 1880 the craft production methods and traditions of an earlier era were still represented by strong contingents of skilled workers in Chicago's furniture plants.

Germans were strongly represented among these skilled workers; they made up almost 40 percent of the more than 3,000 cabinetmakers and upholsterers in the city, according to the 1880 census. If second-generation Germans are added, the trade was over half German.[9] A sample of the German cabinetmakers in 1880 shows that almost two-thirds were heads of household; their median age was slightly over thirty (see Table 1 and Figure 1). Thus the trade still permitted the typical German cabinetmaker to

Table 1. Selected statistics for German cabinetmakers and all German workers employed in the furniture industry: Chicago, 1880 and 1900

	Cabinet-makers		Furniture industry*	
	1880	1900	1880	1900
% all German workers	2.1	1.5	4.2	2.9
% head of household	65.5	86.2	50.0	71.4
% second generation	34.5	17.2	35.6	28.6
N	58	29†	118	56

*Includes cabinetmakers.
†See note 18.

Fig. 1. Age structure of German cabinetmakers and all German workers employed in the furniture industry: Chicago, 1880 and 1900*

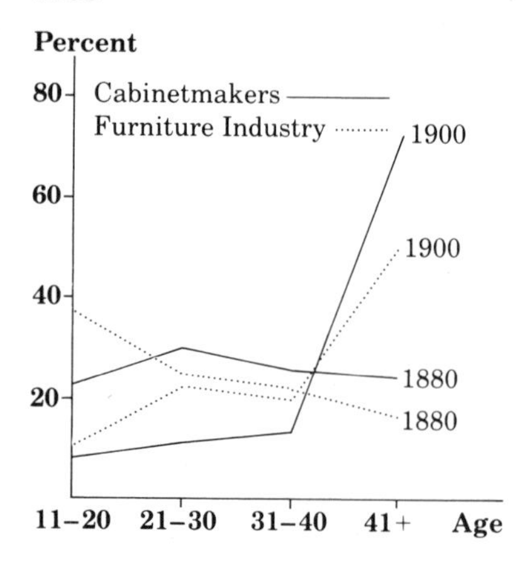

*Source: Samples of the Federal Manuscript Population Censuses of Chicago for 1880 and 1900, taken by the Chicago Project, University of Munich.

head a household and presumably support a family. Moreover, younger men were entering the trade, as evidenced by the fact that more than a third of the cabinetmakers in the sample were second-generation German. Obviously, the trade still had enough advantages to attract them, even though they were likely to have had more vocational options than their immigrant fathers. The industry also had enough attractions to draw workers from non-woodworking backgrounds. In a study of the woodworkers in an 1880 furniture manufacturing district on the Northwest Side, the Chicago Project found not only that a high proportion were second-generation immigrants—more than two-fifths, in fact—but also that the immigrant fathers of these second-generation workers came from a variety of backgrounds: almost 40 percent were the sons of laborers; almost a third had fathers in the woodworking trades; and the fathers of the rest ranged from millers and tanners to teamsters and blacksmiths.[10] Part of the attractiveness of the furniture factories in this district was that they offered year-round work, in contrast to other large local employers like tanneries and lumberyards. They also hired unskilled labor: 27 percent of a sample of the work force of the whole industry was composed of unskilled laborers, some of whom were children.[11] Chicago's furniture industry was, therefore, attracting both unskilled and skilled Germans during its boom period in the late 1870s and early 1880s.

Neither the furniture industry nor its German work force was the same in 1900. By then the industry's share of all employed Germans had shrunk from 2.9 percent in 1880 to 1.6 percent. The age structure of German furniture workers and cabinetmakers also became significantly older, as Figure 1 indicates. The change in the age structure of the cabinetmakers is most striking, with more than two-thirds past forty in 1900; the same trend is also apparent in the sample of the German work force in the entire industry. In addition, the proportion of second-generation German cabinetmakers had declined significantly, showing that Chicago's German cabinetmakers were not training replacements in the new generation to the degree they had done in the past. Among those Germans employed in the furniture industry, it is notable that none in the sample held unskilled positions, compared to over one-quarter in 1880. In 1900 Chicago's furniture factories were not pulling their unskilled workers from the German population; additionally, those Germans already in the industry were either cabinetmakers, upholsterers, or finishers, all skilled positions. Obviously, the furniture industry was shrinking in significance for the German workers of Chicago, even while a reduced number held higher positions within it.

The changing character of German immigration, the relative decline of Chicago's furniture industry, and particularly the mechanization of production help explain the changes in Chicago's German furniture workers. According to the population census, the number of cabinetmakers and upholsterers in Chicago increased from 3,149 in 1880 to 3,763 in 1900, not a large gain compared to the growth of the city. However, their ethnic composition changed significantly. Whereas more than half of all cabinetmakers and upholsterers in Chicago in 1880 were first- and second-generation German, by 1900 they had dropped to 38 percent of the trade; Scandinavians, the next largest group, made up 30 percent, an increase of ten percentage points from 1880.[12] As the proportion of Scandinavians increased among skilled furniture workers in Chicago, German immigration itself changed its character. Immigrants increasingly came from the more rural and less developed German Northeast, rather than from the West and South, which had previously supplied such a high proportion.[13] Thus, the highpoint of German immigration to the United States in the 1880s did not supply the furniture industry with skilled workers to the degree that it had done. In addition, Chicago's furniture industry was past the period of its most dynamic growth, the 1870s and 1880s, when hosts of new workers were pulled into the plants. In 1900 the furniture work force was hardly bigger than in 1890, and it grew modestly in the first decade of this century. By 1900, therefore, the industry was not creating jobs as it once had, and new immigrants and the young had to look to other industries for work.

At the same time Chicago's furniture manufacturers continued to mechanize their industry so that by 1900 the mean capitalization per firm had more than quadrupled over that of 1880.[14] What was happening inside the plants was probably revealed in the *Thirteenth Annual Report* (1898) of the U.S. Commissioner of Labor. Analyzing the contemporary machine production of twelve common maple chairs in 1897, the commissioner found the following kinds of workmen involved in a typical plant: sawyers, sawyers' helpers, rounders, turners, chuckers, laborers, joiners, gluers, planers, shapers, seat finishers, finishers' helpers, varnishers, a foreman, an engineer, a fireman, and a watchman.[15] In contrast, his example of hand production of the same chairs involved four different kinds of workers, all of them skilled. By 1900 there was probably little room for the skilled chairmakers with their own tools who struck at Bruschke and Company in 1880; the term *chairmaker*, in fact, did not appear on the commissioner's list of the workers involved in the machine production of the chairs. A special report on occupations published as part of the 1900 census even classified chairmakers in a second grade of skill and defined a cabinetmaker in a factory as one who "puts together and finishes the finest kinds of work," obviously out of pieces made by others.[16] In addition, the pay of cabinetmakers was modest indeed around 1900: in the first decade of the new century Chicago's cabinetmakers made less per hour than machine woodworkers in planing mills.[17] Lowered demand and reward for their work certainly helps explain the relative decline of Chicago's German cabinetmakers, who were most likely concentrating more and more in the remaining custom shops and smaller factories. Their story is not unique, however; other German crafts, like blacksmithing and tailoring, similarly shrank as their work forces aged and handicraft production and traditional skills declined in the face of industrialization.[18]

Machinists, machine shops, and foundries

THE history of Chicago's machine shops and foundries and their workers was notably different from that of the furniture industry. In 1880 their total value of product was the fourth largest in the city. By 1900 they increased their value of product to the point where they challenged clothing for second place. In the same twenty-year period, their work force grew greatly, from 4,887 to 20,641. Just as important, the number of machine shops and foundries expanded almost as fast as the work force, more than tripling over the two decades to total almost 450 in 1900; and this growth continued. In contrast, the number of furniture manufacturers in the city actually declined slightly during the same period, and the work force grew modestly in comparison, from just over 4,800 to slightly over 7,800. Mechanization made the producer goods from the foundries and machine shops especially important in the economy, helping account for the expansion of this industrial sector when overall employment in manufacturing in Chicago was contracting relative to other economic sectors like trade and commerce.[19]

Despite their tremendous expansion, Chicago's machine shops and foundries maintained a generally modest scale and a high proportion of skilled workers. The average number of workers per firm rose only from thirty-seven to forty-seven between 1880 and 1900, but the average hides a wide range in scale and a significant degree of concentration. Only 6 percent of all machine shops in 1880 employed more than half the workers. On the other hand, smaller plants with from six to fifty workers constituted over two-thirds of all the businesses.[20] Notably, however, the smaller to moderately sized firms did not necessarily have more antiquated production methods compared to the biggest businesses. A special report of the 1880 census on the nation's production of engines and boilers found that medium-sized machine shops with fifty to 100 workers had the most capital invested per operative, compared to larger and smaller firms.[21] The importance and technical advance of the medium-sized firms was mainly a consequence of the variety, sophistication, and distinctive character of so many metal products. Steam engines were often built for a local or regional market in which custom orders were still significant; or the iron work for a particular building was made to order, as were the engines for a large ship or the boiler for a special factory. Other metal products, while perhaps not custom ordered, were so distinctive and frequently new—for example, parts for elevators or special kinds of valves—that only a few firms made them. Such a variety of products aided the existence of medium-sized specialized businesses while at the same time requiring them to employ the latest technology.

Making engines, boilers, valves, tools, or castings of an infinite variety, machine shops and foundries employed an unusual proportion of skilled workers, many of whose tasks were never part of traditional artisanal production because the machines used and the products produced were new to the industrial era. The 1880 census report on engines and boilers calculated that firms making steam engines and boilers typically had work forces in which at least half the workers were skilled, and it cited one big engine and boiler plant in the West with a work force of 20 percent laborers and 74 percent machinists, vise hands, molders, core makers, boilermakers, blacksmiths, and woodworkers. The foundries within such establishments employed the least skilled labor, whereas the machine shops used the most. The census report also describes the high degree of skill, intelligence, and even managerial ability required by some metal workers:

In forging large work [for marine engines] there are a few men who are not only highly skilled but are invested with duties which require such mental qualities that many men would not be capable of fulfilling them. The master-hammer man on such work must not only act correctly and with a skilled perception of the conditions involved, but he must act quickly; high qualities of executive decision are involved which may not be apparent from a mere description of the processes. . . . [For example,] forgings of many tons' weight are handled by a body of men (with no power appliances except a crane and a hammer) in the only practicable way, namely, by balancing. . . . From six to a dozen laborers turn the wheel and shift the work in accordance with the sign motions of the hammerman.

This description may also provide some justification for the report's contention that even unskilled labor in machine shops and foundries required more of workers than other unskilled labor.[22] The character of the work helps explain why—except for the skilled in the very smallest shops—both skilled and unskilled machine shop workers were paid more in 1880 than the comparable furniture workers.[23] The report's analysis also supports David Montgomery's assertion that the knowledge of production processes and training involved in such work gave the skilled workers a real influence in the daily operation of the shops and promoted an independence that was conducive to union organization.[24]

Machinists were one of the largest groups of skilled workers in machine shops and foundries, but they also worked in many other industries, a fact that complicates analysis of their work. The special report of the 1900 census on occupations found machinists working in fifteen different industries producing agricultural implements, railroad cars, chemicals, cigars, clothing, liquor, flour, metal castings and machines, iron and steel, paper, books and newspapers, ships, shoes, leather, and wagons and carriages. The fact that machinists worked in so many different branches of manufacturing is an indication of the broadening scope of mechanization and of the expansion of an occupation associated with it. Nevertheless, the same report found that machinists were of two basic types—those who maintained and repaired machines in any kind of industry and machinists who made metal products. The report divided the machinists who worked with metal into a first and a second class, with a man of the first class being "a skilled worker who thoroughly understands the use of metal-working machinery (such as the lathe, planer, and other machines), as well as fitting and work at the bench with hand tools." Second-class machinists were "able to run only a single machine or perhaps do a little bench work," and the census classified them under machine hands or tenders.[25] The machinists surveyed in the population census—and thus in the samples of the Chicago Project—were skilled workers; but their titles do not clearly specify the industry in which they worked. Nevertheless, the importance of the metalworking machinists justifies analyzing them in the context of one of their largest employers, machine shops and foundries.

The character of a machinist's work helped make it attractive to second-generation Germans who could find employment in an expanding occupation and enjoy the good pay and status of a skilled worker. Thus it is not surprising that machinists increased as a percentage of employed Germans between 1880 and 1900, as Table 2 and Figure 2 show. Just as noteworthy, almost half of the

Table 2. Selected statistics for German machinists, cabinetmakers, and blacksmiths: Chicago, 1880 and 1900

	Machinists		Cabinetmakers		Blacksmiths	
	1880	1900	1880	1900	1880	1900
% all German workers	1.8	4.0	2.1	1.5	1.3	0.7
% head of household	67.3	48.7	65.5	86.2	75.7	78.6
% second generation	28.6	46.2	34.5	17.2	18.9	21.4
N	49	78	58	29	37	14*

*See note 18.

Fig. 2. Age structure of German machinists and cabinetmakers: Chicago, 1880 and 1900*

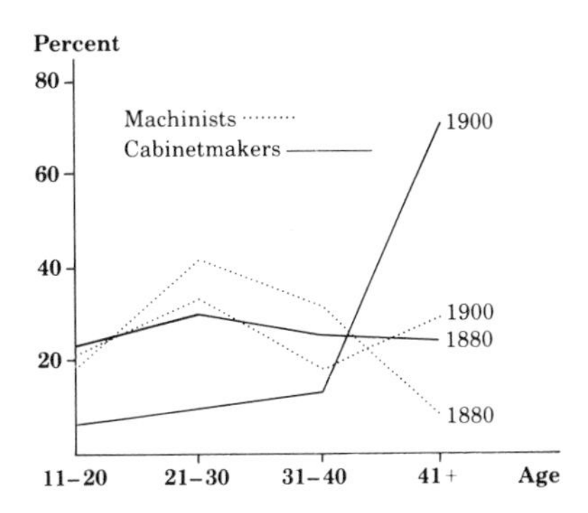

*Source: Samples of the Federal Manuscript Population Censuses of Chicago for 1880 and 1900, taken by the Chicago Project, University of Munich.

machinists in 1900 were second-generation German-Americans, in sharp contrast to less than a fifth of the cabinetmakers. The age structures of the two groups were also distinctly different: about one-fourth of the machinists were more than forty years old in 1900; in contrast, more than two-thirds of the cabinetmakers were in the post-forty age group. Obviously, the machinist trade, much more than cabinetmaking, was attracting younger Germans, particularly of the second generation. The attractions of being a machinist were reflected in the published census figures: first- and second-generation Germans increased their share of the occupation in Chicago from 25 to 28 percent between 1880 and 1900; this growth took place even as the total number of machinists grew from 2,751 to 16,690.[26] However, work as a machinist was not just a matter of good pay in an expanding occupation: work in Chicago's metal shops required a degree of skill and experience with particular machines that may have been available only in Chicago and a few other advanced industrial centers, making such metalworking positions difficult for recent immigrants to obtain. Second-generation Germans, on the other hand, were more likely to have access to the necessary mechanical training. They were also in a position to learn of the opportunities in Chicago's dynamic metal trades.

The metal trades were not, however, uniformly prosperous and attractive for German skilled workers. Some of the same processes taking place in the furniture industry were evident in the metal trades as well. German blacksmiths, for example, were more similar to German cabinetmakers than to German machinists, as Table 2 illustrates. Like the cabinetmakers, blacksmiths declined as a proportion of employed Germans between 1880 and 1900, and both the smiths and the cabinetmakers were substantially older at the turn of the century. Irrespective of industry, the traditional skills for which the Germans were famous became less valuable in the late nineteenth century as the process of industrialization subdivided and mechanized their tasks. But this very process also created new skills and added functions to old trades, as in the case of the machinists, making them attractive to second-generation Germans, whose presence in industrial Chicago and other cities gave them an advantage in acquiring the skills.

Conclusion

THE findings in this essay raise significant questions about the nature of skilled work during America's industrial revolution and about the place of German skilled workers in the economy. Were there, for example, other industries like the machine shops and foundries requiring a high proportion of skilled workers during the Gilded Age? Did the machine shops continue to need so many skilled workers after the turn of the century, and did the medium-sized shops remain so significant in the field? In other words, were the German machinists and the character of their work in the late nineteenth century idiosyncratic or representative of longer-lasting trends? The previously noted article by Bruce Laurie, Theodore Hershberg, and George Alter indicates the latter since these scholars found that by 1880 in Philadelphia the second-generation Germans were increasingly leaving the traditional crafts of their fathers for more lucrative work in dynamic producer goods industries like engine manufacture and boilermaking. The findings here help confirm this trend for Chicago and take it up to 1900, but an issue remains—whether other new industries, like electrical products or automobiles, created similar new skills and had work forces comparable to machine shops and foundries. If, for example, the arguments made here about the machinists have a broader significance, then Chicago's electrical workers in 1900 should have shown a high representation of second-generation immigrants; and in fact they did.[27] Similar questions should be addressed in regard to workers in the new automobile and bicycle industries, which in 1900 were too small to appear significantly in our sample. Further, the structures of the new industries need to be studied and analyzed more deeply in order to see whether they, like the machine shops and foundries, created modern industrial skills. The development of metal work also needs to be pursued further into the twentieth century before substantial conclusions about the nature of modern skilled industrial work can be drawn. Such further research will not only broaden our understanding of industrialization and the changes it brought in the character of work, it will also provide a basis for interpreting the history of America's modern ethnic working class and particularly the relations between the old and the new immigrants.

Notes

1. For a review of the new labor history, see David Brody, "The Old Labor History and the New: In Search of an American Working Class," *Labor History* 20 (Winter 1979): 111–26.

2. These and the following figures on Chicago's industries are from Bureau of the Census, *U.S. Twelfth Census*, 1900, vol. 7: *Manufactures*, pt. 1, 180–86.

3. Hartmut Keil, "The German Working Class of Chicago in 1900,"

Table 6, p. 12 (Paper presented at the Chicago Project Conference on Working-Class Immigrants in Industrializing Chicago, 1850–1920, Newberry Library and the Chicago Historical Society, October 9–12, 1981). As used here, the term *metal trades* does not include the iron and steel industry and its workers.

4. Hartmut Keil, "Chicago's German Working Class in 1900," in *German Workers in Industrial Chicago, 1850–1910: A Comparative Perspective*, ed. Hartmut Keil and John B. Jentz (DeKalb, Ill.: Northern Illinois University Press, 1983), Table 3, p. 28.

5. Bruce Laurie, Theodore Hershberg, and George Alter, "Immigrants and Industry: The Philadelphia Experience, 1850–1880," in *Philadelphia: Work, Space, Family, and Group Experience in the Nineteenth Century: Essays toward an Interdisciplinary History of the City*, ed. Theodore Hershberg (Oxford: Oxford University Press, 1981), 109–16.

6. The calculations of the growth of the furniture work force and the concentration in the industry are based on the firms in the federal manuscript manufacturing censuses for 1870 and 1880, minus all shops with five or fewer workers. These smaller producers were undercounted and may legitimately be considered craft shops instead of manufacturers. In 1870, 20 out of 54 firms were thus eliminated, in 1880, 34 out of 154. The calculation on percentage of plants with steam is a conservative figure, since the shops with 5 workers or less were included to make a proper comparison with Philadelphia: the Laurie article apparently included them in its calculation. Without the small shops, 70 percent of the Chicago furniture manufacturers used steam power in 1880; Laurie et al., p. 97; Bessie Louise Pierce, *A History of Chicago*, vol. 3 (New York: Alfred A. Knopf, 1957), 534; A. T. Andreas, *History of Chicago*, vol. 3 (Chicago: A. T. Andreas, 1886), 734.

7. Bureau of the Census, *U.S. Tenth Census*, 1880, vol. 20: *Report on the Statistics of Wages in Manufacturing Industries*, 438–40.

8. *Chicagoer Arbeiter-Zeitung*, March 20 and March 24, 1880; U.S. 1880 manuscript manufacturing census for Chicago, National Archives microfilm.

9. Bureau of the Census, *U.S. Tenth Census*, 1880, vol. 1: *Population*, 870. The proportion of second-generation cabinetmakers was calculated by using a ratio derived from the sample of the 1880 population census taken by the Chicago Project.

10. The Chicago Project studied all 237 furniture workers in three census enumeration districts just north of Chicago Avenue on the Northwest Side. Over 90 percent of the furniture workers were first- or second-generation German.

11. The proportion of unskilled workers was determined by use of the categories of the Philadelphia Social History Project's occupational dictionary. Of the unskilled workers in the sample, 44 percent were under eighteen years of age.

12. The percentage of first- and second-generation Scandinavians was calculated using the ratio of first- and second-generation German cabinetmakers in the Chicago Project's sample of the 1880 manuscript population census.

13. Wolfgang Köllmann and Peter Marschalck, "German Emigration to the United States," *Perspectives in American History* 7 (1973): 499–554.

14. According to the federal manufacturing censuses, in 1880 the average capitalization of Chicago's furniture plants was $17,159. In 1900, it was $70,303.

15. U.S. Department of Labor, *Thirteenth Annual Report of the Commissioner of Labor, 1898. Hand and Machine Labor*, vol. 2, (Washington, D.C., 1899), 116–17.

16. Bureau of the Census, *U.S. Twelfth Census*, 1900, *Employees and Wages*, "Special Reports," Davis R. Dewey (Washington, D.C., 1903), 1177, 1180.

17. U.S. Department of Labor, *History of Wages in the United States from Colonial Times to 1928* (Washington, D.C.: Government Printing Office, 1934), 451, 471.

18. In this volume Hartmut Keil has enumerated the declining trades in greater detail. In the Chicago Project's sample of the 1900 manuscript population census, the German cabinetmakers, tailors, blacksmiths, carpenters, and brewers had similar age structures. The similarities of the trends in these traditional German trades helps substantiate the figures for individual occupations, some of which appeared in only small samples with high margins of error.

19. Bureau of the Census, *U.S. Tenth Census*, 1880, vol. 2: *Manufactures*, 391–93; *U.S. Twelfth Census*, 1900, vol. 7: *Manufactures*, pt. 1, 180–86. In 1910 there were 669 machine shops and foundries in Chicago, with 35,010 wage earners (Bureau of the Census, *U.S. Thirteenth Census* [1910], vol. 9: *Manufactures*, 296).

20. These figures on Chicago's machine shops are taken from a Chicago Project analysis of the federal manuscript manufacturing census for 1880.

21. Bureau of the Census, *U.S. Tenth Census*, 1880, vol. 22: *Report on Power and Machinery Used in Manufacturing Industries*, "Report on the Manufactures of Engines and Boilers, with a Review of the Principal Types of Engines for Manufacturing Purposes," by Charles H. Fitch, 2.

22. Ibid., pp. 7, 10–11, 18–19.

23. Based on the Chicago Project's analysis of the 1880 federal manuscript manufacturing census.

24. David Montgomery, "Workers' Control of Machine Production in the Nineteenth Century," in *Workers' Control in America: Studies in the History of Work, Technology, and Labor Struggles*, ed. David Montgomery (Cambridge: At the University Press, 1980), 9–31.

25. Bureau of the Census, *U.S. Twelfth Census*, 1900, *Employees and Wages*, "Special Reports," Davis R. Dewey (Washington, D.C., 1903), 1183, 1218.

26. Bureau of the Census, *U.S. Tenth Census*, 1880, vol. 1: *Population*, 870; *U.S. Twelfth Census*, 1900, vol. 2: *Population*, 517–21. The second-generation machinists in 1880 were estimated using a ratio derived from the Chicago Project's sample of machinists for that year.

27. In the Chicago Project's sample of the 1900 population census there appeared fifty-five men involved in electrical work, most of them called "electricians," but the census does not distinguish which industries they worked in. Of these fifty-five men, twenty-seven were second-generation immigrants.

Ethnicity in the Formation of the Chicago Carpenters Union: 1855–1890

Thomas J. Suhrbur

ETHNICITY had a pervasive impact on the formation of the Chicago carpenters union. Since a majority of the city's carpenters throughout the late nineteenth century were foreign-born, union organizers faced a monumental problem in forging class solidarity within a highly heterogeneous work force where language, neighborhood, politics, and culture divided the nationalities and periodically disrupted the unions. English-speaking carpenters virtually monopolized the leadership, and Germans—the largest ethnic group among the carpenters—often complained that they were being misused by their leaders. Nativists, in turn, blamed low wages on the immigrants who flooded the city with cheap labor; and the competition for jobs, especially during economic slumps, encouraged ethnocentrism.

Ethnicity thus seemed to be an insurmountable obstacle facing union carpenters attempting to organize their trade, and the observation in 1880 by P. H. "Pinhead" McCarthy, a carpenter, seemed a simple statement of the obvious: "'Trade unionism could never amount to much in a city like Chicago, the tradesmen of which had come from all parts of the world, precluding the possibility of bringing them together with any degree of confidence in each other.'"[1] Nevertheless, by 1891 the carpenters had successfully organized the most powerful, class-conscious union in Chicago. This essay will explain how they did it.

The phenomenal growth of Chicago following the Civil War increased the city's population tenfold, from 109,206 in 1860 to 1,099,805 in 1890.[2] Although thousands of rural Americans flocked to the city, Europeans accounted for nearly half of its entire population in 1870; they were more than half of Chicago's working class throughout the period from 1870 to 1890. Chicago's growth spurred an extended building boom, which created a demand for construction workers, many of them foreign-born. Among the carpenters, as Table 1 shows, the percentage of foreign-born far exceeded that in Chicago's working-class population as a whole.

The Germans constituted the largest ethnic minority among Chicago carpenters, even outnumbering the native-born Americans in 1870 (see Table 2). However, despite their numerical strength, the Germans never really dominated the leadership of the city's union. Instead, the English-speaking alliance of native-born American, Irish, and British carpenters outnumbered the Germans and controlled the United Brotherhood of Carpenters and the Knights of Labor.[3] In the late nineteenth century, the Scandinavians became increasingly important. Second only to the Germans by 1890, they built one of the largest locals in the city, Local 181. French Canadians, though few in number—only 374 in 1890—represented a tightly knit ethnic minority and in 1886 organized a French-speaking branch in Local 21. The Bohemian and Polish carpenters, who were closely associated with the Germans, were not separately enumerated in the 1890 census. However, the first Bohemian branch was organized in 1881, whereas the few Polish carpenters in Chicago prior to 1890 apparently joined German locals.[4]

1855–1873

THE earliest attempt to organize a carpenters union in the building trades occurred among the German workers who had fled the political repression following the collapse of the 1848 Revolution in Germany. Organized in 1855, the Schreiner-Verein may have served as a bargaining agent, but it was also a social club and debating society. With only a few carpenters organized in Chicago, its function was probably more political and social than economic.[5] The earliest multi-ethnic carpenters unions in Chicago were the Carpenters and Joiners Protective Union, formed in 1863, and the Carpenters and Joiners Consolidated Union (also referred to as the United Order), founded in 1872. Both of these organizations had very low initiation fees and dues. Hoping to secure higher wages and shorter hours, thousands of Chicago carpenters flocked to these unions. The United Order, which was organized in late January following the Chicago Fire, had between

Table 1. Proportions of native- and foreign-born among Chicago's population, work force, and carpenters, 1870 and 1890*

	1870		1890	
	Native (%)	Foreign (%)	Native (%)	Foreign (%)
Total population	52	48	59	41
Persons employed	35	65	45	55
Carpenters	21	79	30	70

*Based on figures reported in or calculated from Bessie Pierce, *A History of Chicago*, vol. 3 (Chicago: University of Chicago Press, 1957), 516; Bureau of the Census, *Ninth U.S. Census*, vol. 1, *The Statistics of the Population of the U.S.* (Washington, D.C.: Government Printing Office, 1872), 782; and Bureau of the Census, *Eleventh U.S. Census*, pt. 2, *Report of the Population of the U.S.* (Washington D.C.: Government Printing Office, 1897), 650.

Table 2. Nativity among Chicago's carpenters compared to the total employed, 1870 and 1890*

	1870		1890	
	Employed	Carpenters	Employed	Carpenters
White native	39,775 (53.2%)	1,315 (21.1%)	198,883 (43.4%)	5,885 (29.3%)
"Colored" native	—	—	8,080 (1.8%)	37 (0.2%)
Germany	25,778 (22.8%)	1,824 (29.3%)	85,429 (18.6%)	4,739 (23.6%)
Ireland	22,337 (19.8%)	756 (12.2%)	41,336 (9%)	934 (4.6%)
Great Britain[†]	7,754 (6.4%)	607 (9.8%)	22,328 (4.9%)	1,423 (7.1%)
Scandinavia[‡]	7,213 (6.4%)	797 (12.8%)	44,503 (9.7%)	4,228 (21%)
British America[§]	4,065 (3.6%)	571 (9.2%)	19,443 (3.7%)	1,275 (6.4%)[‖]
Others	6,820 (6%)	340 (5.5%)	44,663 (9.8%)	1,561 (7.8%)

*Based on figures from the Bureau of the Census, Ninth U.S. Census, vol. 1, *The Statistics of the Population of the U.S.* (Washington, D.C.: Government Printing Office, 1872), 782; and Bureau of the Census, *Eleventh U.S. Census*, pt. 2, *Report of the Population of the U.S.* (Washington, D.C.: Government Printing Office, 1897), 650–51.

[†] Includes England, Scotland, and Wales.

[‡] Includes Norway, Sweden, and Denmark.

[§] Are almost entirely English and French-speaking Canadians.

[‖] French-Canadians represented 374 (1.9 percent) of Chicago's carpenters in 1890.

3,000 and 4,000 members by May, a membership total which was not achieved again until the late 1880s. Despite a brief but intense flurry of organizing, these unions rapidly disintegrated following unsuccessful strikes in 1867 and 1872.[6] The economic depressions in 1867 and 1873 which followed these unsuccessful strikes completed the destruction of the unions. By June 1868, the *Workingman's Advocate* reported that the Carpenters and Joiners

Protective Union was "drooping." By October 1870, the union had dissolved and, except for a Scandinavian and German branch, the United Order suffered a similar fate in early 1873.[7] There would not be another multi-ethnic carpenters union in Chicago until 1878.

Though the carpenters failed in these early efforts to establish a permanent organization in Chicago, several valuable strategies emerged which contributed to the ultimate success of the union movement. One of these was the uniform minimum wage, first adopted in the May 1872 strike. Since it was based on the assumption that class, rather than ethnicity or skills, should be the basis upon which the union should be organized, the uniform wage was one of the most important weapons against ethnic divisions among the carpenters. It also served as a major step toward undermining the differential wages of the piecework system used by the employers to divide and conquer.[8] Piecework was a major factor in the failure of these early unions. As the largest and most diversified craft in the building trades, carpentry was most susceptible to specialization. Large industrial construction allowed employers to subdivide jobs into specialized tasks and subcontract to the semiskilled at piece rates rather than hire skilled carpenters. By greatly expanding the labor pool, employers were able to lower wages and undermine union efforts to improve the carpenters' condition.[9] The 1867 and 1872 strikes were defeated after a large number of "out-of-town" pieceworkers—including many immigrants—flooded the local labor market and replaced striking carpenters. These early efforts at organization also demonstrated conclusively the necessity of a benefit system. While the large English-speaking branches of the United Order collapsed in late 1872, the Scandinavian branch remained intact because of its union benefits. According to the *Workingman's Advocate*, "Out of the general wreck, they preserved their organization and up to the present it is in good working order. This may be from the fact that in the beginning they introduced the beneficial feature which is a tower of strength to any organization which adopts it."[10]

The English Amalgamated Society of Carpenters was an even better example of the beneficial union. Organized in Chicago in 1870, it was the first carpenters union in the city to combine protective and beneficial features. Composed almost exclusively of British immigrants, it relied on ethnic cohesiveness and its ties to its financially solid parent in England. Though the Amalgamated never spread among Americans, its beneficial features provided an important example for American unions. In 1872 the *Workingman's Advocate* carried an article comparing American to English trade unions. Was it not strange, asked the *Advocate*, that English carpenters in the Amalgamated could control their trade with fewer than 10,000 members in the entire country, while the Chicago carpenters union, with over 3,000 members, exercised less influence in the trade than the Amalgamated branch in the smallest English city? The reason for this, explained the *Advocate*, was the Americans' "laxity of discipline" and corresponding unwillingness to pay high dues for a beneficial system. "A union with a membership of a dozen true and tried men, alive to its requirements, who are always on hand in time of danger, is superior to one with a thousand, who are union men just so long as the tide carries them along."[11] The Amalgamated Society's benefit system was substantial. In a letter to the *Chicago Tribune*, Fred Tregay stated that by paying 35 cents weekly dues, a member was entitled to $4.20 per week sick benefits for the first twenty-six weeks and $2.10 thereafter, $700 accident benefits, tool insurance, and a superannuation for retirement of $2.80 per week until death.[12] These benefits bonded the membership, insuring its success. Because of its conservatism, the small Amalgamated Society was often politically isolated from the activist multi-ethnic carpenters unions, but it was the oldest surviving Chicago carpenters union when it finally affiliated with the United Brotherhood in 1924.[13]

Despite the growing conviction that a benefit system was necessary, the majority of Chicago carpenters did not abandon the purely protective union until after the Strike of 1877. Since a beneficial union was more expensive to join than the purely protective union, the low-paid carpenter would have to be convinced of the likelihood that the union would survive before he would risk investing his meager resources in its benefit system. Even in the 1880s, when the Chicago carpenters union officially adopted the principle of a beneficial system, it was very slow to implement benefits. Once the national benefit system was expanded, however, the union was greatly strengthened. Thus the strike benefit was crucial in the struggle from 1886 through 1890 that established an eight-hour day. By the 1890s the benefit system had become so important that the Chicago District Council and the United Brotherhood General Executive Board could use the threat of cutting off benefits to discipline recalcitrant ethnic locals and maintain unity.[14]

1873–1887

AFTER the disintegration of the American-led union in 1873, the *Workingman's Advocate* reported that the Germans attempted to reorganize a "carpenters union of all nationalities."[15] As the call to organize was ignored, the *Advocate* sarcastically remarked: "The American carpenters in Chicago do not consider it necessary to receive good wages and their 'bosses' appreciate their good sense so highly so that they are giving them just enough to keep body and soul together . . . and some are willing to work for even less than that."[16] The German initiative vis-à-vis American carpenters reflected the fact that many of them were Socialists and, consequently, very class-conscious and aggressive trade unionists.

The Germans' commitment to unionism resulted from their socialist perspective. Stressing that the structure of society, rather than individual failure or bad laws, was responsible for the unemployment and poverty of the depression, they called for all workers, regardless of nationality, to organize themselves as a class.[17] The strength of the German unionists was reinforced by their working-class neighborhood associations and ethnic cultural institutions. In January 1876, for example, the *Advocate* commented on the "five or six magnificent halls" built by the Germans. "The Germans have their lyceums, their reading rooms, their lecture and music halls and their gymnasiums where they can meet in social concourse, discuss the political situation, enjoy an intellectual treat and improve their physical condition without money and without practice."[18] Such ethnic neighborhood association encouraged discussion of social issues and facilitated the organization of unions.

The Strike of 1877 was the catalyst that revived Chicago unionism. In response to wage cutting and layoffs during the depression, unorganized railroad workers spontaneously launched a strike which spread across the United States and was soon joined by other trades. In Chicago from July 23 to 26, thousands of working people, predominantly foreign-born, thronged the streets, forcibly closing factories and inaugurating a general strike for a 20 percent wage increase and the eight-hour day. The Socialists provided what little formal leadership there was. In this strike, all the powers of the state, backed by the business community and the middle class, were used to suppress the workers. Chicago police, state militia, and eventually the U.S. Army battled strikers in the streets of Chicago, resulting in at least 30 deaths and 200 wounded.[19] Out of the crucible of 1877 the labor movement in Chicago was reborn. The 1872 defeat and the long depression had killed the old-style carpenter unionism, which had relied largely on the enthusiasm of the moment and lacked a set of stable institutions. After 1877 came a new type of organization, one which combined protective and benevolent features, reflected the growing influence of Chicago's ethnic groups, and signified a new class-conscious unionism inspired by the Socialist critique of capitalist society.

At first, however, the protective and benefit functions of modern unions were represented by two separate organizations of carpenters—the Carpenters and Joiners Benevolent Association ("Benevolents"), formed in 1878, and the Carpenters and Joiners Protective and Benevolent Association ("Protectives"), formed in 1879.[20] In the beginning the growth of these two rivals was slow. The recovery of the building industry from the depression of the early 1870s was not accomplished until 1880; but as the building industry began to prosper, so the competition between the two rival unions became more fierce. By the spring of 1882 the Benevolents outnumbered the Protectives three to one, and the costs of competition were apparent to all. In addition, the inability of the local organizations to control the job market made unity, and even international organization, necessary. For example, French Canadians made annual migrations to Chicago in the spring and worked for rates from 20 to 40 percent lower than the local wage.[21] If Chicago's carpenters were to control their own industry, they had to organize across international frontiers and unify at home.

The Chicago carpenters union turned to the Brotherhood of Carpenters and Joiners for aid. The Brotherhood originated largely out of the efforts of P. J. McGuire, then in St. Louis, to prevent migrant carpenters from other cities from undermining recent gains made by the local unions. In May 1881, a provisional committee headed by McGuire, a prominent Socialist Labor party organizer, petitioned in the first issue of its journal, *The Carpenter*, for unionists across the nation to establish a national brotherhood. The Chicago unions seized the opportunity to host the first national convention, which was subsequently held in August 1881.[22] Under McGuire's leadership, the Brotherhood had an international perspective, advocating cooperation with the European labor movement, especially the English Amalgamated Society; and *The Carpenter* provided a forum for national and international communication. In addition, the Brotherhood organized locals in Canada.[23]

Locally, with McGuire serving as a mediator, the two rival organizations merged into a single body—Local 21—in May 1882. Trying to accommodate ethnic differences, Local 21 allowed the various nationalities to organize ethnic branches. Only a few disgruntled members of the Protective Association failed to join Lo-

Having a significant German membership, the Carpenters and Joiners had become one of the strongest unions in Chicago, as illustrated by their presence in the Labor Day parade of 1897. From *Labor Day Illustrated*, published by the Chicago Building Trades Council. Reproduced with permission of the Chicago Historical Society (ICHi-17258).

cal 21; and when the Brotherhood refused to issue more than one charter per city, these dissidents affiliated with the Knights of Labor.[24] Thus by mid-1882 the Chicago carpenters had apparently developed an organization with the potential to meet their needs. The history of the next few years proved its inadequacy, however, in part because it did not end the ethnic divisions among the carpenters but in fact added one: the leadership of the Brotherhood was overwhelmingly Anglo-Irish while the local membership was more heavily German, Bohemian, Scandinavian, and French. Even more important, many active unionists in Chicago were Germans and Bohemians, whose socialism and ethnic cultures divided them from the Brotherhood's leaders.

The temperance question, for example, was a major source of ethnic tension in the early 1880s between the English-speaking leadership and the German and Bohemian carpenters. J. P. Goodwin, Thomas Doran, and other Anglo-Irish leaders strongly supported the movement to reduce alcoholic consumption through taxation and limiting the licensing of saloons. According to Thomas Doran, an executive council officer in Local 21, the principal cause of the workers' failure to realize their political and economic goals was the "life destroying poisonous alcohol" of the "saloon influence."[25] German and Bohemian carpenters did not agree. They continued to enjoy drinking in their beer gardens and militantly opposed any measures that might infringe on the personal liberty to drink. The German Socialist carpenters clearly understood that the essence of workers' problems was self-discipline, a problem which could not be solved by external controls, even those imposed by the union, such as the prohibition of the sale of liquor at union meetings or picnics. The Americans, they said, needed to learn how to control themselves, "to drink moderately and [to learn] a real temperance instead of howling hell and cold water" like evangelical preachers, such as Dwight Moody and Sam Jones, popular in Chicago of this period.[26]

Another source of conflict between these two groups was the issue of cooperatives. Although most carpenter leaders endorsed the notion that a "cooperative society" would eventually replace the competitive wage system, they differed as to the strategy for achieving this goal. A large group, particularly those coming from the Anglo-American tradition of self-help and self-reliance, thought that the cooperation exemplified in existing working-class institutions was part of an inevitable and gradual evolutionary movement of society toward a new age. This large group of carpenters deprecated class conflict, as embodied in strikes and boycotts, and talk of revolution, while their enthusiasm was aroused by projects for cooperative production. In 1885, Chicago Local 21 proposed that all building trade unions inaugurate a joint stock association to purchase land on the outskirts of the city in order to build low-cost homes for workingmen. Stock shares would be taken up by the various unions of the city; once capitalized, jobs would be provided for unemployed building tradesmen; and most important, profits would go to those who did the work, not to the capitalist middleman.[27] Though this project soon failed, the Anglo-Americans were undaunted; and they were particularly attracted to the Knights of Labor, a universal organization of all "producers" which billed itself as a single great cooperative society. The mostly German and Bohemian Socialists advocated a different version of cooperation. They criticized the formation of cooperative corporations as a diversion of the workers' energy and scarce resources and foresaw that the lack of access to capital and business expertise, combined with the ferocious competition of the market, would doom cooperative production. Instead, they advocated a political solution by which an independent labor party would gain power and secure government aid in establishing a "cooperative state."[28]

The socialism of the Germans and Bohemians was reinforced

by their experience, which was distinctly different from that of the Anglo-Americans. In the late nineteenth century, Chicago Germans generally received lower wages than did American-born co-workers.[29] Within the large ethnic German labor pool, there were numerous recent arrivals who were desperate for work. Contractors, especially Germans, could more readily exploit such a work force. As a German carpenter explained: "German contractors are especially stingy and always try to get greenhands for low wages. This causes low wages for German carpenters in general. German contractors use the low wages to be cheaper than Americans and take a lot of building away from them."[30] Moreover, German carpenters tended to suffer higher unemployment than the Americans, and their sense of being exploited was exacerbated by ethnic problems within the union.[31] American carpenters would criticize Germans for undermining wage rates by working for less. Conversely, Germans often expressed grave dissatisfaction about being "nothing but oppressed dues payers," shunned from participation in union affairs.[32] Thus, throughout these early years of the Brotherhood, German locals remained a vocal dissenting minority within the District Council.

The system of organizing distinct ethnic branches could not contain these differences, although it met real needs. By permitting separate ethnic organizations at the local neighborhood level, the branch system allowed the union to foster a strong class-conscious camaraderie among its members through a variety of social functions, such as picnics, parades, and dances. In addition, the ethnically organized branches were more democratic in that they permitted the members of the group to participate more fully in meetings held in their own language. In fact, the branch system was originally designed to solve the problem of conducting business among many different language groups. As W. T. Henderson, a Chicago carpenter organizer, stated: "We have German, French, Bohemian, Scandinavian, and English-speaking members. Now how can all these different tongues ventilate before one body? It would take you a week to go through a meeting."[33] Each local branch, which met once a week, sent delegates to the central executive council to coordinate the citywide effort. The weekly meetings of the executive council were usually conducted in English and German. Constitutions, executive council minutes, and other documents were published in several languages. Nevertheless, although the branch system reduced language problems, it did not fully eliminate them. First of all, many of the English branches had large numbers of non-English speaking members; and at times, meetings of the branches had to be conducted in more than one language. In addition, many of the less prominent ethnic groups, like the French Canadians, did not have branch organizations. Most important, the branch system ended up institutionalizing ethnic division instead of overcoming it. Strong on the local level, Local 21 was weak at the top.

The political differences, ethnic divisions, and organizational weaknesses of Local 21 became apparent after a disastrous strike in 1884. Encouraged by a successful bricklayers strike the previous year, Local 21 decided to demand higher wages. Despite an apparent victory in May, the combination of non-union pieceworkers, a nationwide depression, and the financial bankruptcy of the union left the union in disarray by early 1885. As the union retreated, ethnic and political differences deepened; and the branch system disintegrated. On June 7, the twelve branches of Local 21 were consolidated into an English-speaking branch and a German-speaking branch which included the Bohemians, but this did not satisfy the dissidents. A large portion of the Bohemians and Germans were attracted to the newly organized anarchist unions, which opposed electoral politics and the reformist wage and hour orientation of the English-speaking leadership. Instead, they advocated revolutionary violence to bring about a "free society" of autonomous cooperatives.[34] The radical Bohemian carpenters, who were closely aligned to the Germans, were the first to secede. Even though the Brotherhood had begun to issue more than one charter per city in 1884, the Bohemian branch was denied a separate charter until it paid a share of the huge debt accumulated by Local 21.[35] Consequently, in 1885 the Bohemians severed all ties to the Brotherhood and the moderate Trades and Labor Assembly, which had roots in the late 1870s, and affiliated as an independent with the anarchist Central Labor Union (CLU) founded in 1884. The Germans left next. In February 1885, *The Carpenter* reported that the Germans also were offered a separate local, but "they have dodged a settlement and under the lead of a few anarchists they want to run on their own hook." Several months later *The Carpenter* noted that "advices reach us that in Chicago there is an armed organization of a dozen carpenters of the Anarchist stripe."[36] By this time the branch system in Chicago was destroyed and the executive council of Local 21 dissolved. In September 1885, the CLU and the Trades Assembly held separate labor day demonstrations. At the Trades Assembly parade only fifty members of the Brotherhood showed up. The CLU, on the other hand, fielded thriving German and Bohemian unions.[37]

Despite these divisions, there was a proliferation of carpenters unions in Chicago after 1885, and membership rose sharply in response to the agitation for the eight-hour day. Carpenters of all nationalities flocked to the Knights of Labor. By 1886, the Knights had five carpenter local assemblies, one of which, Local Assembly 9266, was German. The British Amalgamated Society prospered too, and a radical English-speaking organization called the Progressive Carpenters and Joiners was also started. As for the Brotherhood, it was crippled by defections. Its former German branches formed two separate organizations: the Independent Carpenters and Joiners and the International Society of Carpenters and Joiners, which grew to six branches by late 1886. Bohemian Branch 5 started the Bohemian Carpenters Union with two locals. All of these organizations affiliated with the radical CLU. Except for the addition of the French-speaking third branch in 1886, Brotherhood Local 21 made no gains until after Haymarket.[38] In the months preceding May 1886, the CLU had surpassed the Trades Assembly in membership. The CLU members were almost all German and Bohemian. A survey of Chicago anarchists found that 62.9 percent were German and 15.5 percent Bohemian.[39] The anarchist phenomenon was significant in that a quarter of all identifiable Chicago anarchists were carpenters. More important, these radical Germans and Bohemians were crucial in rebuilding the Brotherhood in Chicago after Haymarket.

1887–1891

THE fate of the Brotherhood changed rapidly after 1886, and the mass defection of Germans and Bohemians in 1885 lasted only two years. The resurgence of the Brotherhood was due in part to a change in the English-speaking leadership of Local 21. The 1884 failure had discredited older leaders such as Doran and McGindley; and during the organizing efforts for the eight-hour day in 1886, a new leadership emerged which included such figures as James "Dad" Brennock, Robert Swallow, and William Kliver. These men were more attuned to the radicalism of the mid-1880s and were more willing to enter into alliances with the German-Bohemian Socialists. While still maintaining their membership in the Brotherhood, some of these leaders, including "Dad" Brennock, Robert Swallow, and J. J. Linehan, had joined the mixed assemblies of the Knights after the 1884 debacle, attracted by the Knights' idea of the unity of all trades and skills. In 1886, this radical leadership devised several strategies for cooperation with the German and Bohemian anarchists. Though they disapproved of anarchism, they strongly supported the defense efforts for the condemned Haymarket prisoners. They also actively participated in the efforts to create an independent political party. The United Labor Party (ULP) campaigned in the city election during the fall of 1886 and the spring of 1887, garnering one-third of the mayoral vote in the latter election. In all, thirty-six delegates from the German, Bohemian, and various English-speaking carpenters unions attended the ULP's founding convention—more, by far, than from any other trade.[40]

Finally, the eight-hour day was an ideal strategy for unifying the carpenters. For many, it simply meant less daily work, more leisure, and time for "personal improvement." Some viewed the eight-hour day as the panacea for the chronic unemployment that plagued the trade. For others it had a much more radical connotation. P. J. McGuire, in calling it "the Lexington of the coming revolution," said that "it would go on until the capitalists were driven from power."[41] From this viewpoint, the ten-hour day was the cornerstone of oppression, since it physically and emotionally exhausted the workers and discouraged them from improving their condition. The eight-hour day was a first step by the working class to strengthen their organizations and change their condition.

With the eight-hour day as a unifying issue and a radical leadership in control, the Brotherhood reasserted its prominent position in Chicago by early 1887. The independent locals, many of them former branches of Local 21, affiliated with the Brotherhood, which, contrary to former policy, issued multiple charters in one city. Previously under the branch system, the Brotherhood suffered large-scale defections among German and Bohemian branches that could no longer abide by the conservative politics of Local 21's leaders. In withdrawing from Local 21, they also left the Brotherhood. The multiple charter system took into account the fragile unity among Chicago carpenters, allowing each local political autonomy and national affiliations. However serious these divisions, they need not have threatened the affiliation with the national body.[42] Thus, four branches of the German International Society and the Independent Carpenters joined en masse as Locals 240 through 244. The Bohemian Carpenters, branches 1 and 2, became Locals 54 and 256 respectively. Large numbers of Knights, including German Local Assembly 9266, joined the Brotherhood as Local 73 out of dissatisfaction with the Knights' leadership and centralized organization, which had proven itself incapable of addressing the peculiar problems in its affiliated trades. Finally, large numbers of new local organizations were organized in response to the agitation for the eight-hour day.

By 1888, the United Brotherhood had twenty-four locals in Chicago and was the unquestionable leader of Chicago carpenter unionism.[43]

The consolidation movement involving Local 1 was a landmark in the carpenters' history. Except when there were too few carpenters to warrant a separate organization, nationality had been the basis by which Chicago carpenters had organized. In early 1889, Locals 240, 241, 243, 244, 284, 291, the Progressive Carpenters Union, and a number of important leaders from Knights Assembly 6570 merged with Local 1. As a result, Local 1 became the largest local in Chicago, containing almost half of the Brotherhood's membership in the city.[44] Although the majority of Local 1 membership was German, its leaders, including Brennock, Linehan, and James O'Connell, were English-speaking. The local belonged to the Central Labor Union as well as the Trades Assembly. Depicted in the *Chicago Tribune* as "the radical" union, Local 1 was the most militant progressive carpenters local in Chicago.[45] In building a political coalition of German- and English-speaking radicals, it was the first carpenter organization to successfully transcend ethnic differences. From its inception, Local 1 was a leader among Chicago carpenters, and its prominence was indicative of the extent to which the Germans and socialism had been integrated into the union.

The spirit of class solidarity following Haymarket inspired the carpenters to a momentous victory in the Strike of 1890. This struggle was unparalleled in magnitude and organization by any other previous event in the union's history. The strike began in April 1890, when 6,000 men, representing the overwhelming majority of Chicago's skilled carpenters, struck for the eight-hour day, higher wages, and union recognition in the form of a permanent joint arbitration committee.

It was not finally settled until the following March, when their employers, the Carpenters and Builders' Association, conceded to these terms in a historic two-year agreement. During the strike, class solidarity was significantly broadened. Initially, the powerful bricklayers union agreed to strike in sympathy with the carpenters on jobs rehiring non-union men. Later a building trades council was organized which, through the tactic of the sympathy strike, provided the additional leverage to win the strike.

The carpenters also relied heavily on the national strike benefit to sustain local members, and the Brotherhood assisted in stemming the influx of non-union men into the city. The *Chicago Tribune* described it this way:

> The strikers have a system that works like a charm. There is not a point of any consequence in the United States from which any man can start with a kit of tools without notice being sent at once to Chicago. In a radius of sixty-five miles around Chicago members of carpenters' unions are stationed at every town along every railroad, and no carpenter can pass them without having the fact wired to the strike committee. In this way the local men can meet every new arrival and most cases capture him for the union.[46]

The fight against strikebreakers was also waged effectively in the city. Squads of strikers visited job sites, intimidating scabs and "losing" their tools. The contractors claimed that thirty-five buildings were raided by strikers and that ninety-seven men were physically attacked during the strike.

Mayor DeWitt C. Cregier and the police were reluctant to act. Following the strong showing of the United Labor party in 1887, Cregier had courted the labor vote in his mayoral campaign. None of the fifty-six carpenters arrested was convicted.[47] Finally, the union mobilized support among progressive middle-class reformers—Clarence Darrow and Henry Demarest Lloyd were two—who raised money and gave speeches exhorting the union's cause. Faced with such a powerful combination and concerned with construction tie-ups that threatened the upcoming World's Fair, the business community gave little support to the contractors. Under these circumstances, the contractors signed the agreement. The victory could hardly have been more complete and, throughout the 1890s, the carpenters remained the most powerful union in Chicago.

By 1891 the carpenters, with between 6,000 and 8,000 men, had organized the largest union in Chicago. Not only did they secure the eight-hour day, higher wages, and better working conditions for their members, but the carpenters held prominent positions in the Building Trades Council and the Trades Assembly. They actively supported organizing efforts by other trades and engaged in radical labor politics. This success demonstrated that class solidarity had to take precedence over ethnic considerations if the workers were to improve their condition.

The carpenters had devised a host of strategies to achieve these goals. The uniform wage, the benefit system, the eight-hour day, the multi-local city organization, and the establishment of an international trade union (the United Brotherhood) contributed, each in its own way, to their success. While the carpenter leadership was mostly English-speaking, union success owed much to other forces. It was the foreign-born, primarily the English, who taught the Americans the necessity of the benefit system. The radical Germans taught the futility of cooperative experiments and reaffirmed the need for the militant general strike following the early American-led defeats in 1867 and 1872. German and Bohemian Socialists were staunch advocates of working-class solidarity and had engaged in independent labor politics pointing to the importance of seeking political solutions to labor problems. The traditions of democracy, cooperation, and the unity of skilled and unskilled as exemplified by the Knights of Labor enabled the Anglo-American carpenters to establish a common ground with the foreign-born Socialists to organize a multi-ethnic union. Ethnicity created many obstacles for organizing the Chicago carpenters; but, in the final analysis, these hindrances were far outweighed by the positive contributions of various ethnic groups to the creation of the Chicago union.

Notes

1. Quoted by L. A. O'Donnell, "From Limerick to the Golden Gate: Odyssey of an Irish Carpenter," *Studies* (Ireland) (Spring–Summer 1979), pp. 76–91.

2. The U.S. Bureau of the Census reported the total population of Chicago from 1860 through 1890 as follows:

1860	109,206
1870	306,605
1880	503,305
1890	1,099,805

3. These men held the following leadership positions in the union: Edward Owen, president, Carpenters and Joiners Protective Union (1872); J. P. Goodwin, president, Carpenters and Joiners Protective and Benevolent Association (1881); Thomas Doran, president, Carpenters and Joiners Benevolent Association (1881); J. P. McGindley, third president, United Brotherhood of Carpenters; James "Dad" Brennock, business agent, officer, and considered one of the founders of the carpenter union in Chicago; J. J. Linehan, president of the Trade and Labor Assembly (1893); J. G. Cogswell and O. E. Woodbury, both presidents of the Chicago District Council.

4. A survey of delegates to the United Carpenters Council, the central body for Chicago carpenters in 1888, reveals Polish surnames in the German locals. Moreover, several Polish carpenters' names also appear among the largely German anarchist carpenters. With much of Poland under Prussian and Austrian control, it would seem that many Polish immigrants probably joined German locals. The sparse available evidence supports this notion. See the *Roll Book of Delegates of the United Carpenters Council*, Chicago District Council of Carpenters, Chicago, Illinois.

5. Bessie Louise Pierce, *A History of Chicago*, vol. 2 (Chicago: University of Chicago Press, 1957), 150–89.

6. For a detailed account of the history of these unions, see ms. in preparation by Richard Schneirov and Thomas Suhrbur.

7. *Workingman's Advocate*, June 13, 1868, p. 3; October 8, 1870, p. 3; and June 5, 1873, p. 3.

8. According to George Vest, president of the Chicago District Council, Chicago is to this day one of the few cities to have a uniform minimum wage: carpenters, drywallers, insulation workers, lathers, tile layers, and others receive a uniform minimum regardless of the levels of their skills or specialization. Other cities have a multicard system, with two or more wage scales paid depending on the categories of work.

9. Robert A. Christie, *Empire in Wood: A History of the Carpenters' Union* (Ithaca, N.Y.: Cornell University Press, 1956), 27–28.

10. *Workingman's Advocate*, June 5, 1872, p. 3.

11. Ibid., September 28, 1872, p. 2; August 13, 1970, p. 3.

12. *Chicago Tribune*, February 16, 1875, p. 7.

13. Chicago District Council of Carpenters, Mill and Factory Workers, *Souvenir of Dedication of Carpenters Council Building* (Chicago, Illinois: 12 East Erie Street, November 7, 1925).

14. *Chicago District Council Proceedings*, 1891–1893.

15. *Workingman's Advocate*, February 14, 1874, p. 3.

16. Ibid., August 22, 1874, p. 3.

17. One German carpenter from Chicago stated: "Unions are not only obliged to discuss wage questions, but it is their duty to fight for the independence from the capitalist class. As soon as they reach this aim they will abolish the existing wage system and replace it with a cooperative society—a just distribution of the yield of work" (*The Carpenter*, April 1882, p. 7).

18. *Workingman's Advocate*, January 8, 1876, p. 3.

19. Richard Schneirov, "Chicago's Great Upheaval of 1877," *Chicago History*, Spring, 1980, pp. 2–17.

20. Before 1881, the *Chicago Tribune* referred to these unions with a confusing array of names, including the C. and J. Consolidated Union, C. and J. Association, C. and J. Protective and Aid League and the United C. and J. Union. (See *Chicago Tribune*, June 17, 1878, p. 5; September 12, 1879, p. 8; September 13, 1879, p. 8; September 15, 1879, p. 8.) By 1881, the *Tribune* used the names referred to in the text. (See the *Chicago Tribune*, January 20, 1881, p. 8; January 29, 1881, p. 8.) This confusion probably stems from both the tentative nature of their existence in these early years and their secretiveness.

21. *The Progressive Age*, March 28, 1881, p. 1. (A Chicago labor newspaper sponsored by the Trades and Labor Assembly.)

22. *The Carpenter*, May–August 1881.

23. In 1891, my great-grandfather, Paul Hudon, a French Canadian in Local 21, was commissioned by P. J. McGuire to organize in the Montreal area. He spent several months in Canada with Local 134 and successfully fulfilled his mission.

24. *The Carpenter*, September 1882, p. 8.

25. *The Progressive Age*, April 15, 1882, p. 4.

26. *Chicago Tribune*, September 18, 1882, p. 2.

27. *The Carpenter*, March 1885, p. 3.

28. Ibid., November 1883, p. 5.

29. *The Carpenter*, June 1898, p. 15.

30. *Chicagoer Arbeiter-Zeitung*, May 25, 1896, p. 4.

31. Ibid., February 5, 1896, p. 4.

32. Ibid., May 25, 1896, p. 4.

33. *The Carpenter*, June 1882, p. 3.

34. Most letters written by German carpenters to newspapers reflect this radical rhetoric.

35. *The Carpenter*, February 1885, p. 8.

36. Ibid., February 1884, p. 8; July 1885, p. 1.

37. *Chicago Tribune*, September 8, 1885, p. 3.

38. The fate of Scandinavian Branch 8 is puzzling. The branch may have joined in the consolidation movement of Local 21 in 1885. There is some mention of an independent Scandinavian carpenters union, but whether it was formerly Branch 8 is unclear.

39. Bruce Nelson, "Culture, Class and Conspiracy: The Foreground to the Haymarket Affair" (Northern Illinois University, ms. in preparation).

40. T. J. Morgan Papers, Illinois History Survey, University of Illinois, List of Delegates to the Founding Convention of the United Labor Party, September 1886, Book 4.

41. *Chicago Tribune*, July 7, 1879, p. 8.

42. Although the Chicago District Council was established in 1889, it was virtually powerless until after the 1890 strike. By that time, the Brotherhood was strong enough to threaten to suspend benefits and revoke the charters of any local that refused to abide by the council decisions once the appeal process had been exhausted.

43. United Carpenters Council, *Roll Book of Delegates*, 1888–1892.

44. Ibid., 1889.

45. *Chicago Tribune*, September 4, 1890, p. 1.

46. Ibid., April 15, 1887, p. 5. This tactic was first employed successfully in the 1887 strike.

47. Ibid., June 1, 1890, p. 6; June 7, 1890, p. 3; and June 8, 1890, p. 9.

Immigrant Workers in Early Mass Production Industry: Work Rationalization and Job Control Conflicts in Chicago's Packinghouses, 1900–1904

James R. Barrett

JURGIS went down the line with the rest of the visitors, open-mouthed, lost in wonder. He had dressed hogs himself in the forests of Lithuania but never had he expected to live to see one hog dressed by several hundred men.—Upton Sinclair, **The Jungle**

The early twentieth century brought a dramatic transformation of both American working-class life and industrial production methods. Clearly, these changes were related. The new immigrants who poured into the country most often worked as laborers and machine tenders in the nation's burgeoning mass production industries. While the cultural component of this transformation—the creation of ethnic subcultures and especially the relations among workers from diverse racial and ethnic backgrounds—remains a problem of concern to social historians, the focus here is on mass production work, an experience which so many in this diverse population shared.

Popular images of mass production work often involve mechanization. A classic example is Charlie Chaplin's 1936 film *Modern Times*, which portrays a lone operative struggling to keep up the pace in a factory filled with machines. Scholarly studies of the early twentieth-century transformation of work have also emphasized this technological aspect of the subject.[1] But the introduction of mass production methods was not simply a matter of getting machines to do the work of men; it involved a change far more fundamental than the mechanization of specific production tasks. Nor was the assembly line a natural product of some face-

process of modernization.[2] Rather, it represented a
e in the ongoing struggle over the control of work.
litical conflict in the broadest sense, because it re-
l power relations at the workplace, specifically the
le what constituted proper behavior and then to en-
ns defining it. How much work? How fast?
rxist scholars have considered this problem of con-
studied workers' roles in the evolution of work, but
ised primarily on craftsmen's defense of their own
nd their resistence to skill dilution.[3] The transfor-
ry work, however, was an ongoing process which
r the introduction of early assembly line methods,
wn actions remained an integral part of this pro-
y describes shop-floor organization and conflict in
htering and meat packing industry, where the bat-
n craft tradition and control had clearly been lost
the century. Here, skilled butchers, machine tend-
non laborers all joined together in the struggle for

sis of work from the shop-floor perspective explores
effects of mass production methods and challenges
at these methods represented a rationalization of the
s. The role played by immigrant butcher workmen
in the evolution of work suggests the potential for sol-
effective workshop organization which existed among
m diverse ethnic backgrounds and skill levels. Finally,
ship between workplace conflicts and the broader char-
ss relations questions the assumption, common to
rians of the Progressive Era, that corporate liberalism
he basis for an ideological consensus between the in-
rking class and the corporate elite in these years.

formation of packinghouse work

VED from the corporate boardroom, meat packing was
e of rationalized business. Executives integrated all the
essential functions into a few huge bureaucracies—
ve. Having minimized competition among themselves
series of marketing pools during the late nineteenth
e largest firms moved in 1903 to consolidate the major
nts into one giant holding company, National Packing.
int, the Big Five and National controlled about 90 per-
erstate meat shipments east of the Rockies and about

95 percent of all beef exports as well. Their control of refrigerated railroad cars, steamships, stockyards, and financial institutions further stifled competition.[4]

As in most industries experiencing rapid expansion, a dialectic developed in meat packing between market and work process. As the market for dressed meat and meat by-products grew, work was "rationalized" to keep up with demand; then increases in output brought a search for new markets. In meat packing, this dialectic was strongest in the last two decades of the nineteenth century, when most of the technological breakthroughs and reorganization of work occurred. Rather than mechanizing their operations, however, which they found difficult because of the irregular shapes and weights of the animals, the packers increased productivity through extreme division of labor coupled with a continuous-flow organization of operations, i.e. an assembly (or in this case, disassembly) line.

A kind of assembly line had been introduced in hog slaughtering as early as the mid-nineteenth century, but until the early 1880s, the entire job of slaughtering and dressing a steer was often done by one man, called the all-round butcher. By the turn of the century, the job was still done by hand, but the all-round butcher had been replaced by a killing gang of 157 men divided into 78 different trades, each man performing the same minute operation a thousand times during a full workday. He cut, or trimmed, or broke, or washed incessantly as the carcasses moved by him on an overhead rail. "It would be difficult to imagine another industry where division of labor has been so ingeniously and microscopically worked out," John R. Commons observed. "The animal has been surveyed and laid off like a map."[5] Though somewhat more mechanized in by-product departments, work throughout the packinghouses was organized along similar lines.[6]

The packers achieved three important and interrelated accomplishments through this reorganization. First, by grossly reducing the amount and quality of skill required to do the job, they destroyed the control which the all-round butcher had exercised over the slaughtering and cutting processes. A few highly skilled positions remained, but these were very specialized. In fact, mass production created a new, more narrowly defined notion of skill. Splitting the backbone of a steer, for example, required great dexterity as well as strength, and only a few men could do the job. Thus, splitters and a few others increased their earnings under the new system. These butcher aristocrats enjoyed high status and wages, but even they had little, if any, control over the character or pace of the work. The intellectual dimension of cattle

This photograph of meat trimmers illustrates that work in the Chicago Stockyards was labor intensive, since it was so difficult to employ machines in the actual slaughtering and cutting process. From *Views in the Chicago Stock Yards and Packing Houses*, 1892. Reproduced with permission of the Chicago Historical Society (ICHi-04076).

slaughtering—the planning and decision making exercised by the old all-round butcher—had been stripped away, appropriated by the packers, and embedded in the technology and organization of the assembly line.

This control, in turn, allowed the packers to greatly increase production speed. In hog slaughtering the foreman controlled the line with a lever. "If you need to turn out a little more," a superintendent explained, "you speed up the conveyor a little and the men speed up to keep pace."[7] The result was a striking intensification of work which affected the skilled butcher as much as the common laborer. Output for splitters, the most highly skilled men on the killing floor, increased by 100 percent between 1884 and 1894, by which time they were handling an average of thirty animals per hour. This figure was up to thirty-five by 1900.[8]

Finally, the transformation of work produced a thorough recomposition of the labor market. The small group of remaining butcher aristocrats was dwarfed by an army of common laborers who made up two-thirds of the industry's labor force by the turn of the century. These unskilled workers were paid a common labor rate, which fluctuated with the supply of labor and general economic conditions.[9]

The social characteristics of the labor force changed as well. Eastern and southeastern Europeans increasingly displaced an earlier generation of Irish, German, and native-born butcher workmen from the unskilled ranks. When the Immigration Commission studied the labor force for the 1907–1908 period, they found that nearly 80 percent of the butcher workmen were immigrants and that dozens of different ethnic groups were represented. Some of the immigrants, notably the Bohemians who rose quickly into skilled jobs, came to Chicago with considerable industrial work experience. The overwhelming majority of Poles and Lithuanians, however, had been farmers or farm laborers. As a group, they were young, single, and recently arrived; many could not speak English. By 1908 these groups accounted for nearly 40 percent of the industry's workers. Young, single women, noted by some labor historians for their docility, also poured into the industry, taking up piece-rate positions as machine tenders and packers. Between 1890 and 1910, the proportion of women in meat packing grew from 1.6 percent to 12 percent.[10] All of this made for a diversity unequaled by any early twentieth-century industry.

Reorganization of work meant not only a deskilling of occupations and greater social diversity in the labor force but also employment instability. Without the artificial pressure of unions, the packers could employ their workers flexibly, taking men and women on for a week, a day, or even for a few hours and then laying them off when they were no longer needed.

Packinghouse work was casual in two ways. Like many other industries of the era, packing was seasonal, though the severity of its seasonal fluctuations were greater than those in most other industries. While refrigeration somewhat reduced its impact, a slack season settled in every summer; and with it came layoffs. Short-term lapses in consumer demand brought more idleness. Whenever cattle shipments or the demand for meat products fell off, those on the lower rungs of the job ladder were thrown out of work, while some of the more skilled men took unskilled jobs in order to keep their places. Thus, both skilled and unskilled suffered under the system.

Even during the busy season, packinghouse employment was unreliable. Working hours varied considerably during the week because the packers hired in relation to cattle shipments. Killing gangs and workers in many other departments reported early in the morning and hung around until they could find out how much work there would be for the day. Men were called to work as the batches of animals entered the pens. The workday began whenever the animals were ready for the slaughter, which might not be until much later in the morning. Then the gang was driven hard until the slaughtering and dressing were done. On a Monday or Tuesday, when most cattle arrived in the yards, this might be 10:00 P.M. or even midnight. On a Friday, when shipments were light, it might be noon. Butcher workmen were paid only for the hours they actually worked, excluding time lost for mechanical breakdowns; and they worked only when they were needed. Most laborers averaged about three days in ordinary weeks, for which they earned about $9 or $10. As economist John C. Kennedy told the Commission on Industrial Relations, "A man never knows if he is hired for an hour or a week."[11]

Even skilled workers had to report by seven in the morning to have a chance for work, but many common laborers were hired on a daily basis. The foreman or a yards policeman would simply go out to the gate and choose the required number of laborers from among those who looked strongest. The lucky men would receive numbered brass checks which were deposited at the end of the workday and picked up again each morning for as long as they remained employed.[12]

The key to the system and the low wage rate was the crowd of unemployed who gathered each morning outside the yards' gates and the employment offices of the various firms. The hiring of common labor was strictly a supply and demand proposition. "They will be glad to take 15 cents an hour," one superintendent reasoned. "Why should we pay more than we have to?"[13] Although the crowds at the gates were greatest during periods of high unemployment, some 200 to 1,000 people were always outside. Thus, wages and working conditions were affected as much by this situation as by what was happening inside the packinghouses.[14]

In management's view, the corporate structure, market organization, work process, and employment system in packing all represented a high degree of rationalization. Yet these same conditions brought chaos to the life of the butcher workman. Not only was his work year rent by a long slack season, but he could not depend on anything like regular hours during the rest of the year. From day to day, his livelihood depended on the number of cattle coming through the gates of the Union Stock Yards. Though the killing day rarely started before ten or eleven in the morning, he had to be standing before the gates by seven; otherwise, he lost his chance for work. Even the skilled man had to expect to work fourteen hours at a grueling pace one day and go without work the next. If a machine or the overhead conveyor broke, the workman lost the repair time. With management in control of the production process and the labor market, the lives of the packinghouse workers and their families were shaped in large part by exigencies of the markets for livestock and dressed meats.[15] The process and practice of unionization was aimed at the heart of management control.

Work rationalization from the bottom up

BETWEEN 1900 and 1904 Chicago's butcher workmen built an impressive union movement which defies many assumptions of historians of labor and ethnicity. Skilled butchers not only helped to organize laborers but welcomed them into their own local unions. Young women organized themselves, led strikes, and fought for equal treatment at work and in the union. Recent immigrants, many of them new to industrial work and unable to speak English, streamed into labor organizations and formed the backbone of the great 1904 packinghouse strike. During the strike, the butcher workmen showed notable solidarity across skill, ethnic, and sexual lines. A full description of these events is beyond the scope of this paper.[16] But an analysis of the strike's background reveals the efforts of immigrant union women and men to rationalize mass production work in their own fashion and to gain a greater degree of control over their lives.

The process of unionization in the Yards generally descended the skill hierarchy and spread from older to newer immigrants as it worked its way through the plants. Cattle, hog, and sheep butchers, all skilled knifemen, formed the first three locals of the Amalgamated Meat Cutters and Butcher Workmen between 1900 and 1901, building on neighborhood and kinship ties within the Irish community. But the Amalgamated had also made a firm commitment to organize the unskilled. Adopting a departmental structure, the union formed a local for each department in the modern packinghouse over the next two years. Every workman engaged in killing or dressing cattle in Chicago, whether he was an aristocratic splitter at Swift or a common laborer at Armour, belonged to Cattle Butchers' Local 87. Other locals included soap and butterine operatives, beef and hog casing workers, livestock handlers, and even stockyards policemen. These Amalgamated locals were transitional forms which embodied elements of both craft and industrial organization. Nominally based on craft, they included all the workers in a department, regardless of skill. By the end of 1903, twenty-two locals had been organized to cover every production worker in the Yards.[17]

Most changes in the character of work rose, not from formal negotiations, but rather from a decentralized, informal process of bargaining in the plants. The keys to this system were the house committees, unofficial shop-floor organizations. Since union locals were based on trades, each one established a house committee in the city's various plants. Committees consisted of three production workers elected semiannually, and care was taken to represent a variety of jobs and skill levels in each department. Committee members were nearly always reelected, a fact that may suggest that rank-and-file workers had a great deal of confidence in them.[18] The official purpose of the committees was to hear grievances from management as well as from the workers and try to settle them at the workplace. In practice, committeemen interpreted the term *grievance* very broadly, and it was through the committees that workers temporarily shifted the balance of power in the packinghouses and began to reshape their work environments.

The range of workers' demands is impressive. Committees in various departments pressed successfully for regular hours, restriction of output, higher wages, layoff and recall by seniority, and increases in the size of work groups. They also fought and sometimes reversed disciplinary measures. Most rationalization initiatives originated with workers discussing problems at union meetings and formulating resolutions aimed at solving them. Often ideas trickled down from those groups, particularly the cattle butchers, who had organized earlier and had stronger shop-floor organizations. Resolutions were voted on by the local membership as a whole at well-attended meetings, and this high degree of democracy explains the broad base of support for the house committees. They were simply delivering to management demands from the rank and file in the various plants.

One of the first problems to which many house committees turned was regularization of employment and control of the casual labor market. Most committees established regular work hours and an overtime differential designed to discourage foremen from keeping men after the regular quitting time. It is clear from local reports and the way in which the rule was enforced that the object was to abolish overtime rather than to increase earnings. The shift to a regular workday came first among the cattle butchers, who often initiated such campaigns. Before unionization it was common for butchers to work from 7:00 A.M. to 10:00 P.M. one day, 11:00 A.M. to 9:30 P.M. the next, and perhaps not at all on the third day. By the summer of 1902, a guaranteed ten-hour day was in effect. If a foreman wanted his men to work overtime, he had to guarantee a full day's work for the following day. The rule provided regular work hours and reduced the length of the workday.[19] E. G. Purcell, an officer of Beef Boners' Local 135, explained how the system worked in his shop:

> Our working hours before we organized were from three, four, five, and six o'clock in the A.M. to all hours in the evening. We have since adopted resolutions regulating our hours of labor, also specifying that work done before 7 o'clock A.M. and after 5:30 o'clock P.M. be considered over time and was to be paid at the rate of time and a half, and it has been the means of doing away with a great deal of unnecessary overtime.[20]

The committees also tried to regularize the work year and stabilize employment. All workers lost under the packers' normal practice of simply discharging about one-third of the labor force during the slack season and spreading the remainder over the entire job structure. Common laborers were thrown out of work, and the skilled men were forced to perform low-paying and disagreeable tasks in order to remain employed. It was another instance in which the fate of the more skilled men was linked to that of the common laborers. Skilled men watched with trepidation as the crowd outside the stockyards gates and employment offices grew during the slack season. The union argued that wages were determined more by the man at the gate than by the man on the floor; the more unemployed, the greater the downward pressure on wages. The trend of wages in the era immediately preceding unionization suggests the wisdom of the argument.[21]

The committees demanded that all workers in a department be retained during slack season, even if this meant part-time work for the gang. Although this demand had some success in the killing gangs, which included a large number of casual laborers, employment had certainly not been regularized in all departments by 1904. But even if the union had not reached its goal of a stable, unionized labor force and regular employment by the time of the strike, its strength represented a threat to the whole system of casual labor, which the industry's seasonality and volatile market seemed to dictate.[22]

The shop-floor organizations enforced seniority systems in the departments where they were strongest. The system in cattle killing was fairly elaborate but amounted to promotion on the basis of time on the job. In hog killing, where seasonal layoffs remained a problem even with the union, workers enforced the last-hired-first-fired concept. As the volume of work picked up once again, they insisted that the oldest man who had been with the house longest should be hired first. This erosion of the foreman's traditional control over employment represented not only an affront to his authority but also the loss of a lucrative source of supplementary income. In the past, workers had paid for the chance to work as well as for promotions. The foremen bitterly resented this incursion on their prerogatives, but the strategy continued to spread up to the time of the 1904 strike.[23]

Certainly the most controversial strategy to regularize work was restriction of output, and this was the one which irritated the packers most. In the cattle- and sheep-killing gangs and most other departments, house committees drew up what workers felt were fair scales of work and wages and presented them to the plant superintendent. The effect of the slowdown on the killing beds was felt throughout the plants, and management sources complained that output had been cut by 30 to 50 percent. Although this figure is probably an exaggeration, there is little doubt that union control over the pace of work hurt the packers. John R. Commons estimated in 1904 that the cut in production ranged from 16 to 25 percent, depending on the plant.[24] But more important than any immediate financial cost, especially since this was probably passed on to the consumer, was the demonstration of collective strength that the tactic represented. The packers' own division of labor was turned against them. Workers at strategic points in the flow of production were given scales of work which were disproportionately low, necessitating the employment of more people throughout the line. Floormen, for example, who had the delicate task of separating the hide from the carcass, handled only fifteen head per hour, while splitters handled twenty-five. A foreman had the option of either hiring two floormen for every splitter or allowing his one splitter to kill time while the floorman caught up.[25]

This restriction aimed not only to slow down the pace of work but also to dry up the labor pool. A member of the Beef Luggers' local explained how the process had improved conditions in his department:

> We used to load 60 or 70 cars of beef with 5 or 6 men, and this was certainly slavery, as anyone who understands the work will admit. This was the first thing we changed, and now we load 60 cars a day with 8 men, thereby putting more carriers to work; and where we had only 37 carriers before we organized, we now have 53, and they do no more loading than the 37 used to do.[26]

The restriction may have been more important to skilled men, but it offered something to the casual laborer as well. In addition to slowing the speed of work, which had reached a deadly pace by the time of unionization, it also produced more jobs. One indication of the effectiveness of restriction was the demise of the pacesetters, well-paid workers placed at strategic spots in the production line who drove others around them to keep up the pace. By vigorously enforcing their scales, the house committees became the new pacesetters.[27]

How did the house committees acquire so much control? The adjustments they made in working hours, wages, advancement, and employment were bound to receive widespread support among workers; but how were they won, and how were they enforced? Aided by relative prosperity and high employment between 1901 and 1904, much of the workers' success was a result of their readiness to engage in short, unofficial strikes around specific issues. These were control strikes, used as levers in the struggle with management to change aspects of the production system. A few examples, drawn from various departments, suggest how they were used to increase workers' power at the point of production.

Many strikes were used to enforce new wage scales. Shortly after organizing, pork casing workers devised a wage scale which amounted to a twenty-five cent per day increase and submitted it to management. When the raise was not immediately forthcoming, a one-day strike brought the concession.[28]

Once the process of unionization was well advanced in a department, a strike or the threat of one could be used to establish a de facto closed shop. By 1903, numerous locals, including those of unskilled workers in a number of by-product departments, were reporting that they allowed only union men and women to work with them. A confrontation in the wool-working department suggests an early racial conflict as well as the pervasiveness of this closed shop drive.

> One of the large packers during the slack season of 1902 started to discriminate by discharging union men or laying them off and putting colored men in their places, who were not union men, and as the union men were idle we refused to let these men work until our men were reinstated, which the firm refused to do. We went on strike and remained out for one week, to uphold the principle, and won out.[29]

Strikes were also used to enforce traditional work rules regarding size of work gangs, for example, or to establish new ones. Regularization of the work year and the workday described above were also introduced into cattle gangs under threat of a strike.[30]

Typically, these unofficial strikes were spontaneous and limited to one department. There was always the possibility, however, that a strike which started in this manner would spread, with workers in other departments or even other houses coming out in sympathy or seizing the opportunity to redress their own grievances. This happened in early 1903 when a Swift foreman laid off part of a beef killing gang in spite of an earlier verbal agreement to keep the whole gang. Killing in every Swift plant in the country stopped at 9:30 the next morning. The Amalgamated's president was called in immediately to accept the company's concession.[31]

Unofficial strikes were increasing in frequency by the spring of 1904. At the union's 1902 convention, delegates passed a resolution authorizing local unions to dispense strike benefits to members involved in small-scale, spontaneous strikes when quick action was needed. During the two years between the summer of 1900 and the summer of 1902, the union tabulated only five strikes and lockouts. In the following year unionization spread through the Chicago plants and in other stockyard centers, and the strength of shop-floor organization grew. Between May 1903 and May 1904, the union counted a total of thirty-six strikes. Part of the explanation for the spread of this system is contained in the strike figures themselves, as well as in local union reports. Of those which had been brought to some sort of conclusion by May 1904, the workers had won nineteen and the employers, five.[32] Clearly, the strikes were successful. The figures for both periods are certainly underestimates, since many short strikes were probably never reported. But even these rough estimates tell us something about the nature of the strike in packinghouse work during these years. The figures, together with local union reports which detail strike causes, suggest that strikes were used in lieu of what we now recognize as the "normal" procedure of collective bargaining and negotiation. Conditions were changed in the packinghouses through unilateral action on the part of the workers. Issues were discussed; resolutions were passed and presented to the superintendent by the house committee. The superintendent's only choices were to accept the demand or face a strike.

To appreciate the significance of this decentralized workers' rationalization process from management's view, we need only put ourselves in the place of the superintendent at one of the largest plants who had to deal with over one hundred of these house committees.[33] Now it was the packers who saw chaos in the ever-changing work environment. They complained that union officials could not follow through on agreements, since the house committees could always disregard them and call a strike. So long as the bargaining procedure remained decentralized, with the house committees responsible for establishing minimum wages and conditions and restricting output, the drift toward higher wages, lower productivity, and greater worker initiative continued. It is this situation which explains the employers' acceptance of a national contract in 1903. By the time the union proposed the agreement, the packers saw it as a chance to stabilize labor relations in the industry. As long as conditions were fluid, i.e., not written into a contract, the committees were free to implement any decision which they had the power to enforce. Both the union officials and the packers looked forward to an agreement which would give them greater control. The struggle on the shop floor, however, propelled the two parties in opposite directions and led ultimately to a bitter strike and the destruction of labor organization in the industry in 1904.

The limits of corporate liberalism

CONTROL conflicts at the workplace and their results in the 1904 strike have direct implications for the view that a significant shift in the nature of class relations took place during the early twentieth century. Several historians have argued that business and labor leaders reached an ideological consensus which embodied a new attitude toward labor relations. The more enlightened employers, usually representing the largest corporate oligopolies, accepted the fact that some form of workers' representation was both inevitable and desirable. Their goal was to foster the development of more responsible labor leaders who were willing to talk out problems rather than resort to strikes. Many trade union officials, the argument contends, agreed that the strike should be scrapped in favor of a system of collective bargaining and arbitration which would place them at the center of the emerging corporate order. The organizational manifestation of this new, supposedly more rational, form of class relations was the National Civic Federation (NCF) and particularly its industrial department, which included representatives from capital and labor. Thus, historians of corporate liberalism argue, American workers were integrated, ideologically and structurally, into the political economy of monopoly capital in its earliest stages.[34]

On the surface, this analysis seems to describe the situation in meat packing admirably. The major packing companies supported the NCF and its program. Indeed, the packers were just the sort of large-scale, highly rationalized firms which have been described as the mainstays of the new corporate liberal movement. J. Ogden Armour and Louis F. Swift, representing the second generation of leadership in the industry's two largest corporations, were both prominent NCF members. And these giants clearly set the tone for industrial relations in packing.[35]

While Amalgamated officials did not see themselves as corporate liberals, their view of labor relations conformed closely to that of the NCF. Homer Call, the union's treasurer and the editor of its journal, was a great admirer of the Federation's "calm, coolheaded businesslike approach" to industrial relations and a foe of what he called "hasty strikes." Call believed that the packers had accepted the Amalgamated as a "business institution in every sense that the word implies." Noting a series of wage increases and other improvements, he argued that these concessions were won through responsibility and conservatism, not strikes.[36]

Michael Donnelly, the Amalgamated's president, devoted considerable time to travelling around the various packing centers to settle unofficial strikes. As a veteran packinghouse worker, Donnelly was clearly more tolerant of these initiatives than Call, who was a meat cutter; but he too, in trying to negotiate a national contract with the packers, worried about the union's image and the trouble the strikes caused.

Pronouncements of the Amalgamated's leadership about the conservative nature of their organization and their desire to run the union on "sound business principles" stood in stark contrast to what was happening on the killing floors and in the packing rooms of the industry. Here, butcher workmen carried on a continual conflict with management over the issue of control. The contrast raises questions concerning the validity of generalizing about working-class consciousness on the basis of statements by trade union officials.

In the end, the Amalgamated's leadership was drawn into the struggle with the packers during the contract negotiations in the spring of 1904 and the general strike in the industry that summer. The national contract was an amalgam of resolutions formulated by local unions—standard work scales, pay scales, and work rules—to be applied on a national basis. While the packers had hoped that the contract would keep local house committees from pressing their own demands and restrict the number of unofficial strikes, the contract in fact placed the strength of the entire organization behind standard scales and rules. In effect, it extended the control struggles initiated by the house committees to the national level. The union's strength proved insufficient in the confrontation over the one factor which continued to threaten employment security and the stability of the union itself—the common labor market. Whatever its formal philosophy, the union as an organization had to assert some degree of control over this market. The Amalgamated tried to do this by writing a minimum common labor rate into the contract, placing the wages of the least skilled workers beyond the play of market forces. Without asserting this kind of control over the price of common labor, the union was living on borrowed time. Maintenance of a large, unrestricted pool of casual labor was crucial, however, in the packers' view. Both sides recognized the importance of the demand, and the result was the 1904 strike.

By integrating the common labor rate into its industry-wide wage scale and setting an absolute minimum, the union served notice of its intention to control the casual hiring system in the Yards. Perhaps most significant was the fact that the more skilled workers, recognizing the importance of this control to the goal of stabilizing their own work situation, were prepared to back the demand.

During the 1904 strike, a spokesman for the packers explained the forces behind the decision to smash the union. By 1904 it had come down to a question of who was running the packinghouses, management or the house committees.

> The domination of the packing plants by the union gradually had become unbearable. The proprietor of an establishment had forty stewards to deal with and nothing that failed to suit them could be done . . . the packer could not run his own plant. It was run by the stewards. Discipline grew lax and the men did not attend to their work as they should have done. . . . As sure as either employer or worker gets control of an industry like meat packing a conflict such as that [which is] now on seems inevitable. The side having the power abuses it and domineers over the other.[37]

Whether or not its policies were domineering, it is clear that from 1901 to 1904 the union, operating through the house committees, was the "side having the power." In 1904, as the union sought to extend its control still further by winning a minimum wage for all common laborers, the packers decided to make their stand. Encouraged by mounting unemployment in the city and a unity of purpose, they dug in for what proved to be a long, bitter strike which they perceived as a just struggle to maintain control over their industry.[38]

The experience in the Chicago plants between 1900 and 1904 suggests several lessons about immigrant workers in early mass production industry. First, the idea of "rationalization" is inseparable from class interest and at best a relative concept. The direction of the process and its ultimate effects depended in large part on the balance of power in the productive relations of the industry. Whether a particular organization of work was "rational" depended on who was doing the rationalizing; management's efficiency could be labor's chaos and vice versa. If we are to grasp the evolution of mass production work, we need to consider more carefully the relationship between management initiatives and those of labor. We need to study the sorts of organizations and strategies created by workers in response to mass production work and, in turn, how these influenced the nature of subsequent management reforms.

The story of shop-floor conflicts in packing can also tell us something about immigrant workers themselves and their relations with one another. What is striking about the highly developed organization in packing is the workers involved. Such strategies and behavior have generally been associated with mature workers, those who had "learned the rules of the game" and created organizations and strategies suited to their problems.[39] Legislation and collective enforcement of work rules was common among highly skilled metalworkers in late nineteenth-century Britain and America.[40] Often, such rules were designed to guard against just the kind of rationalization that occurred in meat packing.

In the case of the butcher workmen, however, we are looking at a strong, sophisticated, and relatively successful shop-floor movement encompassing a very large proportion of recent immigrants, common laborers without industrial work or trade union experience, and young single women—just the sort of workers who ought not to have behaved in this manner. The key to the paradox lies in the relationship between the earlier generation of skilled Irish and German butchers with their craft traditions and sense of solidarity on the one hand and recently arrived Polish and Lithuanian common laborers on the other. In fact, both generations defy conventional historiographical wisdom. The Irish and German "butcher aristocracy" temporarily overcame nativism and craft sectionalism, consciously integrating newcomers into their movement. The Slavic laborers responded enthusiastically and quickly became good union men and women. Part of the importance of this case study, then, lies in a new view of immigrant mass production workers. Given the right situation—a work process which linked the interest of skilled and unskilled and a union structure and strategy which encouraged inter-ethnic class solidarity—recent immigrants were quite capable of developing a class perspective and helping to build strong working-class movements. Such a view of immigrant workers and their relations with groups of older skilled workers might suggest how craft traditions and strategies were transformed by a new generation of workers and how these new forms provided a useful legacy for the industrial union movement of later years.[41]

Finally, this case study underscores the importance of production relations to our understanding of class conflict. Not withstanding the corporate liberalism of union officials and packing executives, conflict within the plants was general and continual. It revolved largely around matters of control and represented a serious threat to the packers' managerial prerogatives. Ultimately, it led to a bitter national strike and the destruction of labor organization in the industry. Nor was this struggle peculiar to meat packing in this era.[42] The persistence of these conflicts undermined any lasting ideological consensus between even the most enlightened and prosperous corporate leaders and America's immigrant workers.

Acknowledgments
The author would like to acknowledge the comments of David Brody, Alf Lüdtke, Anthony LaVopa, and Joseph Hobbs on an earlier version of this essay.

Notes

1. David Landes, *The Unbound Prometheus: Technological Change and Industrial Revolution in Western Europe* (New York and London: Cambridge University Press, 1969), 290–326; Daniel Nelson, *Managers and Workers: Origins of the New Factory System in the United States, 1880–1920* (Madison: University of Wisconsin Press, 1975), 3–23.

2. Peter Stearns, *Lives of Labor: Work in a Maturing Industrial Society* (New York: Holmes and Maier, 1975).

3. Among the scholars of job control are Harry Braverman, *Labor and Monopoly Capital: The Degradation of Work in the Twentieth Century* (New York: Monthly Review Press, 1974); Richard Edwards, *Contested Terrain: The Transformation of the Workplace in the Twentieth Century* (New York: Basic Books, 1977); David Montgomery, *Workers' Control in America: Studies in Work, Technology, and Labor Struggles* (New York and London: Cambridge University Press, 1979). Montgomery, Carter Goodrich, and James Hinton have studied skilled workers' self-defense, in particular. See Montgomery, *Workers' Control in America*; Carter Goodrich, *The Frontier of Control* (London: Pluto Press, 1975); and James Hinton, *The First Shop Stewards' Movement* (London: Allen and Unwin, 1973).

4. Alfred Chandler, *The Visible Hand: The Managerial Revolution in American Business* (Cambridge, Mass.: Harvard University Press, 1977), 299–301, 392–401; Richard Arnould, "Changing Patterns of Concentration in American Meat Packing, 1880–1963," *Business History Review* 45 (Spring 1971): 18–34; David Brody, *The Butcher Workmen: A Study in*

Trade Union Organization (Cambridge, Mass.: Harvard University Press, 1963), 3; Rudolf Clemen, *The American Livestock and Meat Industry* (New York: Ronald Press, 1923), chap. 13; and U.S. Bureau of Corporations, *Report of the Commissioner of Corporations on the Beef Industry* (Washington, D.C.: Government Printing Office, 1905), 66. See also Dorothy Einbecker, "Investigations of Chicago Packing House Combinations, 1898–1906" (M.A. thesis, University of Chicago, 1943), especially pp. 29–32.

5. John R. Commons, "Labor Conditions in Slaughtering and Meat Packing," in *Trade Unionism and Labor Problems*, ed. John R. Commons (Boston: Ginn, 1905), 224.

6. Ibid., pp. 223–25. On the relative lack of mechanization and the extreme division of labor in packing, see Elizabeth Stewart, "Labor Productivity in Slaughtering," *Monthly Labor Review* 18 (March 1924): 14–21; and Harry Jerome, *Mechanization in Industry* (New York: National Bureau of Economic Research, 1934): 116–17. For detailed descriptions of work in all departments of a packinghouse, which suggest the high degree of labor segmentation throughout, see U.S. Department of Labor, *Bulletin No. 252* (Washington, D.C.: Government Printing Office, 1919). Accurate and far more dramatic descriptions of much of the work are available in Upton Sinclair, *The Jungle* (1905; New York: New American Library, Signet Ed., 1973). See, for example, pp. 38–41, 42–45.

7. Quoted by Brody, *The Butcher Workmen*, 5.

8. Commons, "Labor Conditions in Slaughtering," in *Trade Unionism and Labor Problems*, 227. See also Amalgamated Meat Cutters and Butcher Workmen of North America, *Official Journal* 5 (September 1904).

9. Commons, "Labor Conditions in Slaughtering," in *Trade Unionism and Labor Problems*, 243, 245–46.

10. For an ethnic breakdown and demographic characteristics of the various groups, see U.S. Immigration Commission, *Reports*, XIII, *Immigrants in Industry: Slaughtering and Meat Packing* (Washington, D.C.: Government Printing Office, 1911), 199–203, 210, 250–60; and John C. Kennedy et al., *Wages and Family Budgets in the Stock Yards District of Chicago* (Chicago: University of Chicago Press, 1914), 5, 8. On the alleged docility of young immigrant women, see Leslie Woodcock-Tentler, *Wage Earning Women: Industrial Work and Family Life in the United States, 1900–1930* (New York: Oxford University Press, 1979). On the introduction of women into packing, see S. P. Breckinridge and Edith Abbott, "Women in Industry: The Chicago Stockyards," *Journal of Political Economy* 19 (October 1911): 636–44; *Eleventh U.S. Census, 1890, Manufactures* (Washington, D.C.: Government Printing Office, 1895), 144–45; and *Thirteenth U.S. Census, 1910, Manufactures* (Washington, D.C.: Government Printing Office, 1912), 298.

11. Clemen, *The American Livestock and Meat Industry*, 608–9, 71–81; Kennedy et al., *Wages and Family Budgets*, 75–76; and U.S. Commission on Industrial Relations, *Final Report and Testimony*, vol. 4 (Washington, D.C.: Government Printing Office, 1916), 3513–14.

12. Charles J. Bushnell, "Some Social Aspects of the Chicago Stock Yards," pt. 1, *American Journal of Sociology* 3 (1901): 168–69; Commission on Industrial Relations, *Final Report*, 3463–64. See also the description of the hiring given by Antanas Kaztauskis, a Lithuanian laborer, whose autobiography is reprinted in *Workers Speak: Self-Portraits*, ed.

Leon Stein and Philip Taft (New York: Arno Press, 1971), 74.

13. Quoted by Ernest Poole, "The Meat Strike," *The Independent* 57 (July 28, 1904): 180.

14. Commission on Industrial Relations, *Final Report*, 3463.

15. For the impact of casual hiring and other work-related problems on family life and the standard of living in Packingtown, the community adjacent to the Union Stock Yards, see James R. Barrett, "Work and Community in 'The Jungle': Chicago's Packing House Workers, 1894–1922" (Ph.D. diss., University of Pittsburgh, 1981), chap. 3.

16. For descriptions of the Amalgamated organizing, see Brody, *The Butcher Workmen*, chap. 2; and Philip Foner, *History of the Labor Movement in the United States*, vol. 3 (New York: International Publishers, 1964), 191–93. I have described unionization as a process of socialization through which immigrants were assimilated into Chicago's broader working-class movement (Barrett, "Work and Community in 'The Jungle,'" chap. 4).

17. Amalgamated Meat Cutters and Butcher Workmen of North America, *Official Journal*, vol. 2 (August 1902 and September 1902); vol. 5 (May 1904); Clemen, *The American Livestock and Meat Industry*, 696; and Commons, "Labor Conditions in Slaughtering," in *Trade Unionism and Labor Problems*, 223.

18. On the structure and function of the house committees, see Commons, "Labor Conditions in Slaughtering," in *Trade Unionism and Labor Problems*, 249; and Carl Thompson, "Labor in the Packing Industry," *Journal of Political Economy* 15 (February 1906): 100.

19. For a cattle butcher's descriptions of these changes, see George Schick's letter in Amalgamated Meat Cutters and Butcher Workmen of North America, *Official Journal* 2 (August 1902).

20. Ibid., 2 (December 1902).

21. Commons, "Labor Conditions in Slaughtering," in *Trade Unionism and Labor Problems*, 231–32.

22. Amalgamated Meat Cutters and Butcher Workmen of North America, *Official Journal* 5 (May 1904); Thompson, "Labor in the Packing Industry," 103–4.

23. Commons, "Labor Conditions in Slaughtering," in *Trade Unionism and Labor Problems*, 233–35. See also Clemen, *American Livestock and Meat Industry*, 698; and Thompson, "Labor in the Packing Industry," 103.

24. U.S. Commissioner of Labor, *Eleventh Special Report, Regulation and Restriction of Output* (Washington, D.C.: Government Printing Office, 1904), 711; Commons, "Labor Conditions in Slaughtering," in *Trade Unionism and Labor Problems*, 228; *Chicago Inter Ocean*, September 28, 1904.

25. U.S. Commissioner of Labor, *Regulations and Restriction of Output*, 711–16; Commons, "Labor Conditions in Slaughtering," in *Trade Unionism and Labor Problems*, 228.

26. Amalgamated Meat Cutters and Butcher Workmen of North America, *Official Journal* 2 (March 1903).

27. Commons, "Labor Conditions in Slaughtering," in *Trade Unionism and Labor Problems*, 229.

28. Compare Amalgamated Meat Cutters and Butcher Workmen of North America, *Official Journal* 2 (March 1903).

29. Ibid.

30. Commons, "Labor Conditions in Slaughtering," in *Trade Unionism and Labor Problems*, 228, 230, 233.

31. Amalgamated Meat Cutters and Butcher Workmen of North America, *Proceedings of the Sixth Annual Convention, 1904* (Syracuse, N.Y.: Amalgamated Meat Cutters and Butcher Workmen of North America, 1904), 36–37.

32. Ibid., 16, 75; Amalgamated Meat Cutters and Butcher Workmen of North America, *Proceedings of the Fourth Annual Convention, 1902* (Syracuse, N.Y.: Amalgamated Meat Cutters and Butcher Workmen of North America, 1902), 17.

33. Commons, "Labor Conditions in Slaughtering," in *Trade Unionism and Labor Problems*, 249. See also Harry Rosenberg, "The Great Strike" in the Mary McDowell Papers, Chicago Historical Society, Chicago, Folder 15.

34. For relevant analyses of corporate liberalism and its influence on labor relations in this era, see James Weinstein, *The Corporate Ideal in the Liberal State* (Boston: Beacon Press, 1968); "The IWW and American Socialism," *Socialist Revolution* 1 (1970): 3–42; Ronald Radosh, "The Corporate Ideology of American Labor Leaders from Gompers to Hillman," *Studies on the Left* 6 (November–December 1966): 66–67; "Labor in the American Economy: The 1922 Railroad Shop Crafts Strike and the 'B & O Plan'" in *Building the Organizational Society: Essays in Associational Activities*, ed. Jerry Israel (New York: Free Press, 1972); Gabriel Kolko, *Main Currents in Modern American History* (New York: Harper & Row, 1977), 177. For an alternative analysis which has influenced my own, see Montgomery, *Workers' Control in America*, 48–90.

35. Foner, *History of the Labor Movement*, 64; Philip Foner, "Comment," *Studies on the Left* 6 (November–December 1966): 91.

36. Amalgamated Meat Cutters and Butcher Workmen of North America, *Official Journal* 2 (October 1902). See also *Official Journal* 2 (September 1903) and 5 (February 1904).

37. *Chicago Tribune*, August 2, 1904.

38. On the strike, see Brody, *The Butcher Workmen*, 50–58; and Barrett, "Work and Community in 'The Jungle,'" 264–91.

39. The seminal study of work rules among craftsmen is E. J. Hobsbawm, "Wages, Custom, and Workload in the Nineteenth Century," in his *Labouring Men* (London: Wiedenfield and Nicolson, 1964), from which the phrase is taken. On the work culture of this earlier generation of skilled men in the United States, see Montgomery, *Workers' Control in America*, chap. 1.

40. Montgomery, *Workers' Control in America*, 15–18; Hinton, *The First Shop Stewards' Movement*, pt. 1. In more recent times such job control conflicts have been characteristic of some well-organized assembly line workers—notably British and American car workers. See Hugh Beynon, *Working for Ford* (London: Allen Lane, 1975); and Nelson Lichtenstein, "Auto Worker Militancy and the Structure of Factory Life, 1937–1955," *Journal of American History* 67 (September 1980): 335–53.

41. When shop-floor organization reemerged in the Stock Yards during World War I, Polish immigrants composed a large proportion of the rank and file leaders. (See Barrett, "Work and Community in 'The Jungle,'" 315–17.) I am thinking here of the industrial union movement of the 1930s and 1940s which drew so heavily on precisely these groups.

42. On the widespread practice of output and other forms of job control among various trade groups, see U.S. Commissioner of Labor, *Regulations and Restriction of Output* (1904). On the significance of control issues in the high level of class conflict throughout the early twentieth century, see Montgomery, *Workers' Control in America*, 20, 48–90, 97–101; and Bruno Ramirez, *When Workers Fight: The Politics of Collective Bargaining in the Progressive Era, 1900–1915* (Westport, Conn.: Greenwood Press, 1978), 3–13.

Neighborhood and Everyday Life

3.

Chicago's German North Side, 1880–1900: The Structure of a Gilded Age Ethnic Neighborhood

Christiane Harzig

FOR a long time sociologists as well as historians have argued about the nature and social functions of the ethnic neighborhood in America's cities. Social scientists of the Chicago School of Sociology assumed that assimilation in American society took place through a first and second settlement. Recent immigrant arrivals, seeking the proximity and familiarity of their fellow countrymen, were thought automatically to settle in congested low rental areas normally located in transition zones near the center of the city. These areas of ethnic residential concentration were the essential prerequisite of an ethnic identity and culture. With improved social and economic status, outward residential movement began, and with it the dissolution of ethnic residential concentration and, consequently, ethnic identity.[1] More recent studies have questioned the universal applicability of this model, pointing out that

> assimilation by way of a ghetto has always been a limited case in American urban history, limited both in time span and in membership. Most foreign immigrants to American cities never lived in ghettos, and most immigrant ghettos that did exist were the product of the largest cities and the eastern and southern European immigrants of 1880–1940.[2]

If ethnic neighborhoods were nothing more than visible agglomerations of institutions serving an ethnic clientele,[3] then immigrants must have assimilated into American society without the help of an ethnic culture and solidarity based on community ties.

But neither of the two approaches described above adequately reflects the social realities of a large number of ethnic groups. The German-American experience, for example, witnessed "concentration without structural cause, community without measured concentration, assimilation despite community, interest group pressure despite assimilation."[4] As the paradox of the German-American experience demonstrates, we have as yet no useful definition which places the ethnic neighborhood within the urban and industrial development of the city while at the same time taking into account the ethnic culture of the groups under investigation.

The Germans in Chicago were able to create a vital German-American culture and to maintain a stable ethnic identity for a period of more than half a century. Longer than any other area of the city, Chicagoans identified the North Side as a German neighborhood. This essay attempts to identify those elements in the social and economic structure of the North Side which made for this ethnic continuity and stability. Within the analysis a distinction is made between the terms *neighborhood* and *community*. *Neighborhood* is applied to a geographical area defined by the residential and institutional dominance of one ethnic group; it can include nearby industrial areas where the inhabitants work. *Community*, on the other hand, refers to the group solidarity and ethnic identity which result from social and economic structures developed within the neighborhood. Both neighborhood and community are required if an ethnic culture is to arise. This essay, however, is concerned with neighborhood in the limited sense, although it analyzes some structures out of which community was built. So far, neighborhood studies have included larger geographic areas. However, since this essay focuses on the question of how the people themselves were able to shape their environment and how they organized their lives, it concentrates on a small segment of the North Side, relating its occupational structure to that of the larger neighborhood, and describes two German neighborhood businesses as representative agents of community building.

The physical setting and industrial development of the North Side

CHICAGO'S North Side was settled as early as the 1830s, and it profited from the city's rapid commercial and industrial development during the 1850s and 1860s (see map). Lumberyards and woodworking industries, along with iron mills and foundries, settled along the North Branch of the Chicago River, which formed the western boundary of the area. At the same time the North Side housed a disproportionate share of Chicago's rapidly growing immigrant population, with the Germans constituting the largest group, although "Swede Town" developed between Chicago Avenue and Division Street west of Wells.[5] There were also significant concentrations of Irish, and later Poles, near the industrial area along the River, while well-to-do native-born Americans settled along Lake Michigan in the southern and northern portions of the district.

The skills and occupations of the immigrants, and particularly of the predominant Germans, helped shape the North Side's economic and industrial development. Thus, many German artisans "started small bakeries, tailoring, shoemaking, and wood working shops, or brought skills needed in the new industries."[6] Beginning in the 1860s and accelerating after the Great Chicago Fire of 1871, industrial relocation reshaped the North Side, drawing the small packinghouses to the new Union Stock Yards built outside the city limits on the South Side. Grain elevators, lumberyards, and furniture shops remained located along the River, however, while new industries like the tanneries on Goose Island and, across the River, the Chicago Rolling Mills were also added. Other important industries on the North Side were "distilleries and breweries and brickyards, manned largely by Germans."[7] The area south of Chicago Avenue developed into an industrial and commercial district, whereas by 1880 the section between Chicago and Fullerton avenues had become a predominantly residential neighborhood. By the mid-1880s the brewing industry had become less important for the North Side economy, as had the furniture and metal industries. The area maintained a highly diversified business and employment structure with small craft shops and a large number of neighborhood trades where many German North Siders found employment.[8]

The variety and number of retail businesses and service facilities indicate that the area between Chicago and Fullerton avenues was practically self-sufficient. Hospitals, schools, churches, and orphanages were spread throughout the area; traditional places of amusement, like clubs and lodge-houses, had by 1900 been supplemented by newer varieties—five-cent theaters, coffeehouses, palm gardens, and a natatorium. The North Siders could thus rely on their neighborhood for all their basic needs, including recreation. The construction of Lincoln Park in the 1870s added to the desirability of the neighborhood.[9]

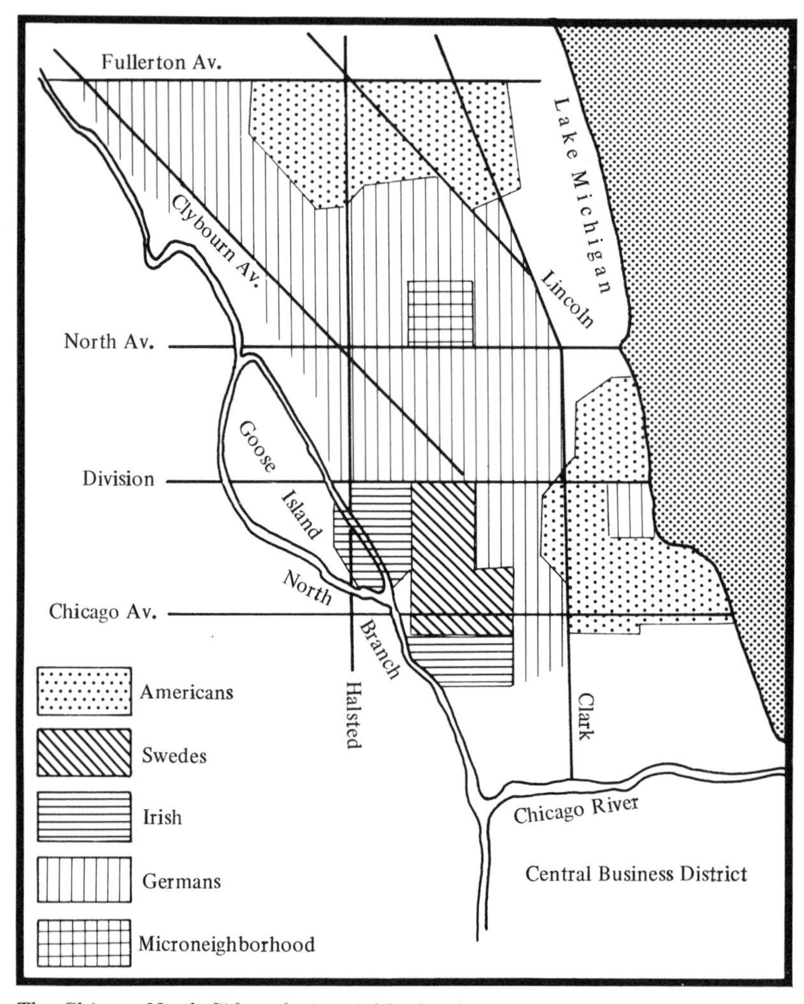

The Chicago North Side: ethnic neighborhoods in 1884. Source: Chicago School Census, 1884.

During the early years of the twentieth century, the settlement patterns of the North Side changed, though not substantially. The Gold Coast had developed along the lake shore, and the area north of Chicago Avenue had become even more residential. Many of the old small frame buildings and wooden stables in the backyards had given way to three- and four-story brick buildings of uniform layout, although "stylistic differences add[ed] variety to these row houses."[10] And despite the beginnings of urban segmentation, small pockets of integrated residential and industrial areas did remain, near the River.

Through its history, the continuity of the North Side was assisted by its mass transit. From the 1860s until the mid-1880s a close network of horse-drawn railways served the North Side, but during the 1880s the area lagged behind the South Side in the development of rapid transportation. Although the Chicago River remained a major obstacle for tying the North Side more closely to the central business district, in 1888 the building of the first cable lines on Clark Street from Diversey to the downtown section improved service to the North Side. By 1890, additional lines were constructed on Lincoln, Clybourn, and Wells. Many North Siders made use of this faster system of transportation for going to work in downtown offices and department stores. Not until 1900, however, did the North Side receive an elevated railway line, which fostered an enormous expansion on the outskirts of the neighborhood. In the next decades the elevated thus contributed to the dispersal of the North Side Germans and furthered the area's decline as an overwhelmingly German neighborhood.[11]

Analysis of a microneighborhood

THE following demographic analysis was made for the area between North Avenue and Menomonee Street, Sedgwick and Larrabee streets (see map, p. 130). It is part of the area now called the Old Town Triangle. During the 1850s Michael Diversey, partner in the Lill and Diversey Brewery, had owned much of the land which was then cultivated by German truck farmers. In the early 1860s small shopkeepers followed to provide goods to the residents, while later in the decade a new wave of German immigrants settled in what was then called North Town, giving it its distinctive German character.[12]

In the 1880s the area of this microanalysis (approximately five acres) had an even stronger residential character than the rest of the North Side, although there were some coal and junk yards, a small broom factory, and some craft and tailor shops. The cultural center of German Catholics, St. Michael's, with its huge church building, priest's house, and two school buildings, dominated a whole block. Folz's Hall, a much frequented saloon, was at the northeast corner of North Avenue and Larrabee Street.

Table 1 shows that the population of this small eight-block area[13] was remarkably homogeneous in origin over a twenty-year period. Nearly 80 percent of the heads of household were of German origin in 1880 and 1900, as compared to some 26 percent for the total population of Chicago.[14] In 1900 one in four German

Table 1. Ethnic composition of heads of households in the microneighborhood

	1880		1900	
	N	%	N	%
Germany	538	74.5	746	61.5
Second-generation German	30	4.2	191	15.8
Austria/Switzerland/Luxembourg	19	2.6	35*	2.9
USA	32	4.4	74	6.1
Ireland	46	6.4	40*	3.3
Scandinavia	29	4.0	42*	3.5
Others	28	3.9	84*	6.9
Total	722	100.0	1212	100.0

*The number includes second-generation residents.
Source: Analysis of manuscript schedules of the Federal Census on Population for the years 1880 (Enumeration Districts 160, 161) and 1900 (Enumeration Districts 655–657), National Archives, Washington, D.C.

households in the microneighborhood was already headed by a second-generation German, nearly a fourfold increase from 1880. The comparatively few non-German residents were evenly distributed throughout the area and did not interfere with its German character.

A further indication of ethnic coherence was the low degree of intermarriage. In 1880, 87 percent of all married couples had a first- or second-generation German partner,[15] while only 10 percent had married outside their ethnic group, with men showing a stronger tendency to do so. (Of those marrying outside, 71 percent were men.) In 1900 the Germans continued to show a remarkable degree of consistency in choosing their partners, since 83 percent of all married couples still involved partners of German descent, and only 15 percent of first- and second-generation Germans had married non-Germans, but now more women made use of this possibility (42 percent of intermarriages were between German women and non-German men.) By the turn of the century, however, the marriage patterns also reflected the increasing impact of the second generation. Whereas 72 percent of all married German couples in 1880 consisted of German-born partners, this proportion had dropped in 1900 to 53 percent, while the marriages involving two second-generation partners had risen from 2.5 percent to 13.6 percent. In contrast to an earlier period[16] the German-born couples in 1900 had not migrated together but had married in the United States, after having arrived as children with their parents during the immigration wave of the 1880s. Their presence in 1900 indicates that the area remained a desirable neighborhood during the last two decades of the nineteenth century.

In 1880 the microneighborhood contained 3,670 persons, who formed 722 households. In 1900 the population had risen to 5,106, living in 1,212 households. A large number of new multiple-family row houses had been constructed to accommodate this population increase, supplementing the one- and two-story frame buildings which had defined the housing stock during the 1880s.

As Table 2 shows, the structure of the households had undergone some important changes during the twenty-year period. Whereas in 1880 the nuclear family predominated among the area's households, by 1900 it made up less than 50 percent of the total. At the same time, the number of single-person households had significantly increased, as had those headed by widows and by persons without children. Taken together, these developments indicate that the neighborhood's residents were quite far advanced in their life cycles. In 1880, 42.6 percent of the heads of households were already past forty years of age; in 1900 the percentage had increased to 51.4. While the number of children still living in the household had decreased by 1900, the percentage of sons and daughters twenty years of age and over still living in the family home had grown dramatically, from 9.2 percent in 1880 to 19 percent in 1900.

The fact that the majority of the heads of household even as early as 1880 were not newcomers to the United States or to Chicago helps account for the relative stability and continuity of this neighborhood. On the average, the German families had come to the country some nine to thirteen years earlier, and most of them

Table 2. Household structure of the microneighborhood

	1880		1900	
	N	%	N	%
Nuclear	443	61.3	591	48.8
Extended	68	9.4	141	11.6
Augmented	69	9.6	129	10.6
Widow and children	62	8.6	142	11.7
Childless	69	9.6	133	11.0
Single	11	1.5	76	6.3
Total	722	100.0	1212	100.0

had headed directly to Chicago.[17] One can also assume that for most of the North Siders in 1880 this was an area of second settlement, since the neighborhood had been totally destroyed by the Chicago Fire nine years earlier.[18] The 1900 census yields more accurate information about the time of immigration: 37 percent of the household heads in 1900 had arrived ten to twenty years earlier; and an additional 36 percent, a goodly proportion of whom must have lived on the North Side even in 1880, had been in the United States from twenty to forty years.

The length of stay and age structure of the heads of household also explain the high rate of home ownership in 1900. If the census taker was accurate in also tallying the buildings in the rear of a lot, there were 478 dwellings and 202 homeowners in that year. Nine-tenths of these homeowners were of German descent, and a staggering 60 percent of the first-generation homeowners had arrived before the Fire of 1871. By contrast, more than 60 percent of all Chicago German heads of household had arrived *after* 1871.[19] Obviously, home ownership contributed substantially to the ethnic continuity of the neighborhood.

Occupations of boarders, sons, daughters, and wives

THE fact that in both 1880 and 1900 the nuclear family was the dominant household form does not imply that the head of household was the only breadwinner in the family. In both years 44 percent of the households with more than one person had more than one person's income at their disposal. What were the additional sources of these family incomes?

Germans on the North Side worked in small-scale industries and craft shops like furniture making and metalwork as well as in printing, publishing, and brewing. Retailing was also a large employer, particularly for women, as was the clothing industry. Significantly, the large industrial belt along the North Branch of the Chicago River did not attract the majority of its work force from the German population, although Germans were represented in the tanning and the iron and steel industries.[20] The industries and trades attractive to German North Siders employed a skilled labor force and offered the possibility for advancement into the ranks of small proprietors and manufacturers.

German businessmen generally employed other Germans, thus also giving new immigrants an opportunity to find work in the neighborhood. They often also passed on their skills to their sons, providing for continuity of the business. For example, all the

North Side carriage and wagonmakers identified in the 1880 population census came from Germany. They often operated their shops in partnership with other relatives, and all had sons who had learned the trade of blacksmith or were currently apprenticed to a smith. Similarly, the clothing and tobacco trades offered fairly easy employment opportunities to newly arrived immigrants. Of the tobacco dealers and cigar makers in 1880, 85 percent were first-generation Germans. Cigar making in the district greatly expanded during the 1880s as growing numbers of immigrants settled there. Also, more than half of the Germans working in printing and publishing lived on the North Side. This prestigious and highly skilled craft certainly helped define the North Side as a center of German ethnic culture. Because the workers in all these trades were not forced to commute out of the neighborhood to get to their jobs, they could easily live the whole of their everyday lives on the North Side.

In the microneighborhood in 1880 the employed persons who were not heads of household probably worked on the North Side as well, since their occupations fit so well with the economic structure of the area (see Tables 3 and 4).[21] In addition, commuting to the city center was still rather difficult. In both 1880 and 1900 these workers composed around half of the employed people living in the microneighborhood. Predominantly boarders and sons and daughters of the household heads, these potentially more mobile workers were employed in neighborhood-based trades and low white-collar positions appropriate to the local retail businesses. Thus a considerable proportion were salesclerks and bookkeepers, while more than two-fifths of the men worked in a large variety of skilled occupations in the neighborhood craft shops, supplying the area with necessary services as painters, plumbers, and blacksmiths. Females, young and unmarried, often worked in the neighborhood-based clothing industry. Close to two-thirds of them worked as tailoresses, dressmakers, or as machine operators in the nearby tailor shops. One has to add to the women workers included in Table 4 those daughters and wives who ran a retail business or craft shop at home. The census taker often just listed under their occupation that they were "at home," when it is very obvious that they worked in the family business.

In 1900 the employment structure had changed to some extent, but it remained very diverse. Among the employed men who were not heads of household, those working in commercial trades had risen to more than 46 percent. The retail trades had become the largest employer in the area. The percentage of sons and boarders working in offices had risen by nine percentage points, while the

Table 3. Occupations of males, other than heads of household, living in the microneighborhood, 1880 and 1900

	1880		1900	
	N	%	N	%
Commerce and trade	**105**	**31.9**	**287**	**46.3**
Office clerks	19	5.8	90	14.5
Bakers and helpers	7	2.1	23	3.1
Barkeepers and bartenders	—	—	13	2.1
Diverse storekeepers and employees	23	7.0	32	5.2
Salesclerks	40	12.2	59	9.5
Errand and delivery boys	1	0.3	18	2.9
Transportation workers	15	4.6	52	8.4
Crafts	**140**	**42.6**	**191**	**30.8**
Metal workers	15	4.6	36	5.8
Tailors, dressmakers, etc.	19	5.8	34	5.5
Pressmen, bookbinders, etc.	24	7.3	27	4.4
Carpenters, furniture makers	24	7.3	19	3.1
Painters	11	3.4	17	2.7
Mechanics, machinists	7	2.1	13	2.1
Furriers, harnessmakers, and shoemakers	10	3.0	9	1.5
Cigar makers	6	1.8	13	2.1
Gasfitters, plumbers, boilermakers	8	2.4	14	2.3
Brickmakers and bricklayers	8	2.4	4	0.6
Diverse	8	2.4	5	0.8
Unskilled workers	**82**	**24.9**	**123**	**19.9**
Laborers unspecified	57	17.3	104	16.8
Diverse unskilled workers	25	7.6	19	3.1
Professionals	**2**	**0.6**	**19**	**3.1**
Total	**329**		**620**	
Dependent males				
Boarders and kin	90	27.3	198	31.9
Sons (under 25 years of age)	225	68.4	312	50.3
Sons (25 and over)	14	4.3	110	17.7

crafts had declined by almost twelve, with the printing and publishing, wood, leather, and building industries accounting for most of the losses. Because the clothing industry had become dominated by other ethnic groups, the German female labor market had changed considerably. Only one-third of the women still worked in the needle trades, whereas salesladies and office girls now comprised one-fourth of the female employed, while another fifth worked as laborers in nearby factories. Meanwhile, the pro-

Table 4. Occupations of females, other than heads of household, living in the microneighborhood, 1880 and 1900

	1880		1900	
	N	%	N	%
Clothing	**158**	**64.5**	**124**	**32.5**
Dressmakers	32	13.1	53	13.9
Tailoresses	87	35.5	16	4.2
Milliners	2	0.8	16	4.2
Seamstresses	24	9.8	15	3.9
Diverse tailorshop workers	13	5.3	24	6.3
Services	**41**	**16.7**	**69**	**18.1**
Servants and housekeepers	37	15.1	47	12.3
Washerwomen and laundresses	—	—	22	5.8
Hairdressers	4	1.6	—	—
Clerical and white-collar	**28**	**11.4**	**111**	**29.1**
Salesladies	17	6.9	65	17.1
Office clerks	3	1.2	26	6.8
Bookbinders	3	1.2	4	1.0
Nurses and midwives	3	1.2	9	2.4
Teachers	2	0.8	7	1.8
Factory workers and laborers	**18**	**7.3**	**77**	**20.4**
Laborers unspecified	2	0.8	12	3.1
Fringe factory workers	—	—	23	6.0
Box factory workers	1	0.4	7	1.8
Shoe factory workers	—	—	9	2.4
Stocking/knitting factory workers	—	—	6	1.6
Diverse factory workers	5	2.0	17	4.5
Diverse unskilled workers	10	4.1	3	0.8
Total	**245**		**381**	
Dependent females				
Married	12	4.9	61	16.0
Boarders, servants, kin	36	14.7	44	11.5
Daughters (under 25 years of age)	187	76.3	223	58.5
Daughters (25 and over)	10	4.1	53	13.9

portion of married women working in gainful occupations had risen from almost 5 to 16 percent. Married women concentrated in the more traditional female trades of tailoring and washing, often working in the family business, but also as salesladies. It is apparent that the married women preferred wage work at home, a work pattern that made it easier for them to also meet the demands of their household labor.

The vast majority of German housewives, however, were not

gainfully employed, and they were also reluctant to take in boarders and lodgers. Rather, the family relied on their adult children for additional income. Children fourteen years and older comprised 76 percent of the working persons other than heads of household in 1880. By 1900 the number had dropped to 70 percent, but a larger number of sons and daughters older than twenty-five still lived in the family. The decline, therefore, has to be explained by the advanced stage in the family cycle. The housewife's time and effort were thus invested in the reproduction of the workforce rather than in boarding and lodging.[22]

Analysis of the occupational structure of the microneighborhood has shown that in 1880 the Germans were able to dominate those occupations and trades which were of structural importance to the continuity of the neighborhood. They often could rely on their own ethnic group for employment or were self-employed in craft shops or in clothing and tobacco. Their skills and businesses served many aspects of neighborhood life and their workplaces kept them in close contact with the area. While in 1900 this pattern continued to predominate in the employment structure of the German North Side, the sons and daughters who had been educated in Chicago's public and parochial schools now made increasing use of employment opportunities in the central business district. Thus for them the locations of their private lives and their work became distinctly separated, and the cultural conflicts resulting from this disjunction may have promoted the neighborhood's decline in the early twentieth century.

The neighborhood trades

MANY of the neighborhood stores and shops concentrated on a local network of business streets which remained stable over a period of more than thirty years. In 1900 every single house on Clybourn and North avenues had a shop on the ground floor, and the vast majority of them were run by Germans.[23] These stores and shops housed retail businesses like groceries and hardware stores; craftsmen like bakers and shoemakers, who produced and sold goods on the same premises; or suppliers of local services, such as barbers and saloonkeepers. Businesses which advertized their German-made products with signs written in German appealed to a predominantly German clientele and gave a distinctive ethnic character to the main streets of the North Side.

Bakeries and saloons are two typical examples of businesses catering to specifically German tastes which helped define the

North Side as an ethnic neighborhood. Baking was one of the handwork trades in which Germans were disproportionately represented, not only in Chicago but in the nation as a whole. Almost half the German bakers in the city lived on the North Side in 1880. Even though the sale of bread depended very heavily on the taste of the buyer, the German bakers supplied the whole North Side in 1880 and thus served other nationalities as well. The 1880 business directory listed sixty-one bakers in the area between Chicago and Fullerton avenues and, of those, 38 could be found in the census for that year, more than four-fifths of whom were of German descent.[24] Beyond the immediate family, the augmented household provided the main source of labor for the German bakers. Sons and daughters as well as boarders and servants worked as bakers, drivers, and sales clerks. All of the North Side neighborhood bakers preferred employees with the same ethnic background.[25]

By 1900 the number of neighborhood bakeries on the North Side had not expanded in pace with the population; and larger bakeries, using more mechanized production methods, began to supply the local market. Yet the trade as it was practiced in the neighborhood shops maintained its basic structure. The same percentage of the master bakers were of German descent, the production had remained household based, the majority of the employees still lived with the family, and half the businesses had sons working as bakers in the family shop.[26] Individual continuity in the trade was also high. Two-thirds of the thirty baker families found in the 1880 city directory were still listed in the directory in 1900 (often they had to be traced through their sons and daughters). Nineteen families had remained in the North Side neighborhood, and four of them had kept their stores at the same address. In eighteen of the thirty cases, the businesses had remained in the family. Thus, during a period of severe pressure on the traditional skilled crafts, baking proved rather stable, and for the majority of members of baker families the neighborhood remained a desirable residential area over a twenty-year period.

Germans also supplied beer to the neighborhood. In 1880 the inhabitants of the North Side patronized German saloons almost exclusively; the business directory listed 238 saloons for the area, 158 of whose owners could be located in the population census. As in the case of the bakers, four-fifths of the saloonkeepers were of German origin. Most of the non-German saloonkeepers—they were from Austria, Switzerland, Scandinavia, Bohemia, Ireland, and the United States—had their businesses in the more cosmopolitan area between Chicago Avenue and Division Street. Al-

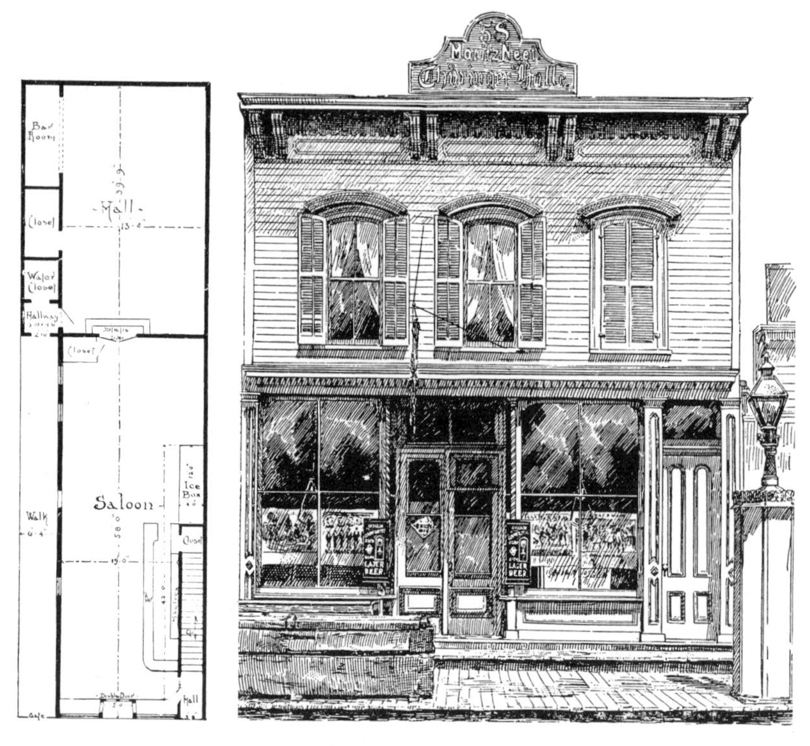

Floor plan, exterior and interior views of Neff's Hall, a typical saloon and meeting hall for German workers' organizations, located in the heart of the North Side German neighborhood. From Michael J. Schaack, *Anarchy and Anarchists*, 1889.

though the trade often attracted newcomers, the German saloonkeepers on the North Side averaged ten years or more in the country, and 75 percent of them were married and had children.[27]

Nonetheless, the pubs on the North Side were subject to the same high turnover in ownership as elsewhere in the city.[28] Yet the saloons remained as neighborhood institutions, spreading out toward the north with the population expansion. Thus their distribution in relation to the density of the population was maintained, and they remained concentrated along the major business streets. In addition, the demographics of saloonkeeping remained stable, since 71 percent of the North Side pubs in 1900 were run by men of German descent, and 90 percent of these had arrived more than ten years earlier, i.e., with the German immigration wave of the 1880s. Since the saloons would have reacted most sensitively to the changing ethnic composition of the neighborhood, the high degree of German keepers is impressive evidence of the continuity of the German neighborhood on the North Side.

Perry Duis has pointed toward the central importance of the saloon to the neighborhood and the development of community. Using the concept of the public city as a framework, Duis analyzes the saloon as a public space in order to explain the relationship between the individual and the neighborhood. The saloon took over important neighborhood functions and served economic, political, and social needs of the inhabitants, thus touching on almost every aspect of their lives.[29] Contradicting the rhetoric of the temperance movement, both the family orientation of the German saloons and the relative respectability of its keepers were evident to many contemporary observers. Unlike the Irish saloons, the German saloons were brightly lighted and tended to welcome the whole family.[30] When comparing the liquor trade in Germany and the United States, the *Chicagoer Arbeiter-Zeitung* in 1896 provided an explanation for the distinctive character of the German saloons. In Germany the liquor business was a very respectable trade, not differing from any other business. Since obtaining licenses was very difficult in Germany—they were granted only after careful examinations of the applicants—liquor licenses were regarded as a privilege; and the saloonkeepers were highly respected. Rooted in this tradition, the *Alte Wirthsverein*, the organization of German saloonkeepers in Chicago, assumed the role of a self-regulating surveillance committee to act against the most notorious scoundrels in their trade.[31] The *Verein* was also, of course, among the leaders of the anti-temperance forces in the name of German traditions and social freedom.

Conclusion

THE Germans who settled on Chicago's North Side during the second half of the nineteenth century helped to develop a diverse industrial and trade structure which formed the basis of a stable German neighborhood. Between 1880 and 1900 Germans controlled neighborhood businesses and institutions and thus impressed their ethnic identity on the area. Their shops and saloons offered a wide variety of contact and communication, both to the women, who did the shopping, and the men, who worked in the neighborhood and drank their beer in the saloon next door. The retail businesses therefore played a vital role in the everyday life of female and male neighborhood residents alike, functioning as catalysts to the formation of community identity. It is thus the continuity of social and economic structures and institutions rather than a continuity of individuals that was of major importance for the processes of North Side community building and maintenance.

Acknowledgments

I want to thank the members of the Chicago Project as well as Donna Bagaccia and Kathy Conzen for their critical reading of earlier drafts of this essay.

Notes

1. See Paul F. Cressey, "Population Succession in Chicago, 1893–1930," *American Journal of Sociology* 44 (July 1938).
2. Sam B. Warner and Collin B. Burke, "Cultural Change and the Ghetto," *Journal of Contemporary History* 4 (1969): 173–74.
3. See Howard P. Chudacoff, "A New Look at Ethnic Neighborhoods: Residential Dispersion and the Concept of Visibility in a Medium Sized City," *Journal of American History* 60 (1973–1974): 76–93.
4. Kathleen Neils Conzen, "Immigrants, Immigrant Neighborhoods, and Ethnic Identity: Historical Issues," *Journal of American History* (December 1979): 609.
5. Vivien Palmer, "Study of the Development of Chicago's Northside," Chicago Historical Society, Chicago, Ill. Palmer's paper was prepared in December 1932 for the United Charities of Chicago. See also Ulf Beijbom, *Swedes in Chicago: A Demographic and Social Study of the 1848–1880 Immigration* (Växjo: Laromedelsförlagen, 1971).
6. Palmer, "Chicago's Northside," p. 12.
7. Ibid., p. 14.
8. The business directory of 1886 lists four breweries and six malthouses of minor size for the North Side. Twenty-eight out of forty-two furniture businesses were retail stores.
9. Commission on Chicago Historical and Architectural Landmarks, *Old Town Triangle* (Chicago: 1976), 8.

10. Ibid., 10.

11. Jerome D. Fellmann, "Pre-Building Growth Pattern of Chicago," *Annals of the Association of American Geographers* 44 (1957): 65–66; Homer Hoyt, *One Hundred Years of Land Values in Chicago* (Chicago: University of Chicago Press, 1933; reprint ed. New York: Arno Press and *New York Times*, 1970), 147, 202, and 210.

13. This area will be referred to as the microneighborhood, in contrast to the larger North Side neighborhood which covers the area between Chicago and Fullerton avenues and the Lake and the River.

14. Percentage from Chicago Project sample of 5,591 households taken from the manuscript schedules of the 1900 federal census on population.

15. The ethnic composition of the neighborhood was determined by the ethnicity of the heads of household. If, however, one takes into account women of German descent who married non-Germans, one gets an even higher degree of ethnic homogeneity in the microneighborhood: 80.7 percent German households in 1880 and 81 percent in 1900.

16. Compare Hartmut Keil, "Chicago's German Working Class in 1900" in *German Workers in Industrial Chicago, 1850–1920: A Comparative Perspective*, ed. Hartmut Keil and John Jentz (DeKalb, Ill.: Northern Illinois University Press, 1983), 19–36.

17. For the 1880 census we have to derive the length of stay of a family in the United States from the age of the first child born in the United States. Since the place of birth was very often Illinois, or Chicago in particular, one has an indicator of the direct migration to the city.

18. Obviously, these Germans did not lose their ethnic identity as Cressey, for example, assumed (see note 1).

19. Chicago Project sample of federal population census of 1900.

20. According to Vivien Palmer, many Polish immigrants, for instance, worked in the tanneries, using skills obtained in their home countries ("Study of the Development of Chicago's Northside," p. 64).

21. An analysis of the fire insurance maps of 1907—the closest to 1900 which are available—shows that the occupations, especially of the women, corresponded very closely with the shops and small factories in the area. There were a large number of box making shops and teaming stables, knitting and candy factories. Right around the corner of the microneighborhood between Hammond Street and North Park Avenue was a weaving, trimming, and braiding factory, which obviously employed many of the female fringe workers.

22. See also John Modell and Tamara K. Hareven, "Urbanization and the Malleable Household: An Examination of Boarding and Lodging in American Families," in *The American Family in Social-Historical Perspective*, ed. Michael Gordon (New York, 1978).

23. Of fifty stores on North Avenue in 1880, forty-three were owned or operated by Germans.

24. Forty-two percent of Chicago's bakers were of German descent; U.S. 10th Census (1880), *Population*, 870.

25. Many problems, such as long working hours and bad living conditions, were related to the boarding system. On the work of the bakers' union on the North Side, see also Hartmut Keil and John B. Jentz, "German Workers in Industrial Chicago: The Transformation of Industries and Neighborhoods in the Late 19th Century" (paper presented at the OAH Conference, Detroit, April 1981).

26. Fifty bakers were traced in the 1900 population census.

27. For a comparable view of the newcomer phenomenon in saloon-keeping, see "Eine Studie über die Ausübung des Schankgewerbes," *Chicagoer Arbeiter-Zeitung*, February 16, 17, 19, 21, 1896, p. 4 of each issue; and *Chicagoer Arbeiter-Zeitung*, February 23, 1896, p. 3.

28. Perry Duis, "The Saloon and the Public City: Chicago and Boston 1880–1920" (Ph.D. diss., University of Chicago, 1975).

29. Ibid., pp. 175 and 551; see also Royal L. Melendy, "The Saloon in Chicago," *American Journal of Sociology* 6 (1900/1901): 289–464.

30. Duis, "The Saloon and the Public City," p. 625.

31. *Chicagoer Arbeiter-Zeitung*, articles on liquor trade, February 1896 (see n. 27 above); Duis, "The Saloon and the Public City," p. 31.

"For Whom Are All the Good Things in Life?" German-American Housewives Discuss Their Budgets

Dorothee Schneider

"WHAT does a working-class family need to live?" In December 1882 the *New Yorker Volks-Zeitung*, a socialist German-American daily, posed this question to its readers, asking them to provide answers from their personal experience.[1] Twenty-three letters were written in response, almost all from German-American housewives, concerning their household expenses and budget priorities. Two themes dominated the letters, which became an exchange of opinions. Most of the women who initially wrote to the newspaper were interested in concrete solutions to the problems they faced in trying to feed, clothe, and house their families within limited budgets; but after a few days the discussion began to shift to the more fundamental question of what standard of living a working-class family in the United States had a right to expect in return for its wage labor. To shed light on both these aspects of the discussion of the standard of living, this analysis of the letters will rely primarily on the views and information supplied by the working-class women themselves. Their voices were rarely heard, yet we can hardly understand the social as well as political implications of the debate without paying attention to them.[2] In order to assess the representativeness of the women who wrote to the *New Yorker Volks-Zeitung*, we will also include income and general expenditure information on immigrant workers from the 1880s in the United States. In order to explore further the implicit frame of reference of these German-American women, we will compare the data provided in their letters with information on German working-class household expenditures measured in the last decades of the nineteenth century.

The *New Yorker Volks-Zeitung*, initiator of the housewives' exchange on the cost of living, was the second largest German-language daily in New York at the time. Although it was only four years old, it already had more than 10,000 readers. Many of the *New Yorker Volks-Zeitung*'s local labor news and feature articles were not written by journalists but by the participating workers themselves, for the editors of the newspaper believed this was a way to include the widest possible circle of readers in the making of the newspaper itself. Readers were also invited to submit commentary and news to the letter column, entitled "Stimmen aus dem Volke" ("Voices from the People").[3] It was under this heading that twenty-one different readers commented on the costs and expenditures of working-class families in December 1882. The discussion was sparked by the letter of one woman who complained about her inability to maintain what she considered a decent standard of living. Instead of answering her directly, the newspaper's editors asked its readers to provide examples from their experience. The twenty-three letters printed as a result of this appeal came from families in a variety of circumstances. Nineteen were written by women, all except one of them housewives (two of them wrote twice); four men also contributed comments. Almost all letter writers described the circumstances under which their own families managed (eight submitted detailed budget calculations), while others only provided general opinions. One man described a neighbor's family, while another, a member of a mutual benefit society, submitted information on all members' families. Altogether, the letters provide us with information about income and expenditures on seventeen German-American families and a collective portrait of the standard of living among the members of one mutual benefit society.

How representative were the letters for New York's German-American community at large? In 1882, when the exchange of letters took place, German immigrants had settled in all parts of the New York metropolitan area, as the letters to the *New Yorker Volks-Zeitung* testify.[4] Although the majority of the paper's readers lived in New York proper—(that is, in Manhattan; the other boroughs had not yet become part of the city), ten of the twenty-one readers who wrote were living outside the city. According to the federal census of 1880, more than 160,000 Germans lived in Manhattan. In other words, 13.5 percent of all inhabitants and 18 percent of all wage earners in New York City were German-born.

By comparison, 14.4 percent of Brooklyn's and 13 percent of Jersey City's wage-earning population was German-born.[5]

The 1880s were years of rapid growth for New York's German community. Germans had been immigrating to New York in sizable numbers since the 1840s. After a temporary drop in immigration during the Civil War and the economic crisis of the 1870s, the number of Germans increased sharply by the 1880s, which were a time of economic recovery from the depression of the previous decade. By 1882 unemployment had lessened for German-American workers, although the competition from large numbers of new immigrants from Germany and other countries still made the search for work difficult. Wages had also begun to rise in most trades between 1879 and 1882. Although 1882 was a relatively prosperous year for the New York economy on the whole, the economic circumstances of German-American workers varied a great deal. New immigrants were worse off than those who had come years earlier, and certain trades were more prosperous than others.[6]

German immigrants could be found in hundreds of different occupations in the metropolitan labor market. All of the more important skilled trades in the city had a sizable number of German workers. The labor-intensive light industries that were so prominent in New York at the time—garment making, cigar manufacturing, furniture making—had a significant number of Germans in their work forces. The same was true for all food trades and for small businesses in general. Germans were slightly underrepresented in heavy industries (relatively few worked as machinists or engineers), as well as in most unskilled occupations; both these employment categories were dominated by Irish immigrants in the 1880s.[7] The predominance of skilled and small business employment did not always permit German immigrants to rank among the better-paid workers of the city. Wages in all skilled occupations varied widely (see Table 1), and German immigrants tended to cluster in those that paid especially little in late nineteenth-century New York: the needle trades, the food trades, shoemaking and cigar making. There were also German immigrants in the better-paying furniture trades and in the building trades, but few were employed in the well-paid trades of metalworking and printing in the city.[8]

Only four of the families participating in the discussion about household budgets stated the occupation of the breadwinner (laborer, cigar maker, carriage driver and seamstress), but the weekly wages quoted by most families conform to the general wage level of German immigrants quoted in Table 1. The earn-

Table 1. Average weekly pay of German immigrants in New York City for selected occupations

Occupation	Year	Weekly pay
Baker	1880	$14.00 to $ 8.00*
Brewery worker	1881	$12.00 to $17.00
Carriage driver	1885	$12.00 to $15.00
Cigar maker	1885	$ 9.67†
Carpenter	1881	$10.00 to $15.00
Furniture worker	1880	$ 7.00 to $10.00
Cabinetmaker	1879	$11.38†
Laborer	1879	$ 8.00
Piano maker	1880	$12.00 to $15.00
Printer	1881	$15.00
Varnisher	1882	$10.00 to $11.00
Domestic servant	1879	$ 2.50*
Seamstress	1880	$ 3.25‡
Embroideress	1879	$ 1.50 to $ 2.00

*Plus room and board.
†Average weekly wage for members of the trade union.
‡Maximum weekly wage calculated from piece wage on the basis of high skill and enough work for a sixty-hour week.
Sources: *New Yorker Volks-Zeitung*, January 7, August 8, December 12, 1879; February 27, March 4 and 21, 1880; January 29, February 9, March 8 and 28, June 3, 1881; April 21, September 29, November 29, 1882; *Western Brewer*, June 12, 1881; and *United States Tobacco Journal*, June 26, 1885.

ings of male wage earners in the *New Yorker Volks-Zeitung* families ranged from less than $9.00 to $16.00 a week; one widowed seamstress, who was the only wage-earning woman among the letter writers, made only $3.00 to $7.00 a week. On the average, the families which reported their incomes to the newspaper made $10.94 a week.

In their letters to the *New Yorker Volks-Zeitung*, all readers maintained that the weekly wages of one wage earner were the sole source of family income, unlike the many other working-class families in New York which had wage-earning wives and children to supplement the income of the father. Close study of the manuscript federal census for New York City, which shows in general that few married German-American women were wage earners in New York, underlines how representative of German-American families the letter writers were in this respect. In a randomly selected sample of 454 German-American families, only twenty-seven families had female wage earners, most of them working daughters.[9] These figures can be corroborated indirectly by the low percentage of German-American women among the city's laundresses and female cigar makers.[10] Of course, there were other, less noticeable ways to increase family income—taking in boarders, for example—but only six percent of the families in the sample did this. While German-Americans were reluctant to let their wives and daughters work for money, grown sons were a different matter; 86 of the 454 families had sons who worked and contributed to the family's income.[11] Thus a majority of the families in this sample subsisted on the income of one wage earner, although a substantial minority profited from the labor of sons. (In this respect they differed from the readers of the *New Yorker Volks-Zeitung*, who reported only one wage earner in all cases.) All things considered, the picture that emerges from the *Volks-Zeitung* was a rather accurate reflection of the income level among German-American working-class families in the metropolitan area; just as the letters suggest, most of them had only one wage earner, who made between nine and fifteen dollars a week. This weekly wage had to stretch through weeks of unemployment that occurred regularly in most trades and was not usually supplemented by the income of other family members.

Just as the incomes of the families in the *Volks-Zeitung*'s debate were fairly representative of New York's German working-class community, so the distribution of expenditures was also fairly consistent with other working-class budgets. Six readers submitted a detailed list of expenditures to the newspaper (see Table 2): on the average each family spent about half its income on food, between 10 and 23 percent on housing, and about a fifth of the expenditures for other items.[12] The same proportions were spent by German-American working-class families in Chicago, according to an 1883 study. The Massachusetts Bureau of Labor Statistics likewise found that workers spent about half their income on food, 24 percent on housing and 10 percent for miscellaneous items. Thus we can assume that the readers of the *New Yorker Volks-Zeitung* differed little from other working-class immigrants in urban America when it came to making a household

Table 2. Six family budgets from the *New Yorker Volks-Zeitung*

Household number	Number of persons	City of residence	Weekly income	Weekly expenses	Food	Fuel	Housing	Clothes	Other
1	6	New York	$16.00	$16.00	$10.00	N.D.	$2.70	N.D.	N.D.
2	6	New York	$15.00	$15.00	$ 6.83	$1.20	N.D.	$0.81	N.D.
3	6	New York	$13.00	$12.72	$ 6.00	$1.00	$2.92	$1.75	$1.05
4	5	Elizabeth	$11.95	$12.64	$ 5.47	$0.62	$2.11	$1.47	$2.97
5	6	Brooklyn	$10.05	$11.57	$ 5.40	$1.00	$1.00	$1.25	$2.92
6	7	Jersey City	$ 9.50	$ 9.50	$ 6.20	$0.40	$1.92	N.D.	N.D.

Source: *New Yorker Volks-Zeitung*, December 6, 9, 11, and 14, 1882.

budget.[13] However, their distribution of expenditures differed measurably from that of German workers of comparable rank in the old country: in Germany, craftsmen and better-paid skilled workers inevitably spent between 55 and 60 percent of their income on food, while the unskilled had to budget up to 70 percent. On the other hand, workers who lived outside large cities spent less than 10 percent of their income on housing.[14] In order to assess the meaning of this difference and the specific choices and problems faced by the German-American working-class families in New York, we need to analyze the budget categories in more detail.

The four major types of expenditure had different degrees of importance for the readers who discussed them. Housing was the most fixed part of the families' expenditures. There were few ways a family could save on housing costs in New York; this part of the budget was therefore not discussed at length in the letters. Most of the budget discussions concentrated on food expenses. The women who wrote to the *Volks-Zeitung* considered this their special realm and thought that the quality of a family's menu directly reflected its general quality of life. Likewise, the expenses for clothing were mostly the women's responsibility. However, the readers of the newspaper treated this item as a minor and irregular expense. The information on clothing expenses is too scant to be analyzed in detail here. On the other hand, any expenses other than those for food, rent, and clothes were hotly debated. Most families' efforts to balance their budgets depended on their ability to keep costs for items beyond food, clothing, and housing to a minimum. The discussion of extra expenses therefore overlapped with the topic of savings and debts in general and will merit close analysis near the end of the essay.

The cost of housing made up a considerable part of those family incomes reported in the *New Yorker Volks-Zeitung*. The survey of housing costs from the letters to the newspaper indicates that they were particularly high in Manhattan itself. Most working-class families could afford only a small tenement apartment, despite the high rent they paid. We do not know where in Manhattan families 1, 2, and 3 of Table 2 lived. Family 1 wrote that they lived in a "quite miserable apartment," possibly one of the three- or four-room tenement apartments—one or two windowless bedrooms, a kitchen, and a so-called parlor—which were quite uniform throughout the city. Family 3, for a bit more than twelve dollars a month, could get a better tenement in one of the newer, airier houses on the Upper East Side or half a floor in a former one-family house.[15] Outside Manhattan, housing was generally cheaper. Rents were one or two dollars lower in Brooklyn and even lower in New Jersey. However, the lower rentals were usually offset by the higher cost of transportation to and from Manhattan: $2.50 to $5.00 a month had to be added to a family's budget if the wage earner had to commute every day.[16] Altogether, housing costs remained a rather static part of the household budget, and few individual efforts could be made to save on the rent.

The cost and quality of working-class housing in New York came closer to the conditions in most larger German cities than to those in other parts of the United States. In many industrial German cities, workers had to pay between 15 and 20 percent of their earnings in return for similarly small dwellings. Overcrowding was also as much a problem in urban Germany as it was in New York's tenement districts. Most of New York's German immigrants, however, came from semirural areas and small towns in the old country where workers lived in small cottages or two-family houses. Housing costs in those areas were usually less than 10 percent of a worker's income, although generalizations are difficult to make.[17] Working-class housing in small-town and rural Germany offered few amenities, but the quality of life in Manhattan's tenements was lower than in non-urban Germany. If they wanted better housing, New York's German-Americans had to spend a larger part of their budgets on rent than their counterparts in the Old World (twelve to eighteen dollars a month) or to assume the costs and time burden of a long commute to work. In the last decades of the nineteenth century, many German-Americans made the latter choice, moving in increasing numbers to New York's suburbs.[18]

The food budgets received much more attention from the readers of the *New Yorker Volks-Zeitung* than the expenses for housing. Altogether, six food budgets and twelve estimates were discussed in detail and hotly debated in the letters. The money spent on feeding a family varied considerably. Six of the women spent no more than seven dollars a week on food. Three others, however, had more than twelve dollars to spend—and their expenses were not considered too high even by those who had less. The thriftiest of those who submitted a detailed budget was Anna Spahn, the wife of a cigar maker earning between $9.00 and $10.00 a week. Anna Spahn fed her seven-member family, each of them with "a healthy appetite," on $6.20 a week. Her food budget included $1.20 (the equivalent of ten pounds of pork) for meat a week, but unlike all the other women in the sample, she spent more money on bread than on meat ($1.30, which bought the equivalent of sixteen loaves of bread at 8 cents each). Milk was also an important part of the family's diet (eleven to twelve quarts a week for 70 cents), perhaps because the Spahns had small children. The main staple besides bread was potatoes. Mrs. Spahn bought about thirty-five pounds a week for 50 cents. She also spent 40 cents a week on vegetables, the types not specified. The family also used over two pounds of lard, a pound of butter, and a pound of sugar, as well as seven pints of beer and five eggs a week; but no mention was made of grains, cheese, or fish. Such a menu made for a very one-sided diet, even by contemporary American working-class standards. This food budget was probably typical for the five other families who spent less than seven dollars on food but did not itemize their menus.[19] For most readers, on the other hand, a food budget such as Anna Spahn's was unacceptable. "It is almost impossible that this Spahn family can be fed properly with $6.20 a week," remarked one woman. Other women resented the fact that their husbands, after seeing Mrs. Spahn's thrifty menu and a similar low-cost food budget by a Mrs. Reinhardt, wanted to curb the food allowance for their families. "My husband wants to send me to Mrs. Reinhardt next week, so that I can learn how to save from her. But I prefer Sing Sing!" wrote one irate housewife.[20]

By traditional German standards, on the other hand, the Spahn family's diet was rather ample. An 1887 inquiry into the standard of living of cigar makers in the province of Baden, the German home of many cigar makers such as the Spahns, showed that those workers had much less to eat. A cigar maker's family in Baden had to get by on one to two pounds of meat a week and one pound of butter; eggs and milk were rare, and sugar was not even a part of the regular diet of those cigar makers.[21] Bread and home-grown potatoes made up a larger part of the diet in Baden than in the United States but were not necessarily more plentiful: fourteen loaves of bread and thirty pounds of potatoes had to suffice for a six-member family. Even better-off workers in the old country had to limit themselves to a diet much less ample than Mrs. Spahn's. In the 1890s the relatively well-paid skilled jewelry workers in the southwest German town of Pforzheim could only afford one pound of meat per adult per week, three pounds of bread, and four pounds of potatoes.[22] Although these diets consisted of the same foods eaten by poorer German-Americans in New York, there was simply much less to eat on the tables of poor Germans in the old country.

Unimpressed by the relative abundance in Anna Spahn's menu, other newspaper readers considered nine to twelve dollars a week the necessary minimum for food. With that amount available, they bought fifteen to seventeen pounds of meat a week; seven quarts of milk; three-fourths of a pound of butter; twenty pounds of potatoes; seven to eight loaves of bread; small quantities of fruit, cheese, or grains other than flour; one to two pounds of sugar; and in most cases a pint of beer a day and over one pound of coffee a week.[23] Many German-American workers in New York City considered these quantities of food—especially the meat, potatoes, and bread—just the necessary minimum; the amounts were not excessive or otherwise unusual. This was demonstrated during an 1877 strike of 10,000 New York cigar makers, about half of whom were German; the other half were Bohemian immigrants. The cigar makers, who were among the poorest workers in the city, set up a store to supply free food to all needy strikers. The weekly ration for a five-member family was designed by the German-American leaders of the strike to provide a modest diet. It consisted of seven pounds of flour, two pounds of coffee, four pounds of sugar, sixteen to seventeen pounds of potatoes, three heads of cabbage, and four quarts of dried beans a week; it also included three pounds of meat and two loaves of bread a day.[24] The food in New York boardinghouses, in many cases the first American diet that working-class immigrants encountered in the United States, was often equally abundant by German standards. A newly arrived cabinetmaker described his first meals, particularly breakfast, in a New York boardinghouse to his friend in Germany: "Beefsteak. Amazing! Meat in the morning! It is really nice in America! On the other side I only had coffee. And then lunch that was even more delicious! Soup, two kinds of meat, different kinds of vegetables—I only had one of a kind on the other side—steamed fruit and last not least a glass of beer after all this! This was fun for me, I must stay here, where could it be better?"[25]

As Werner Sombart noted eighty years ago, the diet of American workers was out of reach for most working-class families in the old country. Even upper middle-class Germans like the six-member family of a manufacturer or the household of a high civil servant in the provincial town of Jena ate only sixteen pounds of meat a week. Only well-to-do Berlin professionals could match the twenty-pound weekly meat consumption described by Friederike S. and other housewives who wrote to the *Volks-Zeitung*. As a rule, workers in Germany only ate a third to a fifth as much meat as most of their American counterparts during the late nineteenth century. Butter, a regular item on German-American tables, was a rarity for German working-class families who consumed only two to eight ounces a week. Only when it came to bread and potatoes did German quantities match those consumed by the German-Americans.[26] Poor families ate more potatoes than richer ones, although the difference was less pronounced in the United States. In general, the overall quantity of food eaten was measurably greater among poor German-Americans than among less well-off Germans.

But did the women in the *New Yorker Volks-Zeitung* still compare their standard of living to that of working-class people in Germany? Only one woman, the thrifty Marie Reinhardt, did so, at least explicitly. She urged her fellow readers who could not manage on less than ten dollars a week to "learn how to save from a housewife in Germany, and you will see that you can achieve equal comfort (*Gemütlichkeit*) with much less." For most of those who wrote to the newspaper, standards of comfort had increased, especially when it came to their daily menus. Mrs. Reinhardt's six-dollar food budget for a family of two, which was probably similar to what a better-off German family of the same size ate in a week's time, was severely criticized by one housewife, who asked, "What does Mrs. Reinhardt eat? As far as I can tell, she makes sauerkraut on Saturdays and reheats it on Sunday." Another woman remarked on the low-cost food budgets of other families: "Many things are missing . . . in one list there isn't even butter!" Clearly, she no longer judged her own standard of living by the standards of her class in Germany.[27] In fact, very few of the *New Yorker Volks-Zeitung*'s readers compared their American eating standards to those of working-class people in Germany. They expected to eat like better-off Americans and resented being forced by their limited means to fall back on the cheaper diet they knew from home.

There was little space in the budgets of most women to make any savings unless families were willing to eat less than other Americans. Most savings, the readers felt, would have to come out of the part of the budget that was spent on items other than food, clothing, and shelter. Such items included anything from small personal luxuries like newspapers or the men's beer money to emergency funds, medical expenses, and membership fees in clubs and benevolent societies. Many of the *Volks-Zeitung*'s readers wanted to discuss how much a family should have spent on these items (and actually did spend); what priorities were set; and what could be done if no money was left after rent, food and household necessities had been paid. A major concern was whether cuts in the food allowance should be made to save money or whether it was justifiable to go into debt in such a case.

Sixteen letter writers mentioned some extra expenses which they regularly incurred, and two budgets list these items in detail. The most frequently mentioned items were newspapers and beer money for the men. A newspaper was, of course, bought by the families who read the *Volks-Zeitung* (a penny a day), but even outside this group, newspaper money seems to have been a regular part of most family budgets. According to the two detailed lists of extra expenses, German-Americans spent about twice as much money for printed matter as was necessary to buy the daily paper; so magazines and books also seem to have been bought regularly by these working-class families.[28]

Beer money was a much more sizable item on most budgets than the amount spent for newspapers and books. Wilhelmine Bauer attested that her husband spent at least $1.80 per week—a day's wages for many workers—on food and drink for himself, and "often more than that." Other women reported fifty cents for beer money; an alcoholic carriage driver spent almost his entire wages on horse feed and beer. It was impossible for most women, though, to assess the exact amount the men spent themselves: "If we ask the men: what do you spend in a week? The answer is, 'that's none of your business, I have to earn it, after all,'" complained Mrs. J. B. The strict Marie Reinhardt maintained that "a husband and father should bring home all his earnings. It seems to me that the pocket money is more generously measured and spent [than household money]."[29]

But some women had to take more drastic measures to cut their spouses' pocket money. The wife of the alcoholic carriage driver stole her husband's money, although this was difficult at times, since he "often puts the money in his socks and goes to sleep in them and does not take them off, until the last cent has been spent on drink." One Emilie Foth asked other women to follow her example and cheat their husbands out of 50 cents in the weekly household budgets to contribute it to the "liberation of women and children"![30] These women's actions demonstrate how dependent they were on their husband's voluntary cooperation when it came to saving money and how little they could do to curb the amount the men decided to spend on themselves.

Two other items were mentioned on the expense lists of the *New Yorker Volks-Zeitung*: medical care and membership fees for organizations. Only four readers of the newspaper mention doctor's fees and expenses for medication. Budget statistics on German-Americans in Brooklyn and Chicago, as well as a study of New York cigar makers (mostly German), show that expenses for medical care occurred in most families during any given year. The families in these statistics had to spend between 2.3 percent and 4.5 percent of their yearly income on medical care, a considerable amount in a tight budget.[31] It is therefore remarkable that only three of the families who wrote to the *New Yorker Volks-Zeitung* listed membership fees in mutual benefit societies as part of their expenses. Such organizations offered the only insurance available to most workers. Studies of the Chicago and Brooklyn German-Americans also indicate that even if workers belonged to such an organization (it is doubtful if the majority did), membership fees made up less than 2 percent of their yearly income.[32]

Very few items other than those already mentioned appeared in the budget discussion at all. Two women listed expenses for their children's education (schoolbooks); another mentioned an occasional trip to the beach in the summer. Trips to the theater, vacations, or other such extras were clearly out of reach for most of these families. "We live very simply," stated one woman; and this seems to have been the motto for the majority of those who wrote to the newspaper. Money for extras was so tight that "I try to avoid going out as if it were purgatory, because I am afraid it might cost something and cause a deficit which would punish us for weeks," one woman wrote.[33]

Despite such principles, many families could not make ends meet, and only those with low housing costs and small food budgets could hope to put aside savings "in order not to become a burden to others during unemployment or other misfortunes." Others who tried to put away savings did not succeed. "Women who are able to make ends meet for less [than $10] without hunger, debt and endless worries, and who are healthy and well dressed, may tell us how they do it. We would like to hear from them," wrote one housewife.[34] But as the discussion went on, it became clear that ending the month on a surplus was impossible for working-class families with three to four children and a wage earner making up to thirteen dollars a week, unless their diet was old-country German in quantity and variety. Few housewives were willing to be so rigorous. Perhaps it is no accident that the two most detailed budgets submitted to the newspaper both showed a deficit. A reader who furnished one of these budgets commented that "workers borrow wildly until none of the little bloodsuckers in the neighborhood will give them any more credit. Then they move to a new neighborhood and start all over again, and I do the same."[35] Three other women expressedly followed these tactics. Two of them had the lowest incomes of any of the families. The wife of the alcoholic wrote that since she had no regular income at all, "I buy everything on credit until I get no more, then I go to another store and do the same there." Another, mother of two children, who as the head of household earned only three to seven dollars a week sewing, had the same problems and solutions. She and her two little daughters—who had "an awfully good appetite"—ate well enough, sometimes more than their budget permitted. This led to unpaid bills and forced moves. But she addressed her problem in more fundamental ways. "Is it really good for a worker to save? I think it is a disgrace if a worker saves something voluntarily through physical self-denial; on the contrary, he should spend everything possible on himself and his family, so that he can withstand the many trials which he has to endure as a working man, apart from the harsh climate, so that if bad times are coming, he and his family don't break off like hollow tree trunks." Mrs. E. H. agreed: "Saving is no good. I learnt from experience: what you save through self-denial is eaten by the cats after a while." She asked the other readers: "For whom are all the good things in life—only for our enemy, the bloodsucker?" Whether they managed with or without debts, almost all women agreed that, whatever their budgets, as wives of working men they could not maintain what they considered a satisfactory standard of living. "To eat, dress and live well, it takes more than fifteen dollars," wrote one of the very thrifty women. Others agreed: "In order to live well you need a good income, and that is what the workingman does not have. The employer takes care of that; he lives well for all of you." Many women agreed with the political implications that were seen by this reader. Mrs. E. H. and other women consequently concluded that "we women should encourage our men to join the union, so that they get better wages. Then we can live decently." Another called on the women themselves to organize in order to better their lot.[36]

How can we measure the standard of living of working-class Germans in the 1880s? In some ways, they were doing well, compared to the Germans they had left behind. As we have seen, food was ample and, for Germans outside Manhattan, housing conditions were also better than in most German cities. Most immigrant families could enjoy these benefits without sending their wives or young children into the work force. Altogether these circumstances came close to fulfilling the dream of many a German social reformer and, indeed, many a worker too. But the readers of the *New Yorker Volks-Zeitung* no longer took German conditions as the only measure of their standard of living. Instead, they considered America's better food and housing part of a normal level of comfort. But varied diet and better housing carried a higher price than figures alone would suggest, as the housewives knew. When immigrant families with modest incomes ate well, they took the risk of incurring dangerous budget gaps. Satisfying their longing for better food and housing left little money for the many rainy days that New York workers almost inevitably experienced, whether as a result of illness or of cyclical unemployment. The housewives were acutely aware that more than just food, housing, and other basics made up their standard of living. They daily faced the choice of saving for the future or providing a decent minimum in the present. The choice always reminded them and their husbands of their insecurity as wage laborers and led them to seek political solutions to their dilemma.

Notes

1. *New Yorker Volks-Zeitung*, December 4, 1882. (Hereafter cited as *NYVZ*.)

2. The most recent work on the standard of living is Peter Shergold, *Working Class Life: The American Standard in Comparative Perspective, 1899–1913* (Pittsburgh: University of Pittsburgh Press, 1982). Unfortunately, I was not able to obtain a copy of it before sending this article to press. The standard of living is also central to numerous studies concerned with immigrant groups and their adjustment to American society. For examples, see Stephan Thernstrom, *Poverty and Progress: Social Mobility in a Nineteenth Century City* (Cambridge: Harvard University Press, 1964); Thomas Kessner, *The Golden Door: Italian and Jewish Immigrant Mobility in New York City* (New York: Oxford University Press, 1977); Virginia Yans-McLaughlin, *Family and Community: Italian Immigrants in Buffalo, 1880–1930* (Ithaca: Cornell University Press, 1977).

3. Karl J. Arndt and May Olson, *The German Language Press of the Americas*, vol. I (Munich: 1976), 406, give a circulation figure of 10,200 for 1880 but no figure for 1882.

4. The dates on which the *NYVZ* printed the letters are December 4, 6, 7, 8, 9, 11, 12, 13, 14, and 15.

5. The percentages for 1880 would be increased to about 30 percent if the American-born children of German immigrants were added to the percentage of German-Americans. See Stanley Nadel, "Kleindeutschland, New York City's Germans 1840–1880" (Ph.D. diss., Columbia University, 1981), p. 82. The 1890 federal census makes a distinction between German-born and American-born children of German immigrants. According to these data, 14 percent of New York's inhabitants in 1890 were born in Germany and 14.3 percent were American-born but had parents who were born in Germany. See Kate H. Claghorn, "The Foreign Immigrant in New York City," in United States Industrial Commission, *Report*, vol. 25 (Washington: 1903), p. 469.

6. Wolfgang Köllmann and Peter Marschalck, "German Immigration to the United States," in *Perspectives in American History* 7 (1973): 499–557. Information on New York's labor market and German immigrants can be found in my Ph.D. dissertation, "Gerwerkschafte und Gemeinschaft—drei deutsche Gerwerkschaften in New York, 1870–1900" (University of Munich).

7. United States Census Office, *Tenth Census of the United States, Census of Population*, vol. 1 (Washington, D.C., Government Printing Office, 1881), 880, 865, and 892.

8. My preliminary research into the population schedules for the Tenth Census for New York City indicates that many second-generation

German-Americans could be found in the well-paid trades of printing and musical instrument making. This impression is partly confirmed by Nadel, "Kleindeutschland," p. 136.

9. United States Census Bureau, *Tenth Census of the United States, Population Schedules for New York County* (New York, 1880); the sample was taken from the tenth, eleventh, seventeenth and nineteenth wards. It includes only households in which both parents (if present in the home) were born in Germany.

10. *Census of Population*, vol. 1, 492; the findings on the low proportion of German-born female cigar makers are from a study of 1,000 cigar makers in the population schedules of the *Tenth Census*, to be discussed in detail in my forthcoming dissertation.

11. U.S. Census Bureau, *Population Schedules for New York County*, 1880; Louise Bolard More, *Wage Earners' Budgets: A Study of Standards and Cost of Living in New York* (New York: H. Holt, 1907), 85. According to More, German-American working-class families were rather strict about having their children contribute most or all their income to the family budget, so that children over fourteen years could be counted on to contribute at least as much money as boarders.

12. *NYVZ*, Dec. 8, 9, and 12, 1882.

13. Peter R. Shergold, "Expenditure Patterns of Workers in Chicago, 1883–1884" (Paper presented to the Munich Conference of the Chicago Project, University of Munich, June 1880); Massachusetts Bureau of Labor Statistics, *Fifteenth Annual Report* (July 1884), 465.

14. Carl Hampke, *Das Ausgabenbudget der Privatwirtschaften* (Jena: Gustav Fischer, 1888), vi, 66–68, 73.

15. *NYVZ*, December 8, 9, and 12, 1882, p. 4 of each issue. For a survey of housing conditions among working-class New Yorkers during the nineteenth century, see Robert DeForest and Lawrence Veiller, eds., *The Tenement House Problem*, 2 vols. (New York: Macmillan, 1903), especially the essay by Veiller, "A Statistical Study of New York's Tenement Houses" (vol. 1, 191–240), and an anonymously written vol. 2 appendix essay, "Tenement House Rentals."

16. Home ownership was beyond the means of most working-class families, even in the outlying areas, in the 1880s. A down payment of at least two hundred dollars and monthly charges of about twenty dollars for the cheapest houses made this option available only to the small group of workers whose financial situation was stable and whose income was above $800 a year (John C. Gebhard, *Housing Standards in Brooklyn* [Brooklyn: Tenement House Committee of the Brooklyn Bureau of Charities, 1918], 38–47; and H. L. Cargill, "Small Houses for Working Men," in *The Tenement House Problem*, vol. 1, ed. DeForest and Veiller, 333–45).

17. On German working-class housing, see Lutz Niethammer, "Wie wohnten die Arbeiter im Kaiserreich?" in *Archiv für Sozialgeschichte*, vol. 7 (1967): 78–81; Heilwig Schomerus, "Die Wohnung als unmittelbare Umwelt," in *Wohnen im Wandel*, ed. Lutz Niethammer (Wuppertal: Hammer, 1979).

18. By 1916 Germans were no longer considered to be a regular part of the tenement population. See Gebhard, *Housing Standards in Brooklyn*, 46–48; and Claghorn, "Foreign Immigrants and the Tenement House in New York City," in *The Tenement House Problem*, vol. 1, ed. DeForest and Veiller, 65.

19. *NYVZ*, December 6, 1882. Since the housewives did not state the quantity of an item they bought but rather only the amount they paid for it per week, the amounts of the purchases had to be calculated using the standard prices for the items. The retail prices used in these calculations were taken from *NYVZ*, January 7, 1879, and New York State Bureau of Statistics of Labor, *Tenth Annual Report* (Albany: B. Lyons, State Printer, 1892), 277–82.

20. *NYVZ*, December 8, 13, 1882.

21. Grossherzoglich badisches Ministerium des Innern, *Die sociale Lage der Cigarrenarbeiter im Grossherzogtum Baden: Beilage zum Jahresbericht des grossherzoglich-badischen Fabrikinspektors für das Jahr 1889* (Karlsruhe: Thiergarten und Raupp, 1890), 117–75.

22. Ibid., and F. Kestner, "Die Bedeutung des Haushaltsbudgets für die Beurteilung des Ernährungsproblems," in *Archiv für Sozialwissenschaft und Sozialpolitik*, vol. 19 (Tübingen: J. C. B. Mohr [Paul Siebeck], 1904), 312.

23. *NYVZ*, December 6, 9, 11, 12, and 14, 1882.

24. *New Yorker Staats-Zeitung*, October 24 and 25, 1879; *New York Sun*, October 25, 1879.

25. *Social-Demokrat*, December 3, 1876.

26. Werner Sombart, *Why Is There No Socialism in the United States?*, trans. and ed. C. T. Husbands and P. M. Hocking (London: MacMillan, 1976), 86–88, 105–6. Sombart's statistical findings are only partially applicable to living conditions of working-class people in New York City around 1880; he is therefore not used as a data source in this article. For the data on German working-class nutrition in comparative perspective, see Kestner, "Die Bedeutung des Haushaltsbudgets," p. 313–14; Hampke, *Das Ausgabenbudget der Privatwirtschaften*, p. 95; and Alfred Grotjahn, "Über Wandlungen der Volksernährung," in *Staats- und Sozialwissenschaftliche Forschungen*, ed. Gustav Schmoller, vol. 20 (Leipzig: Dunker und Humblot, 1902), 42–50.

27. *NYVZ*, December 12, 13, 1882.

28. *NYVZ*, December 8, 9, 14, 1882.

29. *NYVZ*, December 8, 9, and 11, 1882.

30. *NYVZ*, December 14 and December 9, 1882.

31. *NYVZ*, December 8, 9, and 14, 1882; *United States Tobacco Journal*, March 7, 1885, p. 2; and Peter Shergold, "Expenditure Patterns of Workers in Chicago."

32. Peter Shergold, "Expenditure Patterns of Workers in Chicago" and *NYVZ*, December 9, 1882.

33. *NYVZ*, December 8 and 9, 1882.

34. *NYVZ*, December 14 and December 9, 1882.

35. *NYVZ*, December 8 and 14, 1882.

36. *NYVZ*, December 14 and 15, 1882.

Politics and Culture

4.

Free Soil, Free Labor, and *Freimänner*: German Chicago in the Civil War Era

Bruce Carlan Levine

ON January 4, 1854, Illinois Democrat Stephen A. Douglas introduced his Kansas-Nebraska bill into the United States Senate and loosed the dogs of war. Signed into law in May, this legislation eliminated previous federal restrictions on the westward expansion of the slave-labor system, undermining all hope of extending the decades-long era of compromise over this issue. The law produced a wave of revulsion and an unprecedented outpouring of protest throughout the North and West which doomed the old two-party system, eventually bringing forth a new mass-based Republican party whose conquest of the White House just a few years later triggered secession and war.

While rocking the free states as a whole, the Nebraska bill aroused some groups more than others. The large and growing German-American population, which was particularly important in the economy and politics of mid-Atlantic and midwestern urban centers, was swept up in this political storm. German anti-Nebraska meetings seemed to spring up everywhere, most notably in Chicago, Cleveland, Cincinnati, Indianapolis, Pittsburgh, Philadelphia, Newark, and New York City; the dimensions of this response electrified the native-born free-soil forces. The *Free West* of Chicago exulted, "No class of citizens have manifested more indignation at Douglas's scheme for extending slavery over the vast territory of Nebraska than our immigrant and native Germans."[1] To understand the real extent, sources, and meaning of this reaction—and to clarify the specific social strata and broad political concerns it involved—this essay examines developments in one of its principal centers, Chicago.

MID-CENTURY Chicago was a boom town already on its way toward dominating midwestern transportation, commerce, and manufacturing, and its explosive growth was reflected in population statistics. During the decade ending in 1850, the city's residents increased in number from some 4,500 to 30,000. Ten years later, the population was nearly 110,000. By 1870 it was lapping at the 300,000 mark.

Irish and German immigration supplied much of the human material demanded by the expanded economy. And while in 1850 the weight of the Irish-born in the population (20 percent) exceeded that of the Germans (17 percent), a single decade reversed the relative importance of the two groups. By 1860, the Germans made up 20 percent and the Irish, 18 percent of the city's population.

Occupationally, the gainfully employed German population was made up overwhelmingly of skilled craftsmen and unskilled workers; these two categories accounted for 48 and 36 percent, respectively, of all German-born household heads in 1850. The importance of these people in the city's work force becomes clear in Table 1, which is based on statistics compiled from the 1860 federal census manuscripts. While the German-born represented one-fifth of the total population, their significance in many key

Table 1. Percent of work force which was German born in selected Chicago trades, 1860

Occupation	German born (%)
Painters	30
Masons, bricklayers, stonecutters, marble polishers	32
Carpenters	33
Blacksmiths	39
Saddlers and harness makers	53
Tailors	54
Tanners and curriers	55
Wagonmakers and carriage makers	56
Butchers	56
Shoemakers	56
Miscellaneous woodworkers	66
Bakers	68
Cabinetmakers	74
Cigar makers	78

trades was far greater. In addition, 2,000 (30 percent) of the city's approximately 6,700 unskilled laborers were also German-born.[2]

Throughout the country, many of the traditional artisan crafts which appear in Table 1 were undergoing wrenching transformations in these decades as an older mode of production, based largely on a self-employed class of artisan proprietors, gave way to a new system based on wage labor and capital. Strangers to the English language, insecure, owning little property, the Germans were especially vulnerable. In 1854 the *Chicago Daily Tribune* presented one view of the workers' situation. Asserting that it was "without any strong predilections in favor of foreigners of any kind," the *Tribune* continued:

> we confess to a much more cordial feeling toward our German population than to any other class of citizens not "native and to the manor born. . . ." They are industrious, sober (if we except a constitutional and national weakness for Lager Beer) and above all, fitted to do the cheap and ingenious labor of the country.[3]

This last qualification especially gratified the editor, who added happily that "The German will live as cheaply and work infinitely more intelligently than the negro." If remuneration was probably somewhat higher in Chicago than in eastern cities, absolute incomes remained low, employment was often irregular, and living expenses, especially rents, were high indeed. Two financial crises within five years (1853, 1857) considerably worsened the conditions of the laboring population.[4]

The social and political life of these newly arrived Chicagoans was shaped both by conditions encountered in America and by their recent experiences in Europe. The German emigration of the late 1840s and early 1850s was intimately bound up with the general crisis then wracking Germany. Urban artisans were caught squarely in the middle of the conflict between semi-feudal institutions and the pressures of capitalist development. This helps explain why, when crisis led to revolution in 1848, artisans, particularly journeymen, provided the popular movement with much of its driving power. For the same reason, the most extreme democratic leaders and parties found their strongest support among such people. Fearing proletarianization and pauperization (and often equating the two fates) above all, radical artisans and like-minded allies raised demands and behaved in ways that frightened the liberals who dominated Germany's parliament in Frankfurt. The 1848 coalition blew up, opening the way for the counterrevolution.[5]

The Workers Hall (Arbeiter-Halle) on Twelfth Street and the Aurora Turner Hall on Milwaukee Avenue were built in 1864 and 1868, respectively, making them among the earliest meeting places for German workers in Chicago. From *Der Westen*, 15 November 1896 and 9 May 1897.

In the past, historians commonly minimized both the artisans' role in 1848 and the impact of the revolution on the consciousness of craftsmen, including the many who emigrated. The result was a myopic view of 1848 as a revolution of the intellectuals and the equally short-sighted assumption that only an educated elite among those leaving for America identified with radical-democratic doctrines. The social base of the popular movement was thus ignored, and the bond connecting popular leaders with their broader constituency was erased.

But as Carl Wittke has reminded us, while "no estimate of the number of workers among the [emigré] Forty-eighters can be made with any reasonable accuracy," it is clear that

> more of the revolutionary forces were drawn from the rank and file than from the intellectual or upper social classes. Among the German-Americans of whose part in the Revolution we can be certain there were carpenters, cabinetmakers, tanners, weavers, bakers, cigarmakers, butchers, bookbinders, gardners, foundrymen, millers, coopers, coppersmiths and blacksmiths, tailors and representatives of other crafts as well as men who belonged to the unskilled working class.[6]

In his nineteenth-century history of Chicago, Eugen Seeger recalled that "the revolutionists . . . defeated and forced to flee from Germany" included "thousands [who] were simple artisans," as well as "hundreds of professors, poets, musicians, artists, editors and professional men."[7] Education and a degree of social deference often awarded leadership to intellectuals, but a genuine community of concerns, perceptions, and demands linked them to the more numerous artisans, shopkeepers, and other plebeians. Called Jacobinism, the outlook binding all these diverse middle-strata elements together was, in E. J. Hobsbawm's words, "a vaguely defined and contradictory social ideal, combining respect for (small) property with hostility to the rich . . . a universal and important political trend which sought to express the interests of the great mass of 'little men' who existed between the poles of the 'bourgeois' and the 'proletarian,' often perhaps rather nearer the latter than the former because they were, after all, mostly poor."[8] By 1848, this outlook and the heterogenous coalition to which it appealed and whose cohesion it aided was already a familiar phenomenon in Europe, as E. P. Thompson, Albert Soboul, and Gwyn Williams (among others) have demonstrated.[9]

Out of this milieu in German Chicago arose a network of economic, political, and social organizations, all espousing Jacobin doctrines resonating with the issues and rhetoric of 1848. Established in the city in 1852, the Turnverein was one of the most important of these organizations. Born decades earlier in the fatherland as a nationalist group, the Turners by 1848 combined physical and military training with radical-democratic propaganda; members often took the lead in artisan mobilizations that year. The Freimännerverein (Freemen's League), a kindred organization, was founded in Louisville, Kentucky, in 1854 and quickly spread to Chicago and several other cities boasting substantial numbers of recent German immigrants. Educational and mutual benefit societies appeared among Chicago's German tailors, wagonmakers, and carpenters early in the decade. The more inclusive Arbeiterverein, founded somewhat later, was destined to play a pivotal role in the politics of German Chicago.[10]

The doctrines such organizations defended bore unmistakable European birthmarks but also displayed a strong family resemblance to ideas which preoccupied native-born American plebeians during the early stages of industrialization. Their common goal was a society in which all producers enjoyed political equality, social respect, and economic well-being—"prosperity, education, and freedom for all," in the Freemen slogan, permitting the "laboring classes [to] be made independent of the oppression of the capitalist" and securing to labor its "incontestable claim to the value of its products."[11] Inordinate extremes of wealth and poverty would vanish, along with the unequal enjoyment of political privilege. Though hard times in the New World tempered some immigrant illusions, the United States still seemed the one place where this social goal might yet be attained. As an *Illinois Staats-Zeitung* editorial put it,

We crossed the ocean and entered the Land of Promise, to live as human beings and free citizens on a free soil. The glorious banner of Stars and Stripes—not embroidered with pictures of wild animals, as are the standards of despots—attracted us strongly, for in it we saw the symbol of freedom and human rights, the shield of the oppressed of all nations, the sign of victory of a revolution which had eradicated the last vestige of monarchy from the New World, and which fanned a spark across the ocean that ignited such a widespread conflagration in Europe that the citadel of feudalism was completely ruined.

To be sure, the paper observed, the going was often difficult and disenchanting in America:

Many among us fought a severe fight for a material existence; many were bitterly disappointed when their immoderate hopes were not realized, when sanguine expectations proved to be mere bubbles; . . . [but] though the building which was being erected . . . did not afford each one an equally comfortable shelter and did not measure up to each one's conception of beauty and grandeur, the foundation was very good, since it permitted a reconstruction, elevation, and expansion; and everyone who lived in that structure had a right and duty to assist in its erection.[12]

The strong affinity most immigrant Germans felt for the Democratic party early in the 1850s reflected the belief that, in contrast to the aristocratic Whigs, this party did indeed stand in the international democratic tradition. That belief was reinforced by the northern Democrats' comparative openness toward the foreigners, their relaxed attitude toward alcoholic beverages and observance of the Puritan Sabbath, their initially enthusiastic endorsement of land reform (Stephen Douglas championed a homestead bill in 1849), and the verbal support Douglas and his Young America faction of the party gave to the insurgent European democracy.

From the standpoint of the immigrant Jacobin, however, the most glaring single defect of the North American republic was chattel slavery. "Instead of ensuring Liberty to all," raged the Freemen's League in its founding manifesto, "more than three million human beings have been condemned to Slavery, and they [the slaveholders] try to increase their numbers daily." In bondage and the slavocracy, Chicago's German radicals perceived forms of economic and political oppression similar to those they had just escaped in their homeland: the legalized degradation of labor supporting a landed aristocracy which in turn dominated a repressive, stagnant society.

The existence of this labor system anywhere in the United States was shocking, but it seemed at least bearable so long as it remained geographically contained and apparently destined for eventual extinction. Pending its demise, the immigrant could simply settle elsewhere; there was plenty of free soil to go around. But the Kansas-Nebraska Act and the concommitant prospect of slavery's survival and expansion transformed the terms of the issue completely. This became evident, for example, at a convention of northern Illinois German workingmen's and radical societies held in Peoria in May 1854. Convenors and participants included organizations of carpenters and tailors as well as Freemen and Turners. The body adopted a platform containing more than a dozen specific demands, including immigrant rights, public education, complete religious freedom, and a shorter working day; it opposed black-exclusion laws. None of these individual issues, however, was considered more urgent than that of chattel slavery. On the contrary, resolved the assemblage, "We consider the agitation against slavery the most important of all."[13]

In 1854, the Illinois legislature received a petition opposing Douglas's Kansas-Nebraska bill signed by almost 800 Chicagoans, nearly all with German names. More than 60 percent of the signatories whose occupations could be determined were craftsmen, notably shoemakers, tailors, carpenters, cabinetmakers, harness makers, and stoneworkers of various kinds—all leading trades of the immigrant artisanry. If we add those identified as unskilled laborers and small proprietors—mostly grocers and owners of taverns, restaurants, and boardinghouses—the proportion climbs above 80 percent. Individuals engaged in commerce, manufacturing, or finance accounted for just under 4 percent. This breakdown indicates that while opposition to the Douglas bill was a cross-class phenomenon (as it was in the northern population generally), its principal German strength lay among the skilled working people.[14] This fact helps explain the special zeal and volatility of the German anti-Nebraska movement which impressed (or alarmed) so many observers. As the fight against slavery escalated in intensity, the most militant and resolute of its exponents in German Chicago arose from among the plebeian Jacobin organizations and the radical intellectuals associated with them.

One of these people was Theodore Hielscher, a teacher who had played a prominent part in the Berlin uprising of 1848. Forced to flee to America in 1851, Hielscher settled first in Indianapolis, where he edited the *Freie Presse* and became an active member of the local Turnverein. After moving to Chicago, he became a leader of the Arbeiterverein in that city and for some time during the Civil War years served as its spokesman and president. Another Forty-Eighter veteran was Eduard Schlaeger, one of the most radical of the German emigré activists. Schlaeger spent some years in Boston where he co-edited the *Neue England Zeitung*. The *Zeitung* became notorious for its generalized Jacobin radicalism and antislavery fervor and was one of the very few German-language papers in the country to withhold support from the Democrats' presidential candidate, Franklin Pierce, in 1852. Instead, Schlaeger and his associates campaigned for the Free Soil party's John P. Hale. That same year, Schlaeger served as secretary and Boston delegate to the congress of radical German nationalists—the People's League for the Old and New World—held in Wheeling, Virginia. Moving to Chicago, he again became well known as an advocate of extreme democratic views. In 1854 he joined the editorial staff of the *Illinois Staats-Zeitung*, which, under the editorship of Forty-Eighters, sought to speak for German Chicago as a whole while maintaining a special relationship with the Jacobin currents, particularly on the issue of slavery.[15]

Eduard Schlaeger threw himself into the anti-Nebraska cause and on March 12, 1854, organized the first German mass meeting in Chicago to protest Douglas's measure. As in 1852, Schlaeger urged a break with the Democrats, and the meeting adopted his resolution, warning that "we have lost our confidence, and must look with distrust upon the leaders of the Democratic party." Elaborating on this point in his own speech that night, Schlaeger declared that "the time has gone by . . . when it was only necessary to play the fiddle to make the Germans dance to any given tune." It was "high time the German population ceased being led by the nose by the demagogues of the Democratic Party."[16] The *Illinois Staats-Zeitung* took up the call for a new party later in the year.[17]

The outraged sense of betrayal which Douglas's bill created among German craftsmen, small shopkeepers, and laborers burst forth dramatically in the aftermath of the March 12 evening assembly. A large portion of the audience, its ranks soon swollen by what the *Chicago Daily Tribune* called "swarms" of fellow countrymen recruited from the streets, initiated a monster demonstration starting at North Market Hall and ending at Court House Square. Upon reaching their destination, the marchers took hold of a banner bearing the likeness of Stephen A. Douglas, tied it to a rope, hoisted it overhead, and set it ablaze "amidst the hisses, groans, and hurrahs of the largest number of people ever before assembled in the city on any public occasion."[18]

This intemperate display sent a thrill of apprehension through those observers already uneasy about the type and tendency of the recent immigrant influx into the country. "Beggarly sans culottes," cursed the *Cleveland Plain Dealer*, "enemies of peace and order—of government human or divine."[19] "Such acts," warned another writer, "are but the first phase of violence and mob law"; they displayed a spirit threatening "the direst . . . consequences that can well be conceived, to any community where it may occur."[20] Southern senators pointed to the incident in Chicago to justify restrictions on the immigrants' franchise and the exclusion of noncitizens from the benefits of homestead legislation.

Even some anti-Nebraska elements drew back in alarm from the display at Court House Square. "We have yet to hear the first word in approval of that act," reported Chicago's *Daily Democratic Press*, a paper strongly opposed to the expansion of slavery. "Every citizen from whom we have heard an expression of opinion at all in relation to the matter condemns it in unmeasured terms. . . . Excesses of this character are sure to injure the cause they are intended to advance." A letter written by "a German" who professed opposition to the Nebraska bill itself nonetheless denounced the March 16 outburst, charging that "the whole thing was managed by a few abolitionist Germans." That letter, however, was answered by a second German who sneered at the "inconsistency" of the first writer, "who pretends to hate the Nebraska *treason* while he does not dare crush the *traitor*." Fortunately, the reply concluded, "the Germans [are] in general . . . not cold-blooded enough to make such nice distinctions."[21]

As this controversy revealed, German America was by no means politically monolithic in the Civil War era. Some of the wealthiest and most powerful among them, in fact, adamantly opposed social and political radicalism (including antislavery zeal), an attitude they shared with the hierarchies of the immigrant Catholic and Lutheran (especially Missouri Synod) churches. The most widely circulated German-language paper in the country, the *New Yorker Staats-Zeitung*, typified this current. Firmly anchored in the Democratic party, organ of the oldest and richest German mercantile community in the country, the *New Yorker Staats-Zeitung* made war on Jacobinism throughout the 1850s. In 1854, it aggressively supported the Kansas-Nebraska Act and heaped abuse upon the measure's critics.[22]

In Chicago, sponsorship of this political current fell to Michael

Diversey, reputedly the wealthiest German in the city. Alderman, co-owner of the largest brewery in the West, and a conservative Catholic, Diversey was implacably hostile to antislavery and stepped up his support for the Democratic party precisely as its proslavery monolithism hardened. In 1855, Stephen Douglas recognized that the support of the once friendly *Illinois Staats-Zeitung* was permanently lost. Needing funds with which to launch a new and more pliable German-language paper, he naturally turned to Diversey. Just as naturally, Diversey obliged. The *National Demokrat* was launched, and the *New Yorker Staats-Zeitung* celebrated the appearance of an ally in Chicago. Two years later, Buchanan's open proslavery policy in Kansas and the political heat it generated in the free states forced even Douglas to take his distance from the White House. Most regular Illinois Democrats followed his lead, but not Michael Diversey nor the *National Demokrat.* They remained staunch, if increasingly isolated, defenders of Buchanan and his program.[23]

A third current in German Chicago, flanked by radicals like Schlaeger on one side and conservatives like Diversey on the other, professed liberal ideals while struggling to restrain the forces of political polarization and social upheaval. The most consistent, articulate, and influential representative of this current was Gustav Koerner, who had come to the United States in the 1830s among the liberal emigrés of that decade. In this country, Koerner studied law and soon prospered and gained influence as an attorney closely tied to the leading German families of southern Illinois. Extending his ambitions and political constituency statewide, Koerner moved quickly up the Democratic party ladder, becoming state supreme court justice in 1845 and lieutenant governor in 1852.

Koerner's characteristic political outlook expressed itself on a broad spectrum of issues over the years. In 1848, he instinctively identified with the liberal constitutional-monarchist majority in the Frankfurt Assembly, disdaining those who "belonged to the extreme and most radical wing" and who "were full of the most fantastic ideas." Encountering some of the latter in their subsequent American exile, Koerner was again repelled by "the arrogance, the insolence, and charlatanism of these would-be reformers." (In this category, incidentally, he singled out for special mention Eduard Schlaeger, "a half-crazy reformer" who "made a great noise.") Koerner placed much of the responsibility for the rise of anti-German sentiment in this period on the "imperious and domineering conduct of the refugees."

Koerner's reaction to chattel slavery in America grew organically out of this general outlook. "I always hated slavery," he could honestly record in his memoirs but then added with equal accuracy that "constitutionally I saw no way of abolishing it." He greeted the compromise of 1850 with relief, despite its inclusion of the Fugitive Slave Law, as a way to resolve a vexing perennial conflict. Koerner's sounding board in those days, the *Belleviller Zeitung*, excoriated radical German critics of the compromise. In 1854, preferring Southern slavery to remain "a purely local institution," Koerner opposed the Kansas-Nebraska Act because it nullified earlier congressional compromises and therefore portended "agitation, strife, and bloodshed, if not . . . civil war." But, having become Illinois's lieutenant governor on a Democratic ticket expressly designed to soothe downstate proslavery sensibilities, Koerner declined to play a leading role in the anti-Nebraska movement as such.[24] This role he left to Francis A. Hoffmann.

Born in Westphalia, Francis Hoffmann sank his American roots in northern Illinois. The year 1840 already found him a practicing Lutheran minister. By 1847 he was the postmaster of Schaumburg, in Cook County, and he had become Schaumburg's town clerk by 1851. Transferring operations to Chicago, Hoffmann, like Koerner, took up the law and gained admittance to the bar; he then plunged into real estate, won election to the city council, and founded a successful banking house. In 1854 Hoffmann shared Koerner's displeasure with the Douglas bill but felt freer than the lieutenant governor to act.

Hoffmann's prominence and respectability in the German-American population made him a sought-after spokesman at anti-Nebraska meetings, where he sought to exercise a restraining influence on the proceedings. His speeches commonly combined denunciation of slavery with defense of the South's right to maintain it, criticism of Stephen Douglas with reluctance to break from Douglas's party. "We have no inclination whatever to interfere in the rights of the South," he told the March 16 meeting organized by Schlaeger, and "though it may be beyond our comprehension how a freeman can enslave his fellow man, yet we will submit. We peaceably submit to what the politicians call the rights of the South." It was only the Nebraska bill's threat to bring slavery "to the free ground of the North," he explained, which compelled men like him to draw the line and warn, "So far, but no further." But Hoffmann was not yet ready to break with the Democratic party. Yes, he granted, should the party demand that its officeholders and supporters endorse the Nebraska bill, then it would be necessary to "break the chains that fetter us to that party," as the main resolution and Schlaeger's speech that night proposed. But that point had not yet been reached, Hoffmann insisted: "This is not a party test, nor a party measure."[25]

IN the years that followed, inescapable political forces weakened the position in the North of both pro-Southern and conciliationist advocates. As the conflict of interest and outlook between the two contending labor systems grew ever sharper, the whole framework of Northern politics began to shift leftward.

In Chicago, the pro-Nebraska forces among the Germans fought desperately, but ultimately vainly, to reverse the decline of their fortunes. They tried in 1856 to disrupt German Republican meetings; publicly burned *Illinois Staats-Zeitung* editor George Schneider in effigy; and marched on the *Staats-Zeitung* office, threatening to seize the premises and put them to the torch. Only the timely arrival of armed Turnverein members induced the would-be arsonists to reconsider their plans. In 1857, the *National Demokrat* changed tack and sought to embarrass the new Republican city government by championing public works and relief for the unemployed in that depression year. But the growing political polarization over the slavery issue and Buchanan's pariah role left his German supporters unable to capitalize much on such issues. Nor did harping on the nativist associations of some Republicans do more than draw out and complicate the more fundamental political trend. By 1858, the bankruptcy of the Buchanan-Diversey forces in Chicago was clear to virtually everyone.[26]

The same powerful dynamic pushed moderates like Hoffmann and Koerner (the former more quickly than the latter) into the Republican party. Contrary to Hoffmann's hopes, the Democratic leadership in 1854 did declare the Nebraska bill to be a party measure and a party test and proceeded to drive dissenters out of the organization. Election returns that fall registered substantial disaffection with the Democrats among Chicago's German voters. In February 1856, however, Koerner still refused nomination to the Illinois Republican central committee (although by then even the cautious Abraham Lincoln had joined the new party), explaining inter alia that he "could not cooperate with any party" unwilling to "affirmatively maintain that the Constitutional rights of the Southern states should never be interfered with."[27] At last left little alternative to the Republicans, Koerner was pleased to find that party in the hands of kindred spirits like O. H. Browning, who strove to keep the party in this state under the control of moderate men—and conservative influences . . . [for] if we do, the future destiny of the state is in our hands and victory will inevitably crown our exertions; on the other hand, if rash and ultra counsels prevail, all is lost.[28]

For party leaders like Browning, the accession of German moderates was equally welcome. With their aid, the German masses might follow the Republican lead without in the process strengthening the position within the party of "rash and ultra" Germans like Eduard Schlaeger. In 1856, Hoffmann received the Republican nomination for the office of lieutenant governor. As a top Republican spokesman, Koerner, too, worked diligently to rally the German ranks—and keep them in line. His speech the night of June 4, 1856, captured the essence of his campaign message that fall. Addressing thousands of his countrymen after an enthusiastic Republican demonstration led by the Turnverein, Koerner admonished listeners that "the Germans . . . were for free territory, but they were not given to fanaticism of any kind. They would oppose the fanaticism of the North just as they were now opposing the fanaticism of the South."[29]

Chicago's once overwhelmingly Democratic German electorate fractured in 1854 in the wake of the Kansas-Nebraska Act. The taint of nativism and sabbatarian zealotry which clung to the young Republican party briefly sapped its appeal to antislavery immigrants, but by 1860 German Chicago had shifted decisively into the Republican camp—to a far greater extent, in fact, than the rest of the city. James Bergquist's careful study estimates that while Chicago as a whole gave Lincoln a 55 percent majority that year, Germans of the North Side's Seventh Ward voted 75 percent Republican.[30]

Paralleling this shift and reflecting the same underlying forces, the most radical wing of German Republicanism also grew in size and coherence. With its principal social base among the Forty-Eight era artisans and their Jacobin-minded leaders, this militant immigrant Republicanism obtained its strongest organizational support in the Chicago Arbeiterverein. In the 1860 campaign, the Arbeiterverein combined pro-Lincoln agitation with strong lobbying among Republicans for labor's special concerns, expressed in part in the platform adopted at the Deutsches Haus conference of German Republicans that year. In 1861, secession once again revived compromise talk in the North, especially among the upper classes. But Republican societies led by German artisans and laborers denounced "several Chicago meat packers and grain merchants" who, because "they probably are not able to buy as much pork and flour as they were wont," were now "doing everything they possibly can during the current week to support the compromisers in the Senate and House of Representatives."[31]

As the war progressed, German radicals in and out of uniform kept up a steady pressure for a program more aggressive, democratic, and straightforwardly antislavery than the one enunciated by Lincoln, raising demands which often brought them into close collaboration with congressional Radicals. Among themselves, the Jacobins debated, not about the merits of compromise with the South, but rather about whether Lincoln's war policy was antislavery enough to warrant their support.

The order issued by General John C. Fremont in August 1861, emancipating all Rebel-owned slaves in the Department of the West, drew enthusiastic applause in these circles and swelled the ranks of Illinois Germans enlisting under Fremont's command. By rescinding that order and then removing Fremont from command, Lincoln made a great many enemies. The Arbeiterverein's Joachim Kersten, a tailor, chaired the September 1861 meeting at the Arbeiterhalle which resolved, "We are convinced that the slavery existing in the Southern states of the Union is the cause of the present war, and that peace and the Union cannot be restored unless this infamous institution is completely abolished."[32] The Socialer Arbeiterverein of the Tenth Ward branded "Lincoln's mutilation of General Fremont's proclamation" as nothing less than "treason against our country."[33] Only by abolishing slavery could the South be defeated quickly, the verein argued, blaming the government's lack of firm antislavery principles for indecisive, temporizing military tactics which only prolonged the war and its attendant suffering. This hostility toward the Union authorities was often reciprocated. Fremont's replacement, General Henry Halleck, was appalled at the political complexion of his German troops. "Officered in many cases by foreign adventurers or perhaps refugees from justice and having been tampered with by political partisans for political purposes," he wrote McClellan in January 1862, they "constitute a very dangerous element in society as well as in the army."[34]

To achieve a more equal distribution of the war's burdens among all social classes, the Chicago Arbeiterverein called for universal military conscription, shorn of provisions allowing the rich to buy their way out of service. The German-born father of one Union soldier expressed the class resentment beneath this demand, warning that "we plebeians have done our share. The patricians who live on Michigan Avenue need not think that only the sons of plebeians are fit and worthy to be slaughtered and that the wealthy can sidestep their obligations as citizens of the United States and evade the rigors and hardships of military life." Cash bounties were unacceptable substitutes. "What good is a hundred or even a thousand dollars when poor men's sons must sacrifice life and limb under the leadership of these ignorant patrician generals?"[35] A world of difference separated this stance from that of war-weary draft rioters and Copperheads. The Chicago Arbeiterverein declared inciters of New York's draft riots to be "friends of the Rebels" pure and simple and endorsed the restoration of order "with several bullets."[36]

In 1863 and 1864, the Arbeiterverein joined a movement among German radicals nationally which came to endorse John C. Fremont's challenge to President Lincoln's reelection. This movement demanded a war policy aimed at the Confederacy's unconditional surrender, nationwide abolition, congressional reconstruction, laws granting "all men absolute equality before the law," and "confiscation of the lands of the rebels and their distribution among the soldiers and actual settlers."[37] German Fremont clubs sprouted luxuriantly in a dozen states, Illinois prominent among them.

Ultimately, the Fremont boom collapsed. The candidate himself proved less radical than his platform and his German supporters. Specifically, Fremont shrank from land-reform plans requiring large-scale confiscation of private property. But until Fremont actually withdrew his candidacy in late September, the spectre of widespread defections among German voters haunted the White House. Lincoln himself, long sensitive to political shifts among the Illinois Germans, believed their support for Fremont could well cost him that state at the polls. Gustav Koerner, by now a Lincoln adviser, "regretted . . . that so many Germans were found in opposition to Lincoln" in 1864. The leadership of the Chicago Arbeiterverein, however, worked energetically for Fremont; 85 percent of its approximately 1,000 members reportedly supported that policy. Such people, Koerner explained in his memoirs, were simply "highly impractical idealists." They were "most radical on the slavery question, and Lincoln was too slow for them."[38]

THIS essay has reexamined a critical period in American history, one Charles and Mary Beard aptly called the Second American Revolution.[39] It has explored the role of Chicago's German-Americans in the history of local antislavery, the development of the Republican party, and the issues of the Civil War. It has suggested ways in which developing social conditions and class relations shaped the outlooks and conduct of this immigrant group. Finally, the pattern of events recounted here helps clarify a key phase in the evolution of American working-class politics.

In the political development of that class, it has recently been argued, the Civil War represented a kind of detour, diverting labor away from its own interests into a disorienting alliance with its enemy, the northern industrialists. The experience recounted in this essay hardly supports that interpretation. Antislavery was the natural expression of the needs and ideals, formulated on two continents, of the highly politicized immigrant working people examined here. For them, the Civil War was an integral part of the fight for a just and democratic society. Speaking at a pro-emancipation rally organized by the Chicago Arbeiterverein in January of 1863, Wilhelm Rapp explained, "This society recognizes that this battle is a battle of workers and has so indicated in the resolutions made here today."[40] If the pursuit of those goals did indeed involve an alliance with sections of the employer class, these plebeian Jacobins nevertheless proved troublesomely assertive and unruly as allies and distressingly resolute in the war effort itself. Ultimately spurned by the North's political and economic elite, the radical Republicanism championed by the German democrats became a bridge to the still more independent and radical labor movements and programs of later years.

Acknowledgments
I would like to thank the following friends and colleagues for their help in the preparation of this article, Herbert Gutman, Joshua Brown, Stephen Brier, Eric Foner, Bruce Laurie, Frederick Marquardt, Shelley Kroll, and Paul Le Blanc.

Notes

1. *Free West*, May 18, 1854. For a discussion of the German response nationally, see Bruce Carlan Levine, "'In the Spirit of 1848': German-Americans and the Fight over Slavery's Expansion" (Ph.D. diss., University of Rochester, 1980).

2. Elmer A. Riley, *The Development of Chicago and Vicinity as a Manufacturing Center Prior to 1880* (Chicago: University of Chicago Press, 1911), 37–102; A. T. Andreas, *History of Chicago from the Earliest Period to the Present Time*, vol. 1 (Chicago: A. T. Andreas, 1884), 564–73; Arthur C. Cole, *The Era of the Civil War, 1848–1870* (Springfield: Illinois Centennial Commission, 1919), 1–7, 27–29; Bessie Louise Pierce, *A History of Chicago*, vol. 2 (New York: Alfred A. Knopf, 1940), 482; Hartmut Keil, "The German Working Class in 1900" (Paper presented to the Conference on Working-Class Immigrants in Industrial Chicago: 1850–1910, October 1981), p. 9. Table 1 is based on manuscript census totals supplied by Herbert G. Gutman.

3. *Chicago Daily Tribune*, March 7, 1854.

4. Cole, *The Era of the Civil War*, 2, 202–3; *Chicago Daily Tribune*, November 12, 16, 1857; *Weekly Chicago Democrat*, November 14 and 21, 1857.

5. For background, see Mack Walker, *Germany and the Emigration, 1816–1885* (Cambridge, Mass.: Harvard University Press, 1964); and Frederick D. Marquardt, "A Working Class in Berlin in the 1840's?", in *Sozialgeschichte Heute*, ed. Hans-Ulrich Wehler (Göttingen: Vandenhoek and Rupprecht, 1974), 191–210; and "*Pauperismus* in Germany during the *Vormärz*," *Central European History* 2 (March 1969): 77–88.

6. Carl F. Wittke, *Refugees of Revolution: The German Forty-Eighters in America* (Westport, Conn.: Greenwood Press, 1970), 341.

7. Eugen Seeger, *Chicago, The Wonder City* (Chicago: Gregory, 1893), 105–7.

8. E. J. Hobsbawm, *The Age of Revolution, 1789–1848* (New York: Mentor, 1964), 57.

9. E. P. Thompson, *The Making of the English Working Class* (New York: Vintage, 1963), 20–21, 122, 145, 157; Albert Soboul, *The Sans-Culottes* (Garden City, N.Y.: Doubleday, 1969), 30–42; Gwyn Williams, *Artisans and Sans-Culottes* (New York: Norton, 1969), 18, 32. Eric Foner makes a similar point concerning Tom Paine's appeal in revolutionary Philadelphia. See Foner, *Tom Paine and the American Revolution* (New York: Oxford University Press, 1976), 100.

10. Hermann Schlüter, *Die Anfänge der deutschen Arbeiterbewegung in Amerika* (Stuttgart: Dietz, 1907), 18–19, 172–73, 199–203; William F. Kamman, *Socialism in German American Literature* (Philadelphia: Americana Germanica Press, 1917), 51–64; E. Schlaeger, *Die sociale und politische Stellung der Deutschen in den Vereinigten Staaten* (Berlin: Puttkamer and Mühlbrecht, 1874), 13–14; Friedrich A. Sorge, *The Labor Movement in the United States*, ed. P. S. Foner and B. Chamberlin (1891–95; English edition, Westport, Conn.: Greenwood Press, 1977), 96–97, 152; Henry Metzner, *A Brief History of the American Turnerbund* (Pittsburgh: American Turnerbund, 1924), 7–17; Pierce, *History of Chicago*, vol. 2, 166–67.

11. "The Freemen's Louisville Manifesto," *Free West*, May 18, 1854.

12. *Illinois Staats-Zeitung*, July 26, 1861.

13. The resolutions of the Peoria conference appeared in *Der Demokrat* (Davenport, Iowa), June 24, 1854 (transcribed in the F. I. Herriott Papers, Iowa State Historical Department). See also two reports on the conference (brought to my attention by James Bergquist) in the *Belleviller [Illinois] Zeitung*, April 6, 1854, and the *Deutscher Anzeiger* (Freeport, Ill.), July 28, 1854.

14. On the petition, see Levine, "'In the Spirit of 1848,'" pp. 285–90. Compared with their weight in German Chicago, the unskilled were apparently underrepresented (11 percent) among the petitioners. Perhaps this is a statistical mirage; city directories, from which occupational data are drawn, were far more prone to omit the unskilled than any other occupational group. It is therefore possible that the unskilled actually did sign the petition in large numbers but are now hidden among the many signatories whose occupations could not be determined. It is also possible, however, that the unskilled Germans were in general less affected by social radicalism and antislavery doctrines because of their more heavily

rural origins in Germany and their correspondingly stronger attachment to the conservative Old Lutheran and Catholic churches. For this interpretation, see Ernest Bruncken, "German Political Refugees in the United States during the Period from 1815–1860," *Deutsch-Amerikanische Geschichtsblätter*, vol. 4, no. 1 (1904): 33–34; and Carl Wittke, *We Who Built America* (New York: Prentice-Hall, 1945), 225. On the occupational biases of city directories in this era, see Stephan Thernstrom, *Poverty and Progress: Social Mobility in a Nineteenth Century City* (New York: Atheneum, 1971), 31.

15. On the careers of Hielscher and Schlaeger, see A. E. Zucker, "Biographical Dictionary of the Forty-Eighters," in *The Forty-Eighters*, ed. A. E. Zucker (New York: Russell and Russell, 1967), 304–5, 337; J. F. L. Raschen, "American-German Journalism a Century Ago," *American-German Review* 12 (June 1946): 15; Kamman, *Socialism in German American Literature*, 41; Schlaeger, *Die sociale und politische Stellung der Deutschen in den Vereinigten Staaten*, 6, 17; Karl Obermann, *Joseph Weydemeyer, Pioneer of American Socialism* (New York: International Publishers, 1947), 136–39; Pierce, *History of Chicago*, vol. 2, 167, 171–72, 187; T. S. Baker, *Lenau and Young Germany in America* (Philadelphia: P. C. Stockhausen, 1897), 71–73.

16. Schlaeger's speech was quoted in the *Chicago Daily Journal*, March 17, 1854, and the *Chicago Daily Tribune*, March 22, 1854. The meeting's resolution appeared in the *Daily Democratic Press* (Chicago), March 17, 1854, and the *Tribune* of March 20, 1854.

17. The editorial is quoted in the *Missouri Republican* (St. Louis), September 25, 1854.

18. *Chicago Daily Tribune*, March 18, 1854; *Chicago Daily Journal*, March 17, 1854.

19. *Cleveland Plain Dealer*, March 18, 1854.

20. Letter in the *Daily Democratic Press*, March 20, 1854.

21. *Daily Democratic Press*, March 17, 19, and 20, 1854. See also the *Chicago Daily Journal*, March 18 and 20, 1854.

22. See, for example, the *New Yorker Staats-Zeitung* of February 4, 18, and 25; March 11 and 17; and April 8, 1854.

23. On Diversey and the *National Demokrat*, see I. D. Guyer, *History of Chicago; Its Commercial and Manufacturing Interests and Industry* (Chicago: Church, Goodman, and Cushing, 1862), 43; Andreas, *History of Chicago*, vol. 1, 410, 534; Pierce, *History of Chicago*, vol. 2, 219; *Weekly Chicago Democrat*, July 5, 1856; and James M. Bergquist, "The Political Attitudes of the German Immigrant in Illinois, 1848–1860" (Ph.D. diss., Northwestern University, 1966), pp. 187–90, 251. See also the *New Yorker Staats-Zeitung* of February 13, 1856.

24. For Koerner's views, see *The Memoirs of Gustav Koerner: 1809–1896*, vol. 1 (Cedar Rapids, Iowa: Torch Press, 1909), 518, 545–49, 618; Bergquist, "Political Attitudes of the German Immigrant in Illinois," pp. 88, 118–23, 140, 165–67, 315–16; *Daily Democratic Press*, May 13, 1856. For background, see Koerner's *Das deutsche Element in den Vereinigten Staaten von Nordamerika, 1818–1848* (Cincinnati: Wilde, 1880), chaps. 12 and 13; and Cole, *Era of the Civil War*, 102–4.

25. Hoffmann's speech was quoted in the *Chicago Daily Journal*, March 17, 1854. On his career, see Koerner, *Das deutsche Element*, 279–81; [Herman Julius Ruetnik], *Berühmte deutsche Vorkämpfer für*

Fortschritt, Freiheit, und Friede in Nord-Amerika (Cleveland: Forest City Bookbinding, 1888), 432–35.

26. See, for example, the *Daily Democratic Press*, March 8 and 10, 1856; *Chicago Daily Tribune*, March 10 and August 26, 1856; and November 16, 1857; Don E. Fehrenbacher, *Prelude to Greatness: Lincoln in the 1850s* (Stanford, Calif.: Stanford University Press, 1972), 37, 112; Bergquist, "The Political Attitudes of the German Immigrant in Illinois," p. 251.

27. Koerner, *Memoirs*, vol. 2, 3–4. See also Cole, *Era of the Civil War*, 125–26.

28. Browning was quoted in James Lee Sellers, "The Make-Up of the Early Republican Party," *Transactions of the Illinois State Historical Society* 37 (1930): 42, 50–51.

29. Koerner was quoted in the *Daily Democratic Press*, June 6, 1856.

30. Bergquist, "The Political Attitudes of the German Immigrant in Illinois," p. 345. A recent study of statewide voting patterns finds Illinois Germans giving Democrat Franklin Pierce 90 percent support in 1852; in 1860, however, Stephen Douglas, also a Democrat, received only 30 percent of the German vote in the presidential election. See Stephen L. Hansen, *The Making of the Third Party System: Voters and Parties in Illinois, 1850–1876* (Ann Arbor, Mich.: UMI Research Press, 1980), 227, 249.

31. Resolutions of the German Seventh Ward and Seward clubs printed in the *Illinois Staats-Zeitung*, February 19, 1861. See also its issues of January 8, 9, and 23, 1861. Diversey's *National Demokrat* demanded compromise with the seceding South, according to the *Illinois Staats-Zeitung* of January 24, 1861.

32. Resolution quoted in the *Illinois Staats-Zeitung*, September 30, 1861.

33. Socialer Arbeiterverein resolution quoted in *Illinois Staats-Zeitung*, October 1, 1861. Similar opinions were expressed in meetings reported by the *Staats-Zeitung* through late 1861 and well into 1862. Publisher J. L. Scripps expressed concern over the strong German reaction to Lincoln's treatment of Fremont in a November 27, 1861, letter to George Schneider, formerly of the *Staats-Zeitung*. (The George Schneider MSS., Chicago Historical Society).

34. Halleck is quoted in Earl J. Hess, "Sigel's Resignation: A Study in German Americanism and the Civil War," *Civil War History* 26 (March 1980): 12–13.

35. Letter in the *Illinois Staats-Zeitung*, August 1, 1862. See also this paper's issues of November 6, 1861; July 31, 1862; and February 27, 1863.

36. Resolutions and speeches quoted in the *Illinois Staats-Zeitung* of July 22 and 30, 1863. Earlier in the year, a meeting initiated by the Arbeiterverein denounced Illinois's recently passed law barring the settlement of free blacks in the state. It was, the meeting resolved, "a disgrace to a free state and inconsistent with the recently issued glorious decree of freedom," Lincoln's Emancipation Proclamation. *Illinois Staats-Zeitung*, January 13, 1863.

37. Platform adopted by the national Fremont convention, held in Cleveland, published in the *Cleveland Plain Dealer*, June 1, 1864. Related material appeared in the *Cleveland Plain Dealer* on March 31; April 2 and 20; May 31; and June 2, 1864. See also Ruhl J. Bartlett, *John C. Fremont and the Republican Party* (New York: Da Capo Press,

1970), 89–128; Carl Wittke, *Against the Current: The Life of Karl Heinzen* (Chicago: University of Chicago Press, 1945), 189–93; Obermann, *Joseph Weydemeyer*, 104–6, 125–28; *Weekly Chicago Democrat*, May 31, June 1 and 3, 1864.

38. Koerner, *Memoirs*, vol. 2, 410, 432.

39. Charles A. Beard and Mary R. Beard, *The Rise of American Civilization*, vol. 2 (New York: Macmillan, 1930), 54.

40. Rapp was quoted in the *Illinois Staats-Zeitung*, January 13, 1863. The "detour" thesis can be found in Alan Dawley, *Class and Community: The Industrial Revolution in Lynn* (Cambridge, Mass.: Harvard University Press, 1976), 228–29; and Dawley and Paul Faler, "Working-Class Culture and Politics in the Industrial Revolution," *Journal of Social History* 9 (Summer 1976): 474–76.

Class Conflict, Municipal Politics, and Governmental Reform in Gilded Age Chicago, 1871–1875

Richard Schneirov

SO long as the present city-political system prevails in America—a system that practically disfranchises the better portion of the community—we conceive it to be needful to have what we can of a supplemental political organization like this, that will to some extent, represent these disfranchised people.—Franklin MacVeagh, President of the Citizens Association of Chicago, 1874[1]

In recent years historians of nineteenth-century municipal reform have begun to look beyond the reformers' sloganeering about "efficiency" and "clean government" to focus on the political activities of elite businessmen.[2] They have not, however, spent much time investigating the political impact of workers on reform, whether by independent political action or in alliance with ward-based politicians. More importantly, they have not studied reform movements as part of the contest for power between workers and the new urban industrial business elite in the post–Civil War period.[3]

This essay examines the origins and early affairs of the Citizens Association, the first organized and sustained effort in the industrial era of Chicago's top businessmen to renovate municipal government. The Association consisted of leaders of an emerging upper class of large merchants, bankers, and manufacturers who sought to impose social controls upon the new industrial working class and to shape local government to meet the needs of the emerging large-scale industrial order. The history of the Association's urban reform movement developed in a contradictory situation: the new business elite had a relative lack of influence over local government precisely when it was faced with the growing political strength of labor. In the conflict of these class forces it is possible to trace the origins of three important changes in late nineteenth-century Chicago's municipal government: the centralization of the powers of the mayor, the professionalization of the fire department, and the deployment of the national guard in place of independent militias.

BEGINNING in the 1850s, but most importantly in the eight years following the Civil War, local businessmen turned Chicago into a thriving manufacturing center to complement its commercial activities.[4] By the onset of the 1873–1879 depression, Chicago manufacturers in steel, furniture, meat packing, boots and shoes, and men's clothing were rivaling and often outselling their Eastern counterparts.[5] Inspired by this growth, Chicago's businessmen and boosters foresaw Chicago as "the first city on the continent, the reaching of which is merely a question of time."[6] It was this dream and expectation that powerfully animated a core group of Chicago business leaders in the early 1870s, in particular those tied to local manufacturing. These were men such as clothing manufacturer and merchant Henry W. King; two of the city's largest boot and shoe manufacturers, Charles M. Henderson and William Doggett; L. B. Boomer, a bridge and railroad car manufacturer of national importance; Mancel Talcott, owner of the area's largest stone company; and prominent merchants and real estate investors with New York connections like Marshall Field and Levi Leiter.[7]

Chicago's prominent businessmen of this era did not, however, exercise an influence within local government commensurate with their economic power or their visions of national business supremacy. According to Frederic Cople Jaher's study of Chicago's urban establishment, this situation contrasted with the antebellum period, when a largely commercial business elite experienced little difficulty in securing its private goals through direct public office holding.[8] Between 1837 and 1868, for example, all but two of the city's mayoral candidates had been drawn from this stratum of society.[9]

After 1848, as the city grew in size and complexity, formerly private functions were taken over by government, leading to the creation of new public positions and the expansion of old ones, so that political office holding became a full-time and well compensated occupation. In the meantime, as the scope of the city's commercial and industrial enterprises broadened, Chicago's leading entrepreneurs found the major part of their energies absorbed by their business activities. Their direct participation in the city's government diminished, laying the basis for the political dominance of ward-based, professional politicians in Chicago.[10]

The beginnings of ward- or community-based political machines in Chicago—a subject about which not much is known—was undoubtedly facilitated by a city government whose outstanding features were fragmentation and dispersion of power. In 1871 the city's mayor lacked appointive and removal powers. The power of creating and filling offices was lodged in the city council, which was dominated by ward politicians and small propertied elements responsible to the narrowest of constituencies. Rather than being controlled by the city's executive, the city administration was divided among a set of elective boards created in the 1850s and 1860s. Among these autonomous boards was the critical Board of Police and Fire Commissioners.[11] Finally, the structures of city government coexisted with a township system whereby Chicago was divided into three towns. Each of the three possessed a supervisor, a clerk, and five justices of the peace; these officials collectively constituted the town board. Each board could tax, create debts, and pay out funds.[12]

This structure of local government divided the propertied groups of the city and separated them from the political leadership of larger businessmen. The smallest groups, with the help of a malleable working-class constituency, entrenched themselves in comfortable niches within the city council, boards, and town governments. During and after the Civil War, when rings of officials formed for the purpose of retaining offices, Chicago earned a reputation for the corrupt use of patronage that rivalled that of any Eastern city.[13]

The one political institution that might have counteracted this dispersion of power, the political party, was in disarray. In 1869 with the close of Reconstruction and a lack of outstanding national issues, the two major parties collapsed on the local level. For the next seven years, Chicago politics was ruled by an intermittent conflict between rings and a series of shifting reform coalitions. Rather than party labels, these went by such names as Citizens Reform party, Union Fireproof ticket, Law and Order party, Peoples party, and in one case, simply, The Opposition.[14] The fate of the first of these ephemeral coalitions illustrates the nature of local politics in this period. In September 1869 the Citizens Reform party issued an appeal to "Democrats, Republicans, workingmen, temperance men and all kinds of men" to unite against the Republican ring led by German politician Anton Hesing, publisher of the *Illinois Staats-Zeitung*. Overwhelmingly swept into office in November, the new party proved powerless to prevent a continuation of corrupt conditions.[15]

As the 1869 experience suggests, the fluidity and corruption of local politics and the weakness of local government proved inhospitable to movements that sought centralized reform, whether businessmen's civic reform, labor reform, or temperance reform. Nonetheless, within this framework, workers exercised considerable influence. In April 1866, Chicago's ward-based Eight Hour leagues and the Trades Assembly inaugurated what Andrew Cameron, publisher of the *Workingman's Advocate*, called labor's "first contest for political supremacy" in the city's municipal elections. Success was immediate and sweeping: no alderman dared oppose the eight-hour demand. The city council soon passed an eight-hour ordinance, and the state followed with the nation's first statewide eight-hour law. Such unprecedented victories caused Cameron to claim that "here in the Northwest the field is still better and richer than in the East. Our difficulties are less and our power greater."[16]

Nonetheless, between 1867 and 1869, the diverse ethnic and party loyalties of Chicago workingmen, together with the willingness of local politicians to support the political demands of the Trade Assembly, continually undermined attempts to form a labor party. Instead of an independent labor slate and a comprehensive program of labor-oriented civic reform as advocated by Chicago's more aggressive labor reformers, the labor movement retreated to a more defensive posture of endorsing friendly politicians and, where possible, securing regular party support for the candidacy of union leaders.[17]

Nowhere was this policy of alliance with local parties more important than in labor's struggle to control the powerful Board of Police and Fire Commissioners. According to Cameron, the position of commissioner of the board was "one of the most important offices within the gift of the people." In November 1867, labor leaders agreed to support a Republican candidate for treasurer in exchange for the slating of a labor man for the board. "If elected," said Cameron, "he would not allow the police force of the city to be prostituted as it had been too often in the past, to intimidate workingmen." Their own candidate was defeated, but by 1869, labor had a friend on the board in the person of Irish-born Mark Sheridan, a former republican revolutionary in the Young Ireland movement.[18] Another ally in the fire department was German-born Matthias Benner, ex-president of the Cigarmakers Union, and former director and vice-president of the Mechanics Institute; in 1873 he was endorsed by Cameron for fire marshal and appointed by the mayor.[19] Though these and other labor-backed leaders were not advocates of a comprehensive labor reform program, they were still popular reformers, opposed both to corrupt ring politicians and to the business-oriented centralizing reform movement of the early 1870s.

By 1871, on the eve of the Chicago Fire, the city's large property holders were, in important ways, shut out of local government, in contrast to the position they had maintained during the antebellum period. From their viewpoint, city government was fragmented and weak, dominated by a council of ward politicians. Moreover, large employers were confronted with a labor movement that had mounted a general strike in 1867 and demonstrated a political capacity distinctly superior to that of elite business. In view of this, business reformer Franklin MacVeagh's public complaint that local property interests were "disfranchised" was not far from the mark.

THE rebuilding of Chicago after the Great Fire of 1871 brought to a crisis point political issues that had been building since 1867. In order to attract Eastern and foreign capital to reconstruct the city's major commercial and manufacturing interests, local business leaders soon realized the necessity of creating a new political climate conducive to the confidence of outside investors, notably Eastern insurance companies. This in turn implied a wide-ranging structural reform of city government that conflicted with the interests and customs of the city's laboring class, as well as those of entrenched politicians. The pivot of the struggle sparked by this clash of interests soon became the government's attempt to enforce unpopular laws. The ultimate failure of this enforcement planted the seeds of an even greater crisis three years later.

The immediate response to the Fire from all sectors of Chicago's politically active population, including Cameron, was to unite behind a bipartisan reform ticket similar to the 1869 Citizens Reform party. Less than a month later, Joseph Medill's Union Fireproof ticket was elected on the plea that an incorruptible government of what he called the best citizens was necessary to restore the confidence of outside investors. On taking office, Medill received the council's acquiescence in a series of building ordinances designed to create a fireproof city. Meanwhile, Medill lobbied the state legislature with the support of Chicago businessmen for passage of a two-year "Temporary Mayor's Bill." When the bill passed, on March 9, 1872, the Chicago mayor for the first time was able to appoint and remove—with the council's consent—all city officers not subject to election.[20]

But the Medill administration, which had begun so auspiciously, soon ran into serious political difficulties. The onset of a severe winter and a lack of materials delayed the rebuilding of the city, forcing tens of thousands of workingmen to choose between astronomical rents or flight from the city. In January 1872, when the city council, at the behest of Medill and the insurance companies, began considering an ordinance to outlaw all wooden structures, it became apparent that both rents and the cost of home ownership would be bid up to intolerable levels. In the absence of action by the city's unions, Republican boss Anton Hesing, who had been out of power since 1869, led a march of Northside Germans in a demonstration that invaded City Hall. While Medill hid in the cloakroom, the crowd displayed placards to the council reading, "No Barracks," "Homes for the People," and "Leave the Laborer a Home." One sign from the carpenters union depicted a gallows, along with the words, "This is the lot of those who vote for the Fire Ordinance." Much to the dismay of the mayor and the press, the council heeded this threat and revised the act on January 20 to allow wood residences outside the central portion of the city.[21]

The next five months brought further challenges to the authority of the new administration with the revival of the city's dormant trade union movement. The combination of high rents and the need to prevent existing unions from being swamped by out-of-town laborers attracted to Chicago by the promise of work, sparked a flurry of union organizing that began in late January.[22] This led to a confrontation with the Board of Police and Fire Commissioners, which had been under the control of Mancel Talcott since the November election. Talcott was opposed to unions, having crushed a strike of stonecutters in 1866. In the face of opposition from Mark Sheridan, he asked the governor to arm the city's police for defense against expected strikes and riots. The *Workingman's Advocate*, which after the German demonstration had joined Medill and the press in decrying riotous assemblies, now threatened retaliation at the polls.[23]

The tension of impending class conflict deepened when labor leaders announced a May 15 union parade to demonstrate labor's strength to nonunion newcomers engaged in rebuilding the city. Many of the city's large capitalists viewed this as a prelude to a general strike and threatened a lockout.[24]

The clash in Chicago between workers and the militia during the nationwide railroad strikes of 1877 culminated a decade of labor unrest in the city. From Michael J. Schaack, *Anarchy and Anarchists*, 1889.

Invited by Cameron to speak at the demonstration, Medill voiced the fears of these men that the unions were using the fire as an opportunity to "'inaugurate a grand raid on the employers.'" Even more alarming was the possibility that the moderate leadership of labor reformers like Cameron might be overthrown by workmen from nations "'where strikes and lockouts are frequent'" and "where labor considers capital as its enemy." Such an eventuality could lead to a repeat of the 1867 riot which had followed on the heels of a more orderly general strike.[25]

The fear of riot, combined with revival of the trade union movement, led Chicago's "better sort" to prepare for impending class war. It was probably at their behest that Medill had unsuccessfully renewed Talcott's call to Governor John M. Palmer for arms just before the demonstration. When this was rejected, businessmen placed a discreet ad in the *Tribune* reporting that, "Printed blanks are being circulated for the signatures of such merchants and professional men as are willing to join a regiment soon to be organized. . . . The projectors," ran the ad, "men of the highest commercial standing, believe that Chicago at the present time is in peculiar need of such a military body and that every banker, merchant and real estate owner should contribute liberally to its support. . . . The ranks are to be filled by men of character and position."[26]

The attempt to create a private body of militia responsible to business was paralleled by the continued efforts of business to exert control over the politicized police and fire-fighting forces. This was not the first time that large property holders had attempted to reform the fire department. In 1858, Denis Swenie, closely associated with Chicago's business elite, had organized a paid fire department to replace the old volunteer force. This action had come a year after businessmen had organized a brigade in response to the incompetence of whiskey-drinking volunteers during a major fire.[27] Since the 1871 fire, local businessmen, prodded by the fire insurance companies, had complained about an inefficient and patronage-dominated fire department and the unwillingness of police to enforce the new building ordinance. For example, on May 5 the *Tribune* reported that "Police walk by the illegal [wood built] works, chat with workmen and never think of interfering to prevent violations."[28] In mid-May, Commissioner Talcott proposed to weed out applicants for firemen who were members of unions or who had gone on strike. The order became a political issue when it was opposed by Sheridan, who had the warm backing of Cameron. The following month, Talcott continued his divisive policy by replacing Police Superintendent Kennedy with an outsider, Elmer Washburne, who was expected to follow Talcott's orders more pliantly.[29]

Attempts to introduce a greater sense of professionalism and centralized control into the administration of the Board of Police and Fire Commissioners soon hit a major snag. Since the Fire, the city had been plagued by crime, attributed to the large numbers of single laborers who had been drawn to Chicago by the prospect of finding work on the rebuilding of the city. Dismayed by the continuing failure of police to control crime, a group of prominent citizens organized in early September under the leadership of banker Henry Greenebaum. But two weeks later these businessmen were preempted by a committee dominated by religious zealots and led by E. A. Storrs and Charles C. Bonney. Declaring that "the Churches of Chicago are the truest representatives of its power, its principles, its purposes, and its leading men," and that two-thirds of all crime was due to liquor, this "Committee of 70" called for enforcement of the long-ignored city Sunday closing law. One week later, Mayor Medill made the disastrous decision to enforce this law.[30]

Until this time, the businessmen's movement for governmental reform had been successfully justified by reference to the common goal of rebuilding Chicago, an approach that elicited the acquiescence of the *Workingman's Advocate*. Now, it became inextricably mixed with the highly volatile issues of religious and cultural conflict. Medill's support for the temperance-oriented Committee of 70 created a furor among Chicago's foreign-born population, particularly the Germans, who raised charges of Know-Nothingism. No controversy could have been less favorable to the cause of civic reform. Moreover, it even raised legal challenges to the mayor's new powers of appointment and removal from within the government itself, with Mark Sheridan, as head of the Board of Police and Fire Commissioners, leading the challengers.[31]

By the summer of 1873, the rising opposition to temperance and upper-class reform had split the labor movement between Cameron's labor reformers on the one hand and working-class immigrants on the other. The immigrants rallied behind a new political coalition called the Peoples party. Led by Anton Hesing and Irish politician Daniel O'Hara, this party harmonized its long-antagonistic Irish and German constituents at a great unity rally, held a month before the 1873 municipal election. While the party endorsed a Greenback program, the principal theme of unity was defensive and cultural. As Hesing put it most succinctly: drinking a glass of beer on Sunday and listening to outdoor music were "privileges of the poor."[32]

On November 4, the Peoples party overwhelmed the reformers at the polls, electing thirteen of twenty aldermen up for election. All three Peoples party nominees for commissioner also won election. That the campaign had politically mobilized a large sector of the immigrant working class is suggested by the 10 percent increase in turnout over that of the presidential election one year earlier and the doubling of the turnout in the recent mayoral elections.[33] Only one year after Medill had chosen to test his new powers through temperance reform, Chicago's foreign-born workingmen—without the support of Cameron and the Trades Assembly—had unleased a stunning counteroffensive, stopping upper-class reform in its tracks.

As a coalition of Irish and German voters forged by ethnic ring politicians, the Peoples party possessed a fragile unity, dependent on the submergence of class issues that might divide its constituency from its leadership. Indeed, this became an almost immediate problem as the city's economy began to feel the effects of the July 1873 panic. With approximately 25,000 workingmen out of work in December, Chicago's tiny band of Socialists mobilized 3,000 workers in a march on City Hall to demand relief funds from the Relief and Aid Society. A private institution headed by Illinois Central Railroad attorney Wirt Dexter, the society, rather than the corrupt city government, had been selected in 1871 by a bipartisan coalition of top citizens to collect and disperse fire relief funds. In the winter of 1873 and 1874, the society still held $600,000 in its coffers. The demonstrators, led by Francis Hoffmann, an ambitious German lawyer who had earlier spoken at the Peoples party unity rally, confronted the new city administration with the demand that it force Dexter to release these funds. Fearful of losing his German constituency, Mayor Harvey Colvin attempted to appease the crowd by adopting Hoffmann's suggestion that the society turn over its funds to city aldermen for distribution to the needy.[34] Colvin's temporizing with "the mob" confirmed the suspicions of top businessmen that the new administration would not be a bulwark of property.[35]

Despite Dexter's refusal to accept the mayor's proposal, the demonstration was an important triumph for both the Socialists and Chicago workingmen. The amount of money disbursed by the Relief and Aid Society that winter was at least four times greater than that given out during any succeeding depression winter, and the number of families aided more than doubled the average for the succeeding five years. Several workingmen were even appointed as visitors (caseworkers) by the society. The city council responded with two pledges: to improve the Post Office building and to build a new courthouse. Both projects had the obvious intent of providing jobs.

Meanwhile, the first multi-ethnic Socialist party in Chicago, led by German Karl Klings, was organized in February. In calling for state ownership of the means of transportation and communication—and, importantly, of the state banks and fire insurance companies—its platform offered a significant break from the labor reform attitude toward government.[36]

Despite the first crack in the solid front of the Peoples party, the businessmen reformers were still on the defensive. In February the Peoples party refused to support reenactment of the Temporary Mayor's Bill due to expire the next month, and in March the council repealed the Sunday closing law. The success of the new party was celebrated in Hesing's boast—unchallenged by the *Tribune*—that the Republican party had ceased to exist on the city's German North Side.[37]

AN event that occurred on July 14, 1874, suddenly reversed the trend of the previous two years. Once again, Chicago was hit by a runaway fire. Mobilizing themselves as never before, Chicago's large property holders picked up where they had left off in the summer of 1872 and resumed their campaign for a powerful mayor, a reformed fire department, and a militia responsible to business. This time they did not allow the temperance issue to deflect them.

The 1874 fire started among the densely crowded wooden shacks just south of the 1872 fire limits and spread north into the newly built business district. Clearly, the compromise fire limit of January 1872, which had reflected a standoff in the political balance of classes, had become untenable. Once again, Chicago's top businessmen saw their vision of Chicago as the continent's premier city threatened by a flight of capital.[38]

On January 17, Marshall Field, Henry King, and George How, President of the Board of Trade, convened a mass meeting of Chicago businessmen that included Anton Hesing in a prominent role. The new spirit was bluntly summed up by the *Tribune*: "We must no longer decide our fire policy by counting noses. Those who have property to lose feel directly interested in the efficiency of the fire department and there are tens of thousands in this city who have nothing to lose if half the city were reduced to ashes. . . . It is a sad commentary on our form of government . . . almost a confession that, pro tanto, such a government is a failure."[39]

The pressure on city government by Chicago businessmen was backed up on July 24 by an ultimatum to the mayor from the National Board of Fire Insurance Underwriters listing demands for: 1) the extension of the fire limits to the city limits, with no exception for wooden buildings; 2) reform of the fire department; 3) enactment of a stringent building code; 4) increase in water facilities, supplemented by ward fire patrols; 5) removal of lumberyards and other hazardous industries from the city. The board threatened to recommend that its member companies withdraw business from the city unless its demands were complied with by October 1.[40]

Initially, the united power of property interests was unstoppable. Under pressure, the mayor initially agreed to a demand to remove Fire Marshall Benner in favor of business-favored Denis Swenie, and the council extended the fire limits. With the city's labor movement weakened by depression, the only opposition came from Cameron and Mark Sheridan, who supported Benner, and the Socialists, who protested the ban on wooden buildings and accused Hesing of selling out the Germans.[41] Under the impact of the July fire, the Peoples party leadership had begun to split from its constituency.

Nevertheless, from the business reformers' viewpoint, city government was still controlled by irresponsible politicians. The same administration that had extended the fire limits could not be relied upon to enforce them. Though funds were urgently needed to expand Chicago's narrow water mains, the council discussed a new courthouse—the Peoples party's answer to the workers' demand for jobs, as well as a source of political spoils. Several months later, a coalition of aldermen from working-class wards, led by Alderman Schaffner, held up appropriations for new water mains for business and industrial districts until the same could be provided for working-class districts. Most glaring was resistance to reform of the fire department, which on July 29 was the object of a special report released by the national board. The report scored the absence of a qualified engineer in charge of the department, the lack of discipline in the ranks, and the use of political patronage.[42]

The combination of an unresponsive government and the chilling prospect of a limit to Chicago's capital growth led to the founding, on July 24, of Chicago's first ongoing citywide political association of businessmen, the Citizens Association. Though the Citizens Association grew out of the efforts of top business leaders to mediate between the national board and the city administration, its originators were aware, from the beginning, of the need to restructure city government.

In his opening address, on September 11, President Franklin MacVeagh spoke of an irreconcilable conflict between property and democracy in city government:

> American political life has always been partially one-sided, owing to immoderate fancy for the freedom of all human males above the age of twenty-one years. . . . In our effort after this eccentric freedom, we have pretty much succeeded in our great cities at least, in binding hand and foot the best part of the community, and placing political power in the hands of the baser elements of the people. . . . How can you be sure of finding a set of men severely anxious about the protection of property who themselves have no property to protect, unless they are of a class who can be relied upon to rise above personal considerations? I tell you, gentlemen, the men may be bad, but the system is far worse.[43]

The governing structure of the Citizens Association had the effect of solidifying the city's propertied groups in the face of the centrifugal tendencies exerted by the city's ward political system. The association consisted of a committee of 100, comprised of five men drawn from each of the city's twenty wards. Though perhaps a third of these men were small merchants and professionals prominent in working-class wards, actual decision-making power was vested by the association's constitution in a five-man executive board, every member of which was a leading merchant or manufacturer—for example, L. B. Boomer, C. M. Henderson, Henry King. A conservative estimate would be that half of the members of the Citizens Association were prominent businessmen or corporate lawyers.[44]

The Association's policy of refraining from endorsing partisan candidates for office was another way of unifying the city's diverse propertied groups. Rather than engage in partisan political activity, the Association confined itself to scrutinizing the actions of public officials, judging the desirability of proposed ordinances, conducting impartial investigations into matters of general interest, and educating public opinion. In these limitations and functions, the Citizens Association differed from previous reform movements. The 1869 Citizens Reform movement constituted itself as a party, as did Medill backers. On the other hand, the Committee of 70 had been diverted by its emphasis on temperance. Several organizers of the Citizens Association were unequivocal in affirming that, as one man put it, "We will have no temperance or sumptuary nonsense." According to another organizer, "The best men differ on these questions. . . . We hope to avoid the rocks on which other organizations have split."[45]

In September, the Citizens Association began work to forestall the imminent withdrawal of Eastern insurance companies. Their efforts focused on bringing General William Shaler, who had previously reorganized New York City's fire department along military lines, to Chicago. With Shaler in charge of the Chicago Fire Department, Eastern fears that "unscrupulous politicians" ran the department would be allayed. When the Board of Police and Fire Commissioners, as well as Mayor Colvin, agreed to this plan, there was little else that could be done locally to comply with the national board's demands. Only the state legislature could revise either the relationship between the board and the mayor or current building standards.[46] Still, the national board refused to lift its ultimatum, and a faction of businessmen led by Henry King grumbled that "jealous" New York merchants were attempting to ruin Chicago.[47]

Fortunately for the city, the passing of the October 1 deadline led to the withdrawal of only 40 of 150 insurance companies. Several days later, Shaler arrived in Chicago at the invitation of MacVeagh. Within a week he had agreed to reorganize the department for a salary of $10,000, half to be paid by the Citizens Association and half by the insurance companies. Because of rearguard resistance from Sheridan, Shaler's job was made temporary. By the end of the month, the 1874 insurance crisis was over. Most non–New York companies had never left Chicago, and those who left returned within the year.[48]

The resolution of the immediate crisis did not, however, lull the Citizens Association into ending its campaign to oust the Peoples party from office and restructure city government. As executive board member J. C. Dore put it:

"City affairs are in deplorable condition and the solid men in the community are a great deal to blame for it because of their laxity and their want of interest in city politics. . . . In our city government the best minds think it is a mistake to have so many boards and that centralized authority is the most appropriate form of authority. Politics is becoming a matter of business. . . ."[49]

Accordingly, the association began a local campaign to incorporate the city under the state's General Incorporation Act of 1872. When this was approved, the Association had the act amended on the local level, in effect re-enacting the Temporary Mayor's Bill. Also in 1875, the Council abolished the Board of Police and Fire Commissioners and created separate departments under control of the mayor. These developments laid the groundwork for Chicago's modern city government.[50] The Peoples party's rule ended in April 1876 when the party lost control of the council; in July, following a bitter legal battle, a resurgent Republican party reclaimed the mayor's office.[51]

THE long and difficult process by which the Citizens Association secured reforms in the city administration was paralleled by its attempts to create a city militia to be institutionalized as part of a state national guard. The formation of a militia was an overt attempt to contain Chicago's increasingly volatile class conflict, in particular that which threatened to emanate from the Socialist movement.

The abortive attempts to form a businessmen's militia following the union demonstration in May 1872 and also those following the 1874 Socialist demonstrations were both undermined by their organizers' reliance on the legislature to revise the state's existing militia statutes.[52] Under these statutes, militiamen were required to purchase their own uniforms and contribute to the rental of armories in which to drill and store equipment. Moreover, they were expected to drill on their own free time. The state furnished arms only. Militia companies were essentially private, voluntary organizations. Their loyalty to the government was tenuous. The organization of the Citizens Association in August 1874 marked a turning point in the campaign to form a businessmen's militia, for it provided financial backing to would-be militia companies and gave critical support to the political efforts of militia advocates to revise state laws.[53]

Chicago's famous First Regiment was organized at a meeting on August 28, 1874; within ten days it boasted three companies. In October, the Citizens Association formed a militia committee headed by two prominent businessmen and former generals, A. L. Chetlain and Alexander McClurg. There was no doubt as to the purpose of the militia. "It was undertaken," said McClurg, who later became a colonel in the regiment, "solely in consequence of the widespread anxiety among thinking men over the defenseless condition of the city in case of riot and disorder."[54] Having endorsed and provided leadership for the regiment, the Citizens Association committee helped raise $17,000 from Chicago's major businessmen for uniforms and equipment, and by January the regiment had 500 men.[55]

Still, progress toward the long-term goal of state militia law reform required another great scare to galvanize Chicago's so-called best men into action. In February 1875 the Socialists resumed their campaign against the Relief and Aid Society, which had cut its relief disbursements by 80 percent from the previous winter. In the preceding year, according to the *Tribune*, the society's leaders "acted under threats against their own lives and property—permitted by the present city government. . . . It was a disgrace keenly felt . . . but worse than this it was a precedent full of danger which is now imminent." Now, a year later, the city's establishment was prepared. While the militia stood in readiness, the *Tribune* reported that the police mobilized a force "to thwart an insurrection of a whole continent." Out of understandable fear the would-be demonstrators stayed home.[56]

The show of force and the fizzled demonstration of February 1875 gave much needed impetus to militia law reform. On March 1, the legislature began considering a bill giving the governor the power to appoint a general with authority to reorganize the state militia. In May 1877, this culminated in the state's first comprehensive military code, which provided for yearly appropriations, the equipping and drilling of militiamen, the rental of armories, and the exemption of militiamen from jury duty.[57]

Just as important in the professionalization of the Illinois militia was the question of its social composition. Many of the private military companies established after the Civil War were primarily composed of workingmen and were considered unreliable by the city's upper class. The Irish Clan Na Gael Guards, who were refused arms from the state, were an extreme example.[58] To insure loyalty, militia organizers recruited a regiment, 60 percent of whose rank and file consisted of clerks and bookkeepers, but at the same time apparently refused to allow a company of union printers to join.[59] This regiment became a vehicle for character building while also serving as a social club and status badge for Chicago's more fashionable young rich men.

Notwithstanding the martial activities of what one Socialist referred to as "the patent leather mob," the necessity of relying on other groups to man the militia was obvious. In the latter part of 1875, the city's Irish companies coalesced to form the Second Regiment of the militia. It was this regiment, not the First, that helped police quell the riots of July 1877. This demonstrated that the fears of leading citizens had been groundless: a paid and properly drilled and led working-class guard could be relied upon to protect the interests of private property.[60]

The final step in professionalizing the militia grew out of the reaction of Socialists to their experience in February 1875. The use of a class-based militia to intimidate their constituency led the German Socialists to respond in self-defense by chartering their own private militia company, the Lehr- und Wehr-Verein, on April 16, 1875. Meanwhile, Bohemian Socialists joined the Third Regiment, known as The Bohemian Rifles. What one Socialist termed "armed political competition" became a public issue in July 1877 when National Guard General Joseph Torrence disarmed the Bohemians out of fear that they would side with the rioters. After the 1877 riots, both the German Verein and the newly independent Bohemian company gained in numbers and visibility. At Socialist parades and picnics their presence served to dispel fear of the city's new forces of order. To Chicago's upper class, however, they represented defiance and a potential threat in times of disorder.[61]

When the Socialist political presence in the city reached its peak in 1879, the Citizens Association successfully lobbied the legislature for a law prohibiting private militia companies and banning armed drilling without the governor's permission. The Socialists tested the constitutionality of the law in the courts, winning in the county court, but losing in the Illinois State Supreme Court.[62] The state supreme court's decision was an important element in turning the German Socialist movement toward anarchism in the 1880s. It also ended the era of independent militia companies in Chicago and secured for the Illinois National Guard a practical monopoly on the organized means of violence.

HERBERT Gutman has suggested that the economic power of Gilded Age industrialists was not easily translated into the social status and political authority—in short, the legitimacy—assumed by many previous historians.[63] The genesis and history of municipal reform in Chicago indicates that elite businessmen had great difficulty in eliciting the consent of the population to their political rule. Indeed, in his study of the urban establishment, Frederic Jaher speaks of a long-term decline in public office holding by Chicago's top businessmen beginning in the early 1870s. In the absence of such office holding, governmental reforms aimed at centralizing authority and professionalizing crucial municipal functions can be viewed as the elite's means of making the newly expanded local government responsive to the needs of Chicago's industrial economy. Underlining the considerable opposition faced by businessmen in this attempt was the fact that these reforms were conceived outside the sphere of government by a private association. Moreover, only after two fires and an ultimatum by the insurance industry had created an investment crisis in the city could the political standoff between classes be broken and these reforms partially legitimized.

Even the limited success the Citizens Association had achieved by 1875 was highly precarious. The ability of the business elite to institutionalize its political authority was closely dependent on the ebb and flow of class conflict and the course of local politics. In particular, the effective operation of centralized authority and professionalized bureaucracy required the election of a mayor responsive to the needs of the city's leading economic interests. In 1879, following the revival of the labor movement's industrial and political strength, a Democrat, Carter Harrison, was elected mayor in a resurgence of the Peoples party's immigrant coalition, opposed to temperance reform. As a result, many of the 1870s reforms—with the notable exception of the state national guard—were undermined in the 1880s.[64] Meanwhile, Chicago's workingmen remained largely disunited and politically ineffective as a class. Neither the independent labor reformers nor the Socialists were able to garner mass support for an alternative reform program that fused working-class interests with a long-term vision of civic development. Following the precedent of 1873, Chicago's workingmen could only unite around the negative and defensive program offered by the Harrison Democrats.

Despite its failures, the civic reform movement of the 1870s proved to be only the beginning of a thirty-year series of reform efforts which served as a political laboratory for the maturing social consciousness of Chicago's business elite. In this intellectual journey, a number of business leaders began to understand the modern industrial economy as a system which, to be stabilized, required limitations on the use of private property and the formal recognition and political integration of the working class. Franklin MacVeagh, first president of the Citizens Association and later a leading officer of the Chicago Civic Federation and National Civic Federation and Secretary of the Treasury under President William Howard Taft, epitomized this evolution.

In the early 1880s, as Chicago's leading mugwump, MacVeagh had a political perspective that was still confined to the goal of legislating a nonpartisan, professionalized municipal government.[65] After Haymarket, he and banker Lyman Gage, later to become Secretary of the Treasury under President William McKinley, participated along with labor leaders in a series of so-called economic conferences. It was there and in the Sunset Club, which followed, that MacVeagh abandoned his 1870s property-based Tory conception of municipal politics and endorsed "the rational demands of the workingmen. . . . which can be answered through the conservative limitations and corrections, and the normal development of the profoundly elastic and sensitive systems under which we are now living." As a leader in the Chicago Civic Federation, which included social reformers, unionists and Socialists, he wrote, "I believe in democracy and democracy is impossible if in the long run workingmen are not a part of its conservative support. We must not think that every man who thinks us a public enemy is himself a public enemy."[66]

Political authority could not be imposed. Rather, it required the consent of the working class. It was this realization by such reform-minded businessmen of the Progressive Era as MacVeagh that enabled them to transcend the limited vision that had undermined reforms in the 1870s.[67]

Acknowledgments

I wish to acknowledge that my understanding of late nineteenth-century capitalist class formation has been largely shaped by the seminars and lectures of Martin J. Sklar at Northern Illinois University. Sklar, along with James Livingston, Larry Lynn, and Stephen Sapolsky, has made helpful comments on this paper. I would also like to thank John Jentz, Hartmut Keil, and Fannia Weingartner for their help in the editing of this paper.

Notes

1. "Address by President Franklin McVeagh, September 11, 1874," in Citizens Association of Chicago, *Annual Reports, 1874–1901* (Chicago: Citizens Association, 1901), 6.

2. See Samuel P. Hays, "The Politics of Reform in Municipal Government in the Progressive Era," *Pacific Northwest Quarterly* 55 (1964): 157–69; and James Weinstein, "Organized Business and the City Commission and Manager Movements," *Journal of Southern History* 28 (1962): 166–82. The use of the term "business elite" in this essay follows the definition given by E. Digby Baltzell: Only when top members of the business hierarchy can generate a "goal integrating elite"—in the case of Chicago, the Citizens Association—can an upper class establish and maintain its political authority (*Philadelphia Gentlemen, The Making of a National Upper Class* [New York: The Free Press, 1958], 6–8, 32–36).

3. See Herbert Gutman, "The Workers Search for Power" in *The Gilded Age: A Reappraisal*, ed. H. Wayne Morgan (Syracuse, N.Y.: Syracuse University Press, 1968). The lack of such a perspective is a limitation of the only two histories of Chicago political reform during this period. See Donald David Marks, "Polishing the Gem of the Prairie: The Evolution of Civic Reform Consciousness in Chicago, 1874–1900" (Ph.D. diss., University of Wisconsin, 1974); and Sidney I. Roberts, "Businessmen in Revolt: Chicago, 1874–1900" (Ph.D. diss., Northwestern University, 1960).

4. Bessie Pierce, *A History of Chicago*, vol. 2 (New York: Alfred A. Knopf, 1940), 77–117; William Cronon, "To Be the Central City: Chicago, 1848–1857," *Chicago History* 10 (Fall 1981): 130–40.

5. Bessie Pierce, *A History of Chicago*, vol. 3 (Chicago: University of Chicago Press, 1957), 145–92; see also Frederic Cople Jaher, *The Urban Establishment, Upper Strata in Boston, New York, Charleston, Chicago and Los Angeles* (Urbana, Ill.: University of Illinois Press, 1982), 459–60.

6. *Chicago Tribune*, August 15, 1874, p. 7; August 24, 1874, p. 5.

7. Biographical sketches from A. T. Andreas, *History of Chicago*, vol. 2 (Chicago: A. T. Andreas, 1886); see also Jaher, *The Urban Establishment*, 454–539; all these men were prominent in the Citizens Association.

8. Jaher, *The Urban Establishment*, 463, 503–4.

9. Pierce, *A History of Chicago*, vol. 2, 305; Donald S. Bradley and Mayer N. Zald, "From Commercial Elite to Political Administrator: The Recruitment of the Mayors of Chicago," *American Journal of Sociology* 51 (September 1965): 153–67.

10. Pierce, *A History of Chicago*, vol. 2, 77–117; Bradley and Zald, "From Commercial Elite to Political Administrator," 158–59.

11. Samuel Sparling, *Municipal History and Present Organization of the City of Chicago* (Madison, Wis.: Bulletin of the University of Wisconsin No. 23, 1898), 12, 40–58. On the lack of centralization of political power, see also *Chicago Tribune*, December 8, 1871, p. 4. For a description of a ward politician, see the *Workingman's Advocate*, November 13, 1869, p. 3. This newspaper is hereafter cited as *WMA*.

12. Sparling, *Municipal History and Present Organization*, 13, 47; *Chicago Tribune*, January 30, 1874, p. 4.

13. For contemporary discussions of local corruption, see *Chicago Tribune*, October 1, 1869, p. 4; and October 11, 1869, p. 4.

14. For political characterizations of this period, see Pierce, *A History of Chicago*, vol. 3, 340–44; and Bradley and Zald, "From Commercial Elite to Political Administrator," 159–60.

15. On the Citizens party in office, see Pierce, *A History of Chicago*, vol. 2, 297–98; on the Citizens party campaign, see *WMA*, October 16,

1869, p. 3; *Chicago Tribune*, September 6, 1869, p. 4; September 27, 1869, p. 2; September 29, 1869, pp. 2, 4; October 8, 1869, p. 2.

16. On the eight-hour campaign, see *WMA*, April 21, 1866, p. 3; and May 11, 1866, p. 2.

17. On Chicago labor in local politics during these years, see *WMA*, November 2, 1867, p. 3; December 19, 1867, p. 2; April 18, 1868, p. 3; August 8, 1868, p. 3; January 30, 1869, p. 3; October 9, 1869, p. 3; December 29, 1869, p. 3; December 10, 1870, p. 3.

18. Michael Ahern, *The Great Revolution: A History of the Rise and Progress of the Peoples Party in the City of Chicago and County of Cook, with Sketches of the Elect in Office* (Chicago: Lakeside Publishing and Printing, 1874), 139–44; see also *WMA*, October 16, 1869, p. 3; June 8, 1872, p. 3.

19. See Andreas on Fire Marshal Benner (*History of Chicago*, vol. 2, 498). See also *WMA*, September 2, 1871, p. 3; August 30, 1873, p. 3.

20. *Chicago Tribune*, November 5, 1871, p. 4; Pierce, *A History of Chicago*, vol. 3, 11–15; Sparling, *Municipal History and Present Organization*, 81–83; James S. McQuade, *A Synoptical History of the Chicago Fire Department* (Chicago: Benevolent Association of the Paid Fire Department of Chicago, 1908), 58–60. Medill also favored a bill to create an upper house, elected on a general ticket, in the council. See his letter to the *New York Tribune*, March 18, 1872, in *Joseph Boyd Scrapbook of Illinois Politics*, Chicago Historical Society.

21. For workingmen's response to the Fire, see *WMA*, November 11, 1871, p. 3; November 25, 1871, p. 3; February 2, 1871, p. 3; for an account of the German demonstration see *Chicago Tribune*, January 16, 1872, p. 1; January 17, 1872, p. 2.

22. *WMA*, March 2, 1872, p. 3; *Chicago Tribune*, May 8, 1872, p. 2.

23. *WMA*, February 17, 1872, p. 3; March 13, 1872, p. 3.

24. *Chicago Tribune*, May 4, 1872, p. 5; May 11, 1872, p. 6.

25. *Chicago Tribune*, May 16, 1872, p. 4.

26. *Chicago Tribune*, May 14, 1872, p. 4; the ad appeared on May 20, 1872, p. 6.

27. Denis Swenie, *Scrapbook*, Chicago Historical Society, 23; McQuade, *A Synoptical History*, 14, 16. George D. Bushnell gives a history of the volunteer fire force in "Chicago's Rowdy Fire-fighters," *Chicago History* 2 (Fall–Winter 1973): 232–41.

28. *Chicago Tribune*, May 5, 1872, p. 4; see also May 11, 1872, p. 6; and May 12, 1872, p. 7.

29. *WMA*, June 8, 1872, p. 3; *Chicago Tribune*, June 1, 1872, p. 5.

30. On the origins of the Committee of 70, see *Chicago Tribune*, October 12, 1873, p. 8; November 8, 1873, p. 3; see also Andreas, *History of Chicago*, vol. 3, 855–56.

31. Ahern, *The Great Revolution*, 32–44; see also Andreas, *History of Chicago*, vol. 2, 855–56.

32. *Chicago Tribune*, May 24, 1873, p. 5; October 5, 1873, p. 3; Ahern, *The Great Revolution*, 65–99.

33. *Chicago Tribune*, November 6, 1873, p. 4; Pierce, *A History of Chicago*, vol. 3, 539, 542.

34. *Chicago Tribune*, December 22, 1873, p. 1; December 23, 1873, p. 1. See Pierce on the history of the Relief and Aid Society (*A History of Chicago*, vol. 3, 8, 9, 241, 242).

35. *Chicago Tribune*, December 24, 1873, p. 4; January 12, 1874, p. 2.

36. *Chicago Tribune*, January 26, 1874, p. 2; February 23, 1875, p. 4; January 12, 1874, p. 2; Andreas, *History of Chicago*, vol. 3, 608.

37. *Chicago Tribune*, February 4, 1874, p. 3; Ahern, *The Great Revolution*, 108.

38. *Chicago Tribune*, July 15, 1874, p. 1; July 16, 1874, p. 4.

39. *Chicago Tribune*, July 18, 1874, p. 1; and July 19, 1874, p. 6.

40. *Chicago Tribune*, July 28, 1874, p. 2.

41. *WMA*, August 30, 1873, p. 3; *Chicago Tribune*, August 4, 1874, p. 2; July 25, 1874, p. 4; July 24, 1874, p. 2; McQuade, *A Synoptical History*, 60.

42. On the fire department, see *Chicago Tribune*, September 25, 1874, p. 2; and on the obstructive actions of the Common Council, *Chicago Tribune*, July 29, 1874, p. 4; September 29, 1874, p. 2.

43. Citizens Association, *Annual Reports*, 4, 5.

44. Of ninety-three names of Citizens Association members listed in the *Tribune*, I was able to identify sixty-eight. Of these, approximately forty-three were prominent businessmen or corporate lawyers. Though commercial pursuits dominated Chicago's business activities, manufacturers in the association outnumbered wholesale or commission merchants nineteen to seven. Among the forty-three elite businessmen, besides manufacturers and merchants, there were four bankers, four contractors, six corporate lawyers, three real estate men, five with diversified interests, and one U.S. Army officer. The sources of this information are *Chicago Tribune*, August 1, 1874, p. 2; Andreas, *A History of Chicago*, vol. 3; and *Edwards Directory of Chicago* (Chicago: Richard Edwards, 1873). See "Address by Franklin MacVeagh" for a discussion of the purposes of the Citizens Association (Citizens Association, *Annual Reports*, 3–12).

45. *Chicago Tribune*, July 26, 1874, p. 16. The quotations are from Citizens Association members John Hunter and General J. D. Webster.

46. *Chicago Tribune*, September 26, 1874, p. 1; September 27, 1874, p. 4.

47. *Chicago Tribune*, September 25, 1874, p. 2. See *Chicago Tribune*, October 3, 1874, p. 2 on the rivalry with New York merchants.

48. *Chicago Tribune*, October 21, 1874, p. 9; October 25, 1874, p. 4.

49. *Chicago Tribune*, October 11, 1874, p. 2.

50. *Chicago Tribune*, October 17, 1874, p. 3; November 4, 1874, pp. 4, 8; November 13, 1875, p. 1; January 8, 1875, p. 8; January 14, 1875, p. 3; Pierce, *A History of Chicago*, vol. 3, 301–4. Sidney I. Roberts narrates these events in "Ousting the Bummers" (unpublished manuscript, Chicago Historical Society, July 1956): 7–10. Though the April 1875 act was repealed in 1879, the mayor's powers in the area of police and fire protection were successfully established. According to Sparling, "The progress of the city under the law of 1872 has resulted in establishing the position of the mayor as a vigorous fact in the administration. On all sides his discretionary power has been elaborated until a vigorous mayor has abundant opportunity to impress his personality on the life of the city" (*Municipal History and Present Organization*, 93).

51. *Chicago Tribune*, January 4, 1875, p. 4; April 19, 1876, p. 5; Roberts, "Ousting the Bummers," 17–20.

52. *Chicago Tribune*, July 10, 1876, p. 6; August 29, 1874, p. 5; a forerunner of the First Regiment was the "First Regiment of Chicago Volunteers," which patrolled the city for twelve days after the Fire of 1871 un-

der the command of Francis T. Sherman. See *Joseph Boyd Scrapbook of Illinois Politics*, March 4, 1872.

53. Roy Turnbaugh, "Ethnicity, Civic Pride and Commitment: The Evolution of the Chicago Militia," *Illinois State Historical Society Journal* 62 (May 1979): 111; *Chicago Tribune*, July 10, 1872, p. 6; August 29, 1874, p. 5.

54. *Chicago Tribune*, January 3, 1875, p. 9.

55. *Chicago Tribune*, January 15, 1875, p. 8; Turnbaugh, "Ethnicity, Civic Pride and Commitment," 112; Holdridge O. Collins, *History of the Illinois National Guard* (Chicago: Black and Beach, 1884), 12–14.

56. Quotations from *Chicago Tribune*, February 23, 1875, p. 4; February 24, 1875, p. 7. For the actions of the militia, see February 25, 1875, p. 7, and March 5, 1875, p. 8.

57. See *Chicago Tribune*, March 2, 1875, p. 8. For comment on the significance of the February events and the 1877 code, see Collins, *History of the Illinois National Guard*, 17, 41–57; Turnbaugh, "Ethnicity, Civic Pride and Commitment," 114, 115.

58. *Chicago Tribune*, January 3, 1875, p. 9; Andreas, *History of Chicago*, vol. 3, 586; George H. Gibson, *Scrapbook, Militia Notes*, Chicago Historical Society, 9, 100, 177; *Labor Enquirer* (Chicago), June 11, 1887, p. 1; *Chicago Tribune*, May 14, 1885, p. 8.

59. I took a random sample of one of every three privates in companies A, B, C, and D of the First Regiment. Thirty-eight of fifty-five names were identified for occupation. Of these, seventeen were clerks, and six were bookkeepers. The rest were lawyers, salesmen, proprietors, and real estate men. Only one was a skilled craftsman. There were no laborers. The regiment included a number of sons of top businessmen and was generally considered to be a Republican regiment. The sources for this information are Collins, *History of the Illinois National Guard*, 7–9; *Edwards Directory of Chicago, 1873*; and *Lakeside Annual Directory of Chicago*, 1874–1875 (Chicago: Williams, Donnelley, 1875).

60. Joseph Kirkland, *The Story of Chicago*, vol. 1 (Chicago: Dibble Publishing, 1892), 58, 380. On the role of the National Guard in 1877, see *Biennial Report of the Adjutant General of Illinois*, 1877–1878, 106–7; Collins, *History of the Illinois National Guard*, 68, 69.

61. Quotation from John McAuliffe in *Chicago Inter-Ocean*, July 25, 1879. For a discussion of the origins and role of the Bohemian militia in 1877, see Richard Schneirov, "Chicago's Great Upheaval of 1877," *Chicago History* 9 (Spring 1980): 3–17; Collins, *History of the Illinois National Guard*, 27, 65.

62. Collins, *History of the Illinois National Guard*, 86–96; *Chicago Tribune*, September 2, 1879, p. 6.

63. Herbert G. Gutman, "Class, Status and Community Power in Nineteenth-Century American Cities: Paterson, New Jersey: A Case Study," and "A Brief Postscript: Class, Status and the Gilded Age Radical: A Reconsideration," in *Work, Culture and Society in Industrializing America*, ed. Herbert G. Gutman (New York: Vintage Books, 1977), 234–92.

64. For example, see Citizens Association complaints about the politicization of the fire department and the police force under Harrison: Citizens Association, *Annual Reports*, 1882, 9, 10, 15, 16; 1884, 28–31; and 1885, 21, 22; see also *Chicago Tribune*, September 1, 1879, p. 8.

65. *Chicago Tribune*, July 16, 1884, p. 6; September 27, 1884, p. 12.

66. Franklin MacVeagh, "Party Allegiance," in *Echoes of the Sunset Club*, ed. W. W. Catlin (Chicago: Howard, Bartells, 1891), 55–59; MacVeagh, "Socialism as a Remedy," *The Leader*, December 29, 1888, pp. 17–19; and MacVeagh, "The Values of Certain Social and Economic Facts" (Chicago: Address before the Chicago and Cook County High School Association, March 6, 1897).

67. My conception of political authority and consent has been shaped by Hannah Arendt, *On Violence* (New York: Harcourt Brace Jovanovich, 1970); and Robert Bierstedt, "The Problem of Authority" (1950), in *Power and Progress: Essays on Sociological Theory*, ed. Robert Bierstedt (New York: McGraw-Hill, 1974), 242–59.

German Radicals in Industrial America: The Lehr- und Wehr-Verein in Gilded Age Chicago

Christine Heiss

THE Lehr- und Wehr-Verein of Chicago, an armed workers' association for self-defense, was founded in 1875, well before anarchist ideas became prevalent in the Chicago labor movement. Even though the Verein has been considered important in the development of the American labor movement, its organization, ideology, and goals still remain unclear. Described by Friedrich A. Sorge as "a peculiar fruit produced by the heat of the movement in Chicago," the Verein differed in many respects from other workers' associations.[1] Closely connected with the socialist movement in Chicago, it felt called upon to defend a just republic and its constitution and thus fit well into the radical republican current in nineteenth-century American political culture. A purely German organization, it nonetheless made an effort to attract workers of all nationalities by not putting any ethnic restrictions in its requirements for admission.

Unfortunately, lists of members or minutes of meetings of the Lehr- und Wehr-Verein do not exist, a lack of source material typical for labor organizations in this period. The Verein's precarious political and legal situation was also responsible for the paucity of sources. In this period a newly awakened American labor movement was striving to become a recognized force in society, and it was watched with suspicion by the established authorities. Thus it is not surprising that a radical armed workers' organization kept its proceedings secret. Nevertheless, Chicago's German-language labor papers, particularly the *Chicagoer Arbeiter-Zeitung*, do contain significant amounts of information about the Verein, as do the *Chicago Tribune* and the *Illinois Staats-Zeitung*. Information is also available in the proceedings of the Cook County Criminal Court, the Illinois Supreme Court, and the United States Supreme Court in the cases of *Bielefeld* v. *The People of Illinois* and *Presser* v. *The People of Illinois*.

Several questions are of particular importance in analyzing this association. Taking into account the common assumption that radicalism and socialism were imports from Europe, one should ask if there was a tradition of armed workers' associations in the German labor movement in the nineteenth century. Or, given the legal restrictions on workers' organizations during this period in Germany, did any armed workers' organizations actually exist; and, if there is no evidence of them, were they nevertheless discussed? If such traditions existed, how did German workers use them under different conditions in Chicago? Did Chicago's conditions lead German workers to put these traditions into practice? Exactly what role did the Lehr- und Wehr-Verein play in the city's labor movement? Was it considered an elite corps, to be engaged in case a revolution broke out?

Traditions and antecedents

DURING the revolutionary years of 1848 and 1849, Switzerland became a gathering place for German emigrants, largely "petty bourgeois democrats" and republicans who sympathized with the labor movement and who brought under their influence a large number of the workers' organizations in Switzerland. In the course of the revolution this group of immigrants split up and "the more resolute petty bourgeois democrats, above all a part of the political refugees, became more and more radicalized and tried to rely increasingly on the workers' organizations." Johann Philipp Becker, who later was to play a significant role in the First International, was prominent among them. Becker had already advocated arming the people at the Hambacher Festival; in Switzerland he directed his efforts at founding German democratic clubs and a legion, "which in the case of a new revolution in Germany would join the battle for a democratic republic." At the end of March 1848, a Central Committee for Germans in Switzerland, which set up contacts with republicans in the German province of Baden, was founded under Becker's leadership. Under the influence of the Central Committee the organization took part in the Hecker uprising in March 1848 and in the unsuccessful Struveputsch.[2]

After this putsch the Deutsche Republikanische Wehrbund Hilf Dir (German Republican Defense Society Help Yourself), the membership of which consisted largely of German workers who had emigrated to Switzerland and France, was founded on the initiative of Becker. In the call for the founding of the defense society, he and August Willich insisted that "a German republic could only be won with armed power" and that therefore the chief task of Germans living abroad consisted in preparing themselves for participation in a new revolution through military training and organization. At the same time they spoke out against participation in "foolish putsches and unripe uprisings."[3] In 1866, from Geneva, Becker published a monthly journal, *Der Vorbote*, which reported in July 1866 that "the efforts of the German division to introduce the universal arming of the people was received with enthusiasm by all sections. The defense society here is moving along well, and there are four drill sessions weekly." The Defense Section of the Central Committee (German Division) of the International Workingman's Association in Geneva set up the tasks of striving for the universal arming of the people for the defense of the fatherland, encouraging the organization of defense bodies, achieving the combination of these defense bodies into a unified whole, drawing up defense and campaign plans, and trying to obtain contributions from Germans living out of the country, especially those in North America. At another point it was said that the universal arming of the people was the first step toward achieving a free state—doubtless a republic in the tradition of 1848—and that only with the universal arming of the people could genuine universal suffrage be achieved.[4]

Although one cannot find a direct connection between the Hilf Dir defense society or those recommended in *Der Vorbote* and the Lehr- und Wehr-Verein, there is a striking similarity in their readiness to fight for the republic with arms. Since the North American Republic—next to the France of the Second Republic—served as a political model for the German Left in the Vormärz period, it is likely that the United States represented an ideal republic in the light of 1848 for German workers versed in the democratic tradition. Even though the German situation, and particularly that of the German exiles in Switzerland, is not directly comparable to the situation in the United States, the parallels, especially the demands for a universal arming of the people, are nevertheless very striking. In addition, the loyalty to the American Constitution which the Lehr- und Wehr-Verein displayed—and particularly the trust in the constitutionally guaranteed rights of universal suffrage, freedom of speech and association, and the right to bear arms—remind one of the radical liberals and republicans in the German Revolution of 1848. Radical democrats had already called for a democratic-republican revolution in the Vormärz period, a demand that was taken up by both liberal and workers' organizations.[5] German artisans and workers in Chicago who were dedicated to these ideas found themselves in a city in which the suffrage was undermined by election frauds, in which workers' meetings were technically legal but in fact broken up by the police, and in which the constitutionally sanctioned militia system was not really reserved for the people but rather used by the ruling class for its own ends. And this in a country in which the militia—not a standing army—was enshrined in the Bill of Rights. It is therefore understandable that workers felt themselves justified in defending with arms their constitutionally guaranteed rights.

Similar to the Lehr- und Wehr-Verein in many respects, the Turners also had their roots in the political ferment of the Vormärz period. Like educational and singing societies, the Turner clubs had since the 1830s enjoyed increasing popularity among journeymen and workers. The first American Turner club was founded in the fall of 1848 through the direct influence of Friedrich Hecker, who had played a leading role in the revolution in the regions of Baden and the Palatinate. Turner clubs did not simply hold gymnastic exercises; they carried arms and drilled. In the Civil War, Turners made up a whole group of militia. As given in their statement of purpose, the task of the Turners is strikingly similar to the founding principles of the Lehr- und Wehr-Verein.[6] Both stress the necessity of physical and mental fitness for their members "in order that they may become energetic, patriotic citizens of the republic."[7]

The Lehr- und Wehr-Verein also had American antecedents. Since the time of the Mexican War, a tradition of voluntary militia companies in Chicago, a large number of them ethnically organized, had existed. Between the years 1848 and 1860 alone, there were seven militia companies in Chicago. Most important, during the Civil War a whole series of ethnic militia companies, in which a great part of the membership of Chicago's various labor organizations participated, were formed.[8] The Bohemian Sharpshooters, which at this time was admitted as a regular military unit under the name of the Lincoln Guard,[9] was such a workers' militia group. This tradition was used as a counterargument to the hate campaign against armed workers' groups that broke out in the spring of 1878, as well as by the Lehr- und Wehr-Verein in the court proceedings against the militia law which had made it illegal. Arguing that the Constitution mandated that the militia be open to all social groups, the Verein was drawing upon a living tradition of preindustrial America. A further parallel is evident in the social functions held by the ethnic militia companies in peacetime—balls, picnic excursions, shooting contests, and dress parades. As we shall see, the Lehr- und Wehr-Verein exercised similar functions for the working class.[10]

The 1870s: Founding, success, and controversy

INITIATING a period of social unrest, the panic of 1873 ended the economic expansion stimulated by the rebuilding in Chicago after the Great Fire of 1871. Labor's discontent was revealed in demonstrations against the Relief and Aid Society, a charity organization responsible for the administration of public donations to the city of Chicago for the repair of damage caused by the Fire. In the fall of 1873 a newly organized temporary committee of workers led a huge demonstration to the Chicago City Council, demanding immediate relief for the unemployed. According to Sartorius von Waltershausen, some members of the Chicago section of the First International—armed with revolvers—participated in the demonstration.[11] When questioned, they did not deny that there were plans to arm the workers and to organize them into military units. Intimidated by the vehemence of the demonstration, the Relief and Aid Society promised to meet the demands; but in fact relatively little was distributed compared to what had been promised.

By the fall of 1875 conditions had not improved. Tension grew considerably, and the authorities feared that angry workers would attack the Relief and Aid Society. At the instigation of Charles S. Diehls, the First Regiment of the Illinois State Guard was formed on August 28, 1874, equipped by the city administration. The regiment carried arms for the first time in March 1875; its purpose was to prevent an anticipated socialist attack on the Relief and Aid Society.[12] Though arms proved unnecessary, a speaker and several other people were clubbed by the police when the crowd assembled in front of the city hall was dispersed. Reporting the event, the Chicago *Vorbote* stressed that workers legally expressing their demands were illegally prevented from doing so by the police and militia. Therefore, the *Vorbote* argued, it would be more than legitimate for workers to back their demands by means of force. Noting the formation of additional militia units, the *Vorbote* went on to draw parallels between the reactions of the contemporary American authorities and German authorities during the Revolution of 1848.[13] The extreme hardships that workers, and especially immigrant workers, had to face in Chicago in the years following the panic of 1873, the reluctance of the Relief and Aid Society to accept the workers' demands, and the willingness of the authorities to intimidate workers by force led a considerable number of workers to the conclusion that they could back up their demands for immediate relief only if they were armed and organized. In addition, the ideological confusion of the socialist movement in the early 1870s in Chicago, reflecting all factions of the socialist movement in Europe and lacking a clearly defined direction, fostered the formation of a "revolutionary romanticism,"[14] which contributed greatly, according to Hermann Schlüter, to the formation of armed bodies of workers. The Lehr- und Wehr-Verein can legitimately be seen as one illustration of the desperate conditions in Chicago and the tendency of Chicago's labor movement toward radicalism in this early period.

On April 16, 1875, the Lehr- und Wehr-Verein was incorporated by the office of the Illinois secretary of state as the lawful association of its founders, Carl Finkensieper, Ferdinand Stamm, and August Timroth. Finkensieper was a member of the Illinois Workingmen's party, and the others were probably either members of that party or affiliated with a section of the International in Chicago. All of them declared themselves to be citizens of the United States. According to the records of incorporation, the association was formed "for the purpose of improving the mental and bodily condition of its members so as to qualify them for the duties of citizens of a Republic." To this end, members would obtain a knowledge of the laws and political economy and an instruction in military and gymnastic exercises. Eligible for membership was any "able-bodied man, having reached his eighteenth year, of good repute, who has declared his intention of becoming a citizen of the United States of America." The *Vorbote*'s announcement, however, explicitly stated that the association was formed exclusively by workers. It said furthermore that the association's foundation was a workers' reaction against the formation of additional militia units designed to be used against them. The drills of the same militia units, the *Vorbote* continued, were openly directed against the Illinois Workingmen's party. In "Our Way to Liberation," the editorial of the same issue of the *Vorbote*, Conrad Conzett called for the organization and training of workers. "It is our duty," he said, "to train ourselves in order to be able to lead the coming uprising of the people in such a way that the victory of the oppressed cannot fail."[15]

This illustration of a group of the Lehr- und Wehr-Verein shows the uniforms and arms of the association. From Michael J. Schaack, *Anarchy and Anarchists*, 1889.

A group of anarchists—the man in the center of the illustration is in the uniform of the Lehr- und Wehr-Verein. Taken from Michael J. Schaack, *Anarchy and Anarchists*, 1889.

The years from 1875 to 1877 can be seen as the organizing period of the Lehr- und Wehr-Verein. In the summer and fall of 1875 the emphasis was on raising funds for weapons and uniforms and advertising the association among the workers. Lists of voluntary contributions to the Lehr- und Wehr-Verein appeared in the *Vorbote*—most donations came from socialist clubs or members of the Illinois Workingmen's party—and the paper repeatedly urged workers to join, emphasizing again and again the threat of the militia buildup. And yet it seems that in the first two years of its existence the Verein did not attract a large number of members. In 1875, for instance, not a single general meeting of the membership was held.[16]

The administration of the Lehr- und Wehr-Verein lay in the hands of its General Council; the members of the council held officers' ranks and were also required to take part in the drills. Theoretical instruction was given by three so-called supervisors, who did not belong to the General Council and whose positions could be taken up by persons not belonging to the association. A Lehr- und Wehr-Verein Court Martial had the responsibilities of settling disputes and imposing punishments. The purchase of weapons by members was facilitated by an installment plan—a method picked up and recommended later by the International Working People's Association. The Verein was financed by voluntary contributions; admission fees were fifteen cents and monthly dues ten cents for its members.[17]

Concerning the tactics of the Lehr- und Wehr-Verein, the association's constitution and bylaws said only that "the drills are the society's own." The *Chicago Tribune* hinted that the drills were similar to those of the militia and federal troops, enriched by "a fair sprinkling of modern movements made up by the officers of the Lehr- und Wehr-Verein." This was confirmed by the *Vorbote*, which spoke of a mixture of the newest Prussian and American drills, calling them "extremely practical in street fighting and field service." The uniforms were reminiscent of the imaginative uniforms of the volunteer militia in Chicago before and during the Civil War: "Presently the uniform consists of a blue linen blouse, black Sheridan-hat, in summer white linen pants, or dark ones in the colder season. The further equipment consists of a strong white linen haversack (sailcloth), and a cloth covered tin canteen." In weaponry the Lehr- und Wehr-Verein obviously tried to maintain the same standard as the militia. Statutes of the association spoke only of breech and muzzle loaders, but the *Vorbote* reported in April 1879 that the Verein was the best equipped unit among the militant workers' organizations, armed exclusively with Springfield and Remington rifles, and that its equipment had therefore reached the same standard as that of the militia. The meetings of the association were public, as were the drills, which were held two to three times a week by various divisions; the time and place were announced a week earlier by the labor press. In the court proceedings that surrounded the militia law, the Verein insisted repeatedly that the drills had always been public and that the association was entirely within the law.[18]

Despite the militant calls for arms published by the *Vorbote* after the association's foundation, visitors to the Verein's first big public rally, the dedication of the association's banner on November 4, 1876, were promised an evening of entertainment without a single mention of the political importance of the event. In 1878 the Verein held a series of balls to raise money for uniforms and weapons. Apart from dance and drink, the drill parades were particularly popular. Political speeches were often embellished with *tableaux vivants*, most of the time depicting events from the class struggle in Europe. Marching and fighting songs served to spread "utmost Gemütlichkeit" and create a "suitable festive military mood" in the audience.[19] The songs, described by the *Vorbote* as patriotic or military, were often composed by prominent members of the Chicago labor movement—Gustav Lyser is one example—and recall the singing tradition of the labor movement in Germany.[20]

Besides evening entertainments and picnics which integrated

the Lehr- und Wehr-Verein smoothly into the "staged culture"[21] of the German labor movement in Chicago, one of its main functions for the working class was the organization of parades and processions. Apart from the proud way in which the labor press reported about the "proletarian militia,"[22] the significance of this public demonstration of force became obvious in the controversy over the militia law, which forbade any armed parades of workers. The *New Yorker Volks-Zeitung* claimed on this occasion that "'the possibility of bearing arms in open street parade in and by itself represents an important right.'"[23] Another function of the Verein was to take a role similar to that of neighborhood police, keeping order at mass meetings or celebrations of the working class, sometimes even in cooperation with regular German policemen. At election meetings of the Socialist Labor party, members of the association served as guards.[24] Although one of the Verein's functions was to prevent police raids on workers' meetings, it never entered a fighting confrontation during its whole existence. The essential function of the association for the labor movement seems to have been psychological: its military appearance at the head of parades of socialist unions and clubs gave the workers a feeling of strength and self-confidence. The violent reactions of the middle-class press, which started a hate campaign against military workers' organizations after the strike wave of 1877, confirm the Verein's symbolic importance.

In 1877 the depression that began in 1873 came to its climax. The year before had been marked by wage reductions and dismissals, and the number of unemployed grew daily. Chicago had about 30,000 unemployed workers, about 18 percent of the city's labor force. When the nation's railroad workers struck in 1877, paralyzing almost every important railroad line and instigating violence in major eastern cities, riots were expected in Chicago as well; and the militia was called out. A day after the June 23 mass meeting of the Illinois Workingmen's party, the switchmen of the Michigan Central went on strike, addressing their strike appeal to all industrial workers. At the instigation of the Chicago Board of Trade, influential citizens, and factory owners, several volunteer police and militia units were formed; and several thousand additional policemen were sworn in. Numerous industrial concerns formed plant guards of their own or hired special detectives. The newly formed Veterans' Corps and Citizen Patrols, as the special police units were called, provided around 20,000 men, prepared to suppress a riot. Finally, on July 26, a street fight broke out between police and demonstrators, injuring around twelve of the latter. The trouble was already over when police dispersed a legal union meeting of furniture workers, killing one member in the process.[25]

This incident reinforced the apparent necessity of a workers' self-defense society to defend constitutional rights like the freedom of assembly, which had on July 26 been gravely violated. The assault on the furniture workers' meeting, working-class papers argued, showed clearly that civil rights for workers in the United States existed only on paper. According to the *Vorbote*, police clubs and militia rifles outweighed the Constitution; and freedom of assembly and speech in reality existed, as in Europe, only for the ruling class. A proposition of Mayor Monroe Heath to institutionalize the Citizens' Guard was seen by the workers as a direct threat. The *Vorbote* warned them not to stand patiently by and see their right to vote being curtailed, as had been the case with the right of assembly. Rather, they were urged to use the following year for organization. Bitter that they could not claim civil rights without encountering repression by police, militia, or even federal troops, workers did turn to armed groups, the membership of which increased substantially. This was especially the case with the Lehr- und Wehr-Verein. At the same time, the question of the use of force had become a prominent issue within the socialist movement in Chicago. The brutal attempts to quell the strikes of 1877 and the disregard of workers' civil rights had generated a rebellious mood in the city, reinforced by ideas imported from Europe in a wave of political refugees. For many, bearing arms seemed now to be the only solution to the labor question.[26]

The growing popularity experienced by the militarily organized groups after the strike wave of 1877 had to lead to differences within the Socialist Labor party. Criticism of the political strategy, as it had been practiced from the beginning by members of the First International, coincided with criticism by members of the armed organizations, who had been unsatisfied with the slow progress of the party anyway. On the other hand, the Socialist Labor party leadership declared that armed groups, because of their militant appearance, would split the party and discredit the socialist movement in the eyes of the public.[27] The editors of the *Vorbote* took up the defense of the armed organizations, emphasizing their defensive character and the constitutional guarantees for their existence.[28] The occasion for the open break between the national executive and the Chicago section of the party was the latter's organization of a parade of socialist unions and clubs on July 5, 1878, which was to be opened by the Lehr- und Wehr-Verein. The national executive of the Socialist Labor party, led by Phillip Van Patten, called upon its own Chicago section and the

Lehr- und Wehr-Verein "to avoid any military display and instead ridicule the authorities by appearing in a manner as innocent as that of a religious procession."[29] After the Chicagoans rejected this suggestion and marched with weapons, the national executive withdrew the party's recognition of the Verein, despite the opposition of its Chicago section. This national executive decision began the split of the Socialist Labor party into radical and reformist wings. The coalition with the Greenback Labor party, which the national executive planned, only deepened the gap between the English- and the German-speaking sections in Chicago. The obvious election scandal in Chicago's spring election of 1880, in which the votes for two Socialist candidates for the city council were undercounted, as well as the acquittal two years later of the election officials who had falsified the vote, convinced a large group of workers "that there were no rights for politically independent workers and that it would be futile in the future to achieve anything by legal means."[30]

The same growth in membership and popularity of the armed groups which divided the Socialist Labor party aroused the established authorities of Chicago. The Lehr- und Wehr-Verein was able to marshal four companies in 1878, each of which consisted of several divisions. The *Chicagoer Arbeiter-Zeitung* attributed forty-two men to one division. The companies located on the North and Northwest sides were reported to have the largest membership. The other two, located on the South and Southwest sides, seemed to be smaller. When the Verein began drilling in formation in the spring of 1878, the attention of the authorities and the press was focused on the armed "socialists and communists." The March 23, 1879, Spring Festival, held in the exhibition building under the auspices of the Socialist Labor party, attracted more than 20,000 people, a larger number than had ever been seen at any socialist mass meeting in Chicago. The members of the Verein functioned as guards, and a big drill exercise was planned. In the beginning even some conservative factions had considered the association's drills harmless. This attitude disappeared, however, when it became evident that the Verein planned to take part—in full uniform and bearing arms—in a march organized by the Chicago section of the Socialist Labor party. In the spring several newspapers had already spread the rumor that the Socialists wanted to occupy the city in order to form a commune (as had occurred in Paris in 1871). March 23 was supposedly fixed as the day the revolution would erupt. Although the demonstration was conducted peacefully—as was generally conceded by the press—it marked the beginning of attempts to outlaw armed organizations. Alarmed over the strength of the Verein, the press published exaggerated reports, helping accelerate the passage of a law which prohibited armed workers' organizations.[31]

The railroad strikes of 1877 led to a redefinition of the role of the militia.[32] A militia bill was introduced in the lower house of the Illinois State Legislature and received its first reading on January 17.[33] The *Vorbote* reported that socialist representatives saw in the law "a dangerous step in the direction of a costly military supremacy in the place of the voluntary organization of militia companies paid for by their own members" and objected to "increasing the tax burden of the people in order to create a militia which would aid the people's exploiters in repressing and holding down the wage slaves." Charles Erhard, another socialist representative, had emphasized that the Lehr- und Wehr-Verein was ready to join the state militia.[34] The main cause of the socialist protests were the paragraphs in Article XI of the proposed bill, which forbade private groups not a part of the state militia from associating "themselves together as a military company or organization, or to drill or parade with arms in any city, or town of this State, without the license of the Governor thereof. . . ."[35] A protest demonstration against the militia law held by the Verein and other armed groups on April 20 only helped convince the public and the press even more of the necessity for a stronger militia.[36]

The basis of the Verein's case against the militia law was that it contradicted the second amendment to the federal Constitution. In addition, appealing to the Militia Act of 1792, the labor press referred to the unlimited power of the federal government over the militia and argued that such militia laws by individual states presented the possibility "of the federal government's being robbed of any aid from the state militias, simply because the laws forbid them to assemble with weapons, to undertake military exercises, and to parade." Moreover, a commentary on the federal Constitution by Judge Story was quoted; the judge saw the militia not only as a natural defense against external enemies and unrest but also against "domestic usurpations by holders of power."[37] In the proceedings of the Criminal Court of Cook County on July 28, 1879, the defense stressed that the right of the citizens to bear arms "'had always been recognized in connection with a militia system, as contradistinguished from a standing army, and by militia was to be meant the whole body of the people, not a certain number of them selected by one man to suit his own ideas.'" A well-selected and organized militia was the alternative to a standing army, and its composition could never be left to the arbitrariness of a governor.[38]

The decision of the Criminal Court of Cook County in the case came on September 2, 1879. The Criminal Court of Cook County put the status of the law in jeopardy when it determined that no sentence of the Constitution bound the right to bear arms to the existence of an organized militia. This judgment was overruled, however, on February 9, 1880, by the Supreme Court of Illinois in a case initiated indirectly by the First Regiment of the Illinois National Guard. In order to take the case to the United States Supreme Court, the Lehr- und Wehr-Verein initiated the case of *Presser* v. *The People of Illinois*, which lasted six years and was finally decided in 1886 in favor of the Illinois militia law. The Verein had attempted in vain to obtain the recognition of its rights as a militia group of the people.[39]

Analysis of membership and ideology

IN 1879 the Lehr- und Wehr-Verein had reached the peak of its strength. The *Chicago Tribune* reported that at least 470 armed Socialists took part in the March 23 Spring Festival,[40] a figure that probably included members of the other armed ethnic groups, like the Bohemian Sharpshooters, the Jägerverein, and the Irish Labor Guard. Although the *Chicagoer Arbeiter-Zeitung* estimated the total number of the "proletarian militia" in 1879 to be 1,000, the *Vorbote* spoke only of 668 armed men.[41] The lack of more detailed information makes it impossible to systematically analyze the membership of the Verein. Until 1880, at least the names of the officers could be found in the working-class papers. Subsequently, only titles, such as officer or secretary, were attached to the meeting announcements.[42] Descriptions in the newspaper reports were also vague. The *Chicago Tribune* hinted that "there were many boys in the ranks, but also men whose erect bearing and steady marching showed, that either in this country or in Europe they had seen powder burnt and heard shots fired in earnest." It expressed amazement that "although almost all the members are labouring men, working ten hours a day at hard manual labour, their drills are very well attended."[43]

The few members who could be found in the manuscript population census of 1880 were laborers or artisans, as Table 1 shows.[44] At least these men were not recent arrivals in the United States or in Illinois: they had been in the state an average of 6.7 years; and even that is probably an underestimate, given the method of determining the length of stay. Thus it is unlikely that radical socialist immigrants recently arrived from Germany were responsi-

Table 1. Nine members of the Lehr- und Wehr-Verein of Chicago: Origin, years in Illinois, occupation in 1880

Origin	Years in Illinois*	Occupation
Hannover	11	Currier
Hannover		Works in shoe factory
Hannover		Works in frame factory
Prussia	5	Parlor bracket maker
Prussia	6	Laborer
Prussia	4	Teamster
Saxony	6	Carpenter
Saxony	2	Instrument maker
Holland	13	Plasterer

*Determined by the age of the first child born in Illinois.

ble for the more radical position that the Verein assumed after joining the International Working People's Association. Most important, the occupational character of these men reminds one that the German labor movement at the beginning of the nineteenth century was supported by a great number of artisans with staunch republican ideals—such as those of the Lehr- und Wehr-Verein—and that the only armed association linked with the labor movement in Germany—the Wehrbund Hilf Dir—was comprised to a large extent of craftsmen.

The Lehr- und Wehr-Verein's ideology, expressed particularly in its loyalty to the American Republic and its Constitution, became evident whenever its leadership considered it necessary to justify the existence of the association. In an open letter to Hermann Raster, the editor of the *Illinois Staats-Zeitung*, Hermann Schulz, the incumbent secretary of the Verein, declared "that the Lehr- und Wehr-Verein does not intend to take action as long as the rights guaranteed by the constitution, especially that of free union and free association, are not attacked by the bourgeoisie." Schulz further stressed that the "'preparations of the workingmen . . . are not . . . limited to the German-speaking element.'"[45] At an anniversary celebration in May 1879, Frank Bielefeld gave his speech in English and reaffirmed the loyalty of the Verein to the Constitution.[46] The overthrow of the Republic, the association repeated again and again, must not be expected from armed workers' groups but instead from the bourgeoisie, who tried to curtail the people's rights and did not respect the Constitution. In a speech in January 1879, when the impressions of the violent events of 1877 were still fresh, Gustav Lyser defined the purposes of the Verein as follows: "The Lehr- und Wehr-Verein was not founded to support putsches from time to time, but to maintain law and order when exploiters and swindlers of the people threaten to stage such putsches so as to install reactionary tendencies."[47] In the opinion of the Verein, the growing accumulation of capital in the 1870s and 1880s, which concentrated power in the hands of a few and limited the workers' rights, led directly to the decay of the Republic. To prevent this, Bielefeld declared in 1880, it was necessary that the people be armed, because "only a people fit for military service is a free people."[48]

Socialists, anarchists, and the 1880s

FROM the beginning there was close cooperation between social revolutionaries and armed organizations. The General Council of all armed groups, created in 1880 and comprised of the officers of the Lehr- und Wehr-Verein, the Jägerverein, the Bohemian Sharpshooters, and the Irish Labor Guard, had been involved in the split of the social revolutionaries from the Socialist Labor party. In addition, important leaders of Chicago's social revolutionary movement, like August Spies and Paul Grottkau, were at one time or another members of the Lehr- und Wehr-Verein. The decision of the Illinois Supreme Court in February 1880 had once more confirmed the opinion that workers could not gain anything through legal channels, and officers of the Lehr- und Wehr-Verein now pointed to the increasingly critical situation and emphasized that only through arms could the workers attain their liberation. One of these officers even warned of a "violent attack by the upper ten thousand upon the freedom of the working people" and called on the workers to buy weapons for defense instead of losing money in strikes.[49] Even if the Verein had lost a majority of its members as a result of the Supreme Court's decision, the same decision, rejoiced the *Chicagoer Arbeiter-Zeitung*, "had made possible a modern organization of armed groups, an organization whose strength and extent could no longer be determined and which could therefore be suppressed neither by law nor by force."[50] Within Chicago's Socialist movement the resort to arms was finally defended. Although the revival of the anarchist International had great significance for the armed groups in Chicago, within the International Working People's Association there was a divided opinion about the role of armed, organized troops of the "people's militia." On the one hand, their usefulness was not contested; on the other hand, it was debated whether this form of armed organization was not too time-consuming and costly and, moreover, whether it too could be crippled through the law, as had happened in Illinois. On the local level, in Chicago, the question of whether the workers had to be able to attack and not simply to defend themselves was raised—a contrast with previous statements of the Verein. The officers of the Verein even adopted a military arrangement which gave numerical representations for the strength of a whole army corps and would make it possible "in any town, beginning with a company, to form organizations which at the assigned moment could rise as one."[51] Although it took no aggressive actions, however, the question of whether the Lehr- und Wehr-Verein gave up its defensive position in the years following the Supreme Court decision can be answered only hypothetically.

When the social revolutionary movement in Chicago declined as a consequence of the repression following the Haymarket bomb, armed groups also disappeared. Late in 1886 attempts to reorganize these splintered groups were made; but the effort apparently met with little interest among the workers.[52] Haymarket ended an era in the politics of the Left in Chicago in which the Lehr- und Wehr-Verein had played a prominent part. Violent labor conflicts in the city did not end, of course, as the Pullman strike illustrated, but Chicago's workers turned to politics and labor unions as weapons, not to arms. A child of the bitter 1870s, the Verein was driven to extremes in the defense of traditional republican values, a stance that put it in common with so many others of the time, including the Knights of Labor and those who participated in the eight-hour uprising of 1886. Only the Verein's exotic and sensational methods—which in fact were never used to attack established authorities—made it look like the peculiar fruit of a foreign land.

Notes

1. Friedrich A. Sorge, "Die Arbeiterbewegung in den Vereinigten Staaten 1877–1885," *Neue Zeit*, February 10, 1892, p. 203.

2. Rolf Dlubek, "Zur politischen Tätigkeit von Friedrich Engels in der Schweiz Ende 1848—Anfang 1849. Zwei unbekannte Briefe von Friedrich Engels," *Beiträge zur Geschichte der Arbeiterbewegung* (1956): 749–50.

3. Ibid., p. 751.

4. *Der Vorbote*, Geneva, July 1866, "Der Entwicklungsgang unserer Assoziation," p. 101; "Adresse des Wehrausschusses des Central-Comites (deutsche Abtheilung) der Internationalen Arbeiterassociation in Genf an den Landesvertheidigungsausschuss in Frankenthal"; ibid., June 1866, "Allgemeine Volksbewaffnung."

5. Eckhart G. Franz, "Das Amerikabild der deutschen Revolution von 1848/49: Zum Problem der Übertragung gewachsener Verfassungsformen," *Beihefte zum Jahrbuch fur Amerikastudien* 2 (1958): 104.

6. Augustus J. Prahl, "The Turner," in *The Forty-Eighters: Political*

Refugees of the German Revolution of 1848, ed. A. E. Zucker (New York: Columbia University Press, 1950), 93 and 98.

7. *Act of Incorporation of the Lehr- und Wehr-Verein*, April 15, 1875, Secretary of State, Corporation Division, Dissolved Charters File, Record Group 103112, State of Illinois (Chicago, 1920).

8. Alfred T. Andreas, *History of Chicago from the Earliest Period to the Present Time*, vol. 1 (Chicago: A. T. Andreas, 1884: reprint ed., New York: Arno Press, 1975), 284–86.

9. *Chicago Tribune*, April 27, 1878.

10. Robert Reinders, "Militia and Public Order in Nineteenth Century America," *Journal of American Studies* 11 (April 1977): 87.

11. A. Sartorius von Waltershausen, *Der moderne Sozialismus in den Vereinigten Staaten von Amerika* (Berlin: Verlag von Hermann Bahr, 1980), 90.

12. Alfred T. Andreas, *History of Chicago from the Earliest Period to the Present Time*, vol. 3 (Chicago: A. T. Andreas, 1886; reprint ed., New York: Arno Press, 1975), 585.

13. *Vorbote*, February 27, 1875; ibid., January 1, 1875.

14. Hermann Schlüter, *Die Internationale in Amerika: Ein Beitrag zur Geschichte der Arbeiterbewegung in den Vereinigten Staaten*, Deutsche Sprachgruppe der sozialistischen Partei der Vereinigten Staaten (Chicago: 1918), 308.

15. For the membership of Carl Finkensieper, see Michael J. Schaack, *Anarchy and Anarchists* (Chicago: F. J. Schulte, 1889; reprint ed., New York: Arno Press, 1977), 49; *Act of Incorporation*, April 15, 1875; and Conrad Conzett, "Our Way to Liberation," *Vorbote*, May 1, 1875.

16. *Vorbote*, May 26 and August 7, 1875.

17. *Act of Incorporation*, April 15, 1875; *Freiheit*, February 14, 1885.

18. *Chicago Tribune*, March 24, 1879; *Vorbote*, April 5, 1879; *Constitution and By-Laws of the Lehr- und Wehr-Verein of Chicago, Adopted December 30th, 1878* (Chicago, 1878), Illinois State Archives.

19. *Vorbote*, March 1, 1879; ibid., January 1, 1879; ibid., September 21, 1875; ibid., November 11, 1878.

20. Vernon Lidtke, "Lieder der deutschen Arbeiterbewegung, 1864–1914," trans. Hans J. Ginsburg, *Geschichte und Gesellschaft* 5 (1979): 54–82.

21. Hartmut Keil and Heinz Ickstadt, "Elemente einer deutschen Arbeiterkultur in Chicago zwischen 1880 und 1890," *Geschichte und Gesellschaft* 5 (1979): 103–24.

22. "Unser Fest," *Chicagoer Arbeiter-Zeitung* (hereafter *ChAZ*), June 26, 1878.

23. Quoted by *ChAZ*, March 9, 1883.

24. "Unser Fest," *ChAZ*, June 26, 1878.

25. Howard B. Myers, "The Policing of Labor Disputes in Chicago: A Case Study," (Ph.D. diss., University of Chicago, 1929), pp. 112, 114.

26. *Vorbote*, August 4 and 11, 1877; see also Henry David, *The History of the Haymarket Affair* (1936; New York: Russell & Russell, 1964).

27. See "Proceedings of the National Convention of the Socialist Labor Party Held at Turner Hall, Allegheny City, Pa., 1879," Socialist Labor Party Papers, National Conventions 1877–1950, State Historical Society of Wisconsin, reel 35.

28. "Antwort der Redaktion auf das Eingesandt von Geo. Block," *Vorbote*, May 11, 1875.

29. "Proceedings of the National Convention of the Socialist Labor Party, 1879."

30. "Der erste Mai, Der Geburtstag der Arbeiterbewegung," *ChAZ*, May 18, 1887.

31. *ChAZ*, June 23, 1879; *Chicago Tribune*, April 27, 1878.

32. See Reinders, "Militia and Public Order," p. 92.

33. *Journal of the House of Representatives of the Thirty-First General Assembly of the State of Illinois* (Springfield, January 8, 1879), 66.

34. "Originalkorrespondenz aus Springfield," *Vorbote*, March 29, 1879.

35. *The Revised Statutes of the State of Illinois, 1880*, ed. Harvey B. Burd (Chicago: Legal News Company, 1887).

36. *Chicago Tribune*, March 24, 1879.

37. "Die Milizbill," *Die Fackel*, July 27, 1879.

38. The defense was quoted by the *Chicago Tribune*, September 2, 1879.

39. *Chicago Tribune*, September 2 and 22, 1879; February 9, 1880.

40. *Chicago Tribune*, April 21, 1879.

41. *Vorbote*, September 7, 1879; "Der Geburtstag der Arbeiterbewegung," *Vorbote*, May 18, 1887.

42. In 1885 the Verein began to identify its members by numbers; see *Freiheit*, February 14, 1885.

43. *Chicago Tribune*, April 21, 1879.

44. Most of the names of the members indicated in the papers were common, like Meier or Müller; it was thus impossible to identify the persons with certainty in the city directories.

45. Quoted by *Chicago Tribune*, April 28, 1878.

46. *ChAZ*, May 5, 1879; *Vorbote*, May 4, 1879.

47. *ChAZ*, January 25, 1879.

48. *ChAZ*, March 16, 1880.

49. "Eingesandt von Franz Kanneberg," *ChAZ*, March 3, 1880.

50. *ChAZ*, January 13, 1886.

51. "Glossen zur Bewaffnungsfrage," *ChAZ*, May 28, 1884; "Zur Volksbewaffnungsfrage," *ChAZ*, April 21, 1881.

52. *ChAZ*, November 11, 1886. Announcements of the Lehr- und Wehr-Verein were inserted in the labor papers until April 1887, after which information on the association peters out, with no official reference concerning its dissolution. The Verein was not formally dissolved until 1920. A 1901 law that provided that associations incorporated under Illinois law had to submit yearly reports and pay a fee of one dollar finally uncovered the sham existence of the Lehr- und Wehr-Verein. Since the association did not meet these obligations, it lost its legal existence in the state; compare *Act of Incorporation*.

German Socialists and the Roots of American Working-Class Radicalism

Paul Buhle

To speak with the octogenerians of the European-American Left today—the Slavs, the Hungarians, the Finns, and especially the Jews—is to recognize that they represent the end of a tradition more than a century old. The social forms of their radicalism—literary culture, musical societies, holiday celebrations, bake-fests, and neighborhood block parties—grew out of long-disappeared German-American radical practice. Until the U.S. government's destruction of the International Workers Order in the early 1950s, such activities had for generations supplied the working-class Left with a cultural infrastructure and funds. Even now perhaps a majority of the ethnically oriented radical papers are a remnant of that older movement.

As I have ranged across the country for the American Left Project, the veterans have expressed to me in a variety of languages and contexts an essentially similar message: their political movement rested upon a cultural base, and the cultural activists spanned the gap between the Left proper and the immigrant community at large. Indeed, even when the immigrant radicals saw their tasks in straightforward political and economic terms, the cultural side of their work maintained a millennial vision amidst turgid Marxist orthodox rhetoric and economistic trade unionism. The most conscious of the cultural activists have also articulated the goal of a pluralistic America common to every immigrant radicalism: "Culturally, as well as politically, the melting pot has a scorched bottom. It is anti-democratic and anti-American to follow the jingoistic theory of complete cultural assimilation. . . .

Cultural democracy means necessarily language democracy as well," as Jewish fraternal leader Itche Goldberg argued in the 1940s.[1] The German militants who had long before developed the essential insights could not have put it better themselves. When scholars analyze German-American radical culture in the late nineteenth and early twentieth centuries, they are thus studying the earliest and the formative pattern of a far larger movement.

In addressing the nature of radical German-American culture here, we are describing first of all the *subjectivity* of the social movement—not the formal, essentially ideological expression of Marxism as the belief in scientific social analysis but rather the means available when ordinary Socialists expressed their own perceived position in society and their hopes for the future. Ambivalences between this latter subjective response and the formal political structure of the Marxist organization are omnipresent. The many mediations between the two therefore depended upon the actual situation, even upon the particular personalities who directed the movement and helped to provide its symbolism.

Second, we are not treating a group in isolation from the surrounding society and culture; instead, we are describing one in dynamic and swift-changing relation to the dominant society and culture at historical points where those entities might literally go one way or the other. When we seek to explain the efflorescence of German-American culture in the 1880s and the fading of the political movement—but not its cultural component—thereafter, we face a moment analogous to that passed through by Jewish "1905er" immigrants, by Slavs and Finns in the decade between 1910 and 1920, and by a plethora of immigrant groups at a later stage of development in the 1930s. Although the promise of such moments was not fulfilled (and much of the evidence is afterward erased or forgotten), the expectations they create defined a unique approach to American civilization hardly imaginable before or after the crises.

Finally, we are considering a form of mass culture, a mass aesthetic, which has never been properly appreciated. The point at which a centuries-old tradition of artisan consciousness, free thought, and messianic anticipation meets the most vibrant popular commercial culture in the world is a creative time indeed. Immigrant workers provided the audience for and the participants in sports, theater, music halls, moving pictures, and the commercial press. They also developed their own unique forms—for example, plays about the banal ethnic nouveaux riches, musical repertoires including workers' songs and black spirituals—

mixtures of American experiences and European tradition which made a special contribution to the evolving pluralist culture.

The prime difficulty of analysis from the old Marxist standpoint lies in the unplanned and unanticipated character of these latter developments. Since the European Socialist movement failed for decades to come to grips conceptually with its own cultural auxiliaries and never fully acknowledged the persistence of pre-modern religious and romantic folk traditions in its own culture, its American counterpart could hardly be expected to interpret the significance of America's mass popular culture. Nevertheless, Socialists and sympathizers living in American neighborhoods, learning American habits while seeking to retain aspects of old-world culture, had to adapt; and in a bemused, if sometimes pessimistic, fashion, they shared a fascination with a society that produced Houdini, moving pictures, and the Brooklyn Bridge. Their aesthetic contained an awareness, mixed anxiety, and pleasure at the ongoing process of modernization—a taste, a feeling for the possibilities at hand, which are only *represented* by formal politics and economics. German-American Socialist culture was, at points, a statement about the way the new society, the one just before the participants' eyes, could be brought to a revolutionary conclusion.

RADICAL German workers in Gilded Age America had a self-understanding which reached backward to the distant origins of artisan culture and forward to the eclipse of the class order. Liberation theologians, such as José Miranda and Ernesto Cardinal, have recently popularized what generations of Marxist-oriented historians have felt embarrassed to articulate: the transference of religious and deep mystical principles into Socialist historical consciousness.[2] Using Marxism, German Socialists added what were intended to be scientific claims to messianic visions they had picked up from such varied sources as religious mysticism, the classical poets, and the popular mythology of folk tradition. Most important, this Socialist millennialism had a solid foundation in the craft tradition. As Thorstein Veblen shrewdly noted, the artisanal heritage continued to impart a sense of self-confidence which helped shape the response of the skilled workers, like cabinetmakers and machinists, to the challenge of changing production methods.[3] The repository of deeply held craft values par excellence, German working-class culture was prepared to interpret industrial conflict and social crises as the most recent phase of an age-old conflict that would lead to the ultimate vindication of human brotherhood.

In Germany the uses of Socialist music, theater, poetry, and recreation conformed to no theoretical prescription, no conscious political strategy. While providing for the leisure, entertainment, and spiritual needs of the proletarian constituencies, Social Democratic culture drew its resources from a mixture of folk culture, contemporary popular culture, and the national legacy of high culture. Historians' arguments about the exact nature and function of this culture in Germany are beside the point here. The activities existed first of all to make the lives of participants—family, co-workers, and others—more tolerable and more beautiful. By every reasonable measure, they succeeded in that end.[4]

In America, immigration presented such cultural activity with potentially insuperable problems; but it also presented opportunities for carrying out the poignant role of preserver of age-old sensibilities, transmitter of key values to a pluralistic order. The American press, the public school system, and a thousand other mechanisms operated to discredit, especially among the young, the European ideologies, the old. As the Yiddish Socialist journal *Tsukunft* recorded in 1909, the presence of Socialist convictions was considered in many families evidence of a *grüner* who could not adapt.[5] And yet, opposed to these attitudes, something of great importance also obtained. Joseph Stipanovich, historian of the South Slav Socialists, put the matter well:

> Paradoxically, the socialists . . . were best able to harmonize the sense of social responsibility, at both abstract and practical levels, with the primary value of their cultures. The South Slav clerics and entrepreneurs, on the other hand, were able to harmonize their sense of responsibility with the values of indigenous American culture only at the expense of their South Slav cultures. Very early in the history of the South Slav immigrant communities the social and economic interests of the clergy and the merchants began to supersede their interest in maintaining their cultural identity.[6]

The implications hold for Germans as well as for Jews, Hungarians, Ukrainians, Italians, Finns, and others. It was never literally true that, as Yiddish Communists would later claim, Yiddish was a proletarian language, *Yiddishkeit* a proletarian culture. Small businessmen, newly arrived immigrants, factions of pious religious folk, and a scattering of cultural devotees from all backgrounds and vocations—all held to the old language and customs, and for a variety of reasons.[7] But because the cleric or businessman offered integration only on the terms of the existing order, his perpetuation of the ethnic culture remained fundamentally superficial. The Socialists, and later the Communists, had no such restraint. Despite their emphasis upon internationalism and, at times, a desire to assimilate to reach American workers, they found themselves defending immigrant culture in the only possible genuine way: affirming a valid second identity within a transformed nation.

In the context of the United States, the effective use of German Socialist culture required an intelligentsia able to contain and move between two worlds. Quoting in bold and rebellious style some of the greatest German writers, emigré Socialists laid claim to the best of their country's national culture as they tried to build a viable tradition in America. To Socialists, the romantic Schiller and Goethe—their Sturm und Drang embrace of the common people against well-fed and arrogant rulers, their heroizing of the rebel pitting energies against all existing laws and institutions—had more than a whiff of the Socialist millennium. While the exaltation of subjectivity and the inner man over against a philistine world could be used by cultural reactionaries as a signal for a retreat into the past, something important for the revolutionary had been justified as well. Threatened by industrialization, the poet's world could be reclaimed by an appeal to true reality beyond everyday appearances: "What is the artist in the salon of today's swindler, factory owner, speculator or banker?" asked prolific German-American Socialist feuilletonist August Otto-Walster. "A poor slave. If he follows artistic ideals, he is an impractical man, a fantastic dreamer, an ideologue, unsuited for the times."[8] Only as a Socialist could the artist be vindicated.

Marx and Engels might object that this sentimental attitude created poetry for, and not by, workers. Certainly it spoke in romantic tones of a pre-industrial idyll seemingly out of place in the emerging order. But such objections, often repeated by a variety of immigrant political leaders, failed to appreciate both the unique cultural status of the immigrant and the special qualities of popular culture. Even those proletarians who, at the very hub of American production, were considered most politically advanced, still clung to their youthful memories of Europe, maintaining their radical commitment through a fusion of their older sentiments and their New World experiences. Thus memories of working-class culture in Europe summoned up decades later helped provide images of what Socialist society might be like; and popular theater, music, and sports kept alive or adapted heroic archetypes, so that even a German-American second baseman might take the likeness of Wilhelm Tell. Because pure Socialist-proletarian culture existed nowhere in the real world, practical activists learned to make adaptations of Socialist culture, using whatever vernacular was available.

Thus teachers, physicians, and other intellectuals who threw their energies into the cause played a crucial role. Newspaper editors, public speakers, playwrights, and theatrical critics were the thinkers "who attempted to merge the hopes and aspirations of the immigrants with practical forms of organization and behavior which could bring them to fruition."[9] This intelligentsia feared that history might not vindicate them, their cultural initiatives, their constituency's expectations. Defeat would consign their old-world legacy to the nostalgia of future generations. The older Socialist, with years of ups and downs in America, naturally reverted toward the romantic self-consciousness of youth and held up its values against philistine acquaintances and neighbors and sometimes even against the rest of the family. The intellectual and political leaders who remained in the movement after the glory days became evermore like dear comrades to the ranks aged in the struggle. They shared with their like-minded constituency a desperate eagerness to rescue elements of the past from total obscurity in order to provide the foundation for a distinctly American revolution.

THE apocalyptic nature of the German-American Socialist movement set the context for the combative syndicalism whose effectiveness was unequaled until the beginnings of the Industrial Workers of the World. Gustav Lyser, editor of the Sunday edition of the *Chicagoer Arbeiter-Zeitung* in the early 1880s, could sing in these martial strains:

When will the last strike be?
When the spirit of Man rises
When in the Lehr- und Wehr-Verein
And in the Bund of Jägers
Ten thousand shall be found;
When the ranks of proletarians
Struggle no longer 'gainst each other
But close ranks among themselves.
Then, oh friend, then,
Then will the last strike be![10]

Lyser was the son of a Vormärz poet and an actress who played at royal court. Expelled from the German Social Democratic party, he edited a New York Socialist paper in the mid-1870s before he was driven out for his extremism. Afterward, he made his way to

Milwaukee, where for a time he published a bitter satirical review. Lyser condensed in his own character, one might say, the incendiary quality of the Chicago revolutionary Socialist movement of the 1880s. Like a lesser Johann Most—a difference being, of course, that Most was internationally notorious—Lyser brought to crowds and to readers the spirit of rebellion "against everything," against bourgeois culture and morality, conservative trade unionism, and above all, against the state.

A lyrical romantic, Lyser thrived briefly within a milieu where lessons had been drawn from the brutal facts of class conflict and political manipulation. Insurrectionary confrontation seemed the logical consequence of the experience of Chicago's streets. Did his radical imagery limit Lyser to a small band of fanatics, isolated from the broader strands of American culture? Yes and no. The social revolutionary movement proper never had more than a few thousand members. But when some of its bravest spirits led a movement into the trade unions and joined the eight-hour agitation, they brought to bear an inclination toward workers' control deep in the American grain. Their activity did not stop at the factory gate but was continuously linked to public demonstrations and neighborhood organizing—almost everything but the faulted electoral system. Indeed, revolutionary unionists had more to teach future trade unionists than anyone else. They believed in unions—not as a job trust, a la Gompers, or as a mere defense mechanism until politics could save the working class—but rather as an all-encompassing movement which became politics in the largest sense. The IWW and later the CIO imbibed this message.

The social revolutionaries grasped at the real prospects for change alive in the streets of Chicago, and they comprehended perhaps better than anyone else the crisis in American civilization. They had too little comprehension of their potential allies in America. They understood, for example, next to nothing about the starkly different traditions of agrarian radicalism or feminism. So perceptive about the real character of class rule, they could not render in native vernacular their own rudimentary understanding of national tradition. Nevertheless, living only a decade away from Pullman, Homestead, and the invasion of the Philippines, the revolutionaries saw most clearly the end of America's democracy of small property holders.

Haymarket proved, in the most punishing way possible, that the warnings against barbarism were correct. One of the obscured cultural figures who spoke over the martyrs' graves, Robert Reitzel, editor of the Detroit weekly *Der Arme Teufel* and the foremost literary personage of radical German-Americans, perhaps saw

Die Fackel or "The Torch" was the Sunday edition of Chicago's German labor paper. Its purpose was expressed in the caption: "Independent organ for instruction, entertainment and enjoyment: giving the serious and the funny its due, and despising nothing but the base." From *Die Fackel*, 25 May 1879.

best how an era had closed for the German-American Left. As he wrote shortly after the hanging, "We write now for the future. One must struggle, as Heine said, against stupidity, against venality, in which we find ourselves trapped; that is our solitude. But with the best skill one must still ask the question: why?"[11]

That "why" addressed the meaning of Haymarket beyond all specifics of police repression, the judge and jury's prejudice, the low level of American labor support, and the nation's indifference to judiciary injustice. The house of Robert Reitzel's parents had been raided by German police in 1848; he was named for the martyr Robert Blum. For a second time, he and elder statesmen of German-American socialism lived through a period of revolutionary hope turned sour. This time they had nowhere to run. The German contribution to American socialism would be made subsequently upon other grounds.

THERE was another sense in which Lyser and his fellow militants reached an audience wider than their own pure revolutionary kin. In the long run, the movement's cultural base proved more resilient than the particular politics it had upheld. This was not, strictly speaking, a matter of conservative drift, as Carl Schorske would later claim for the German Social Democracy in the early twentieth century, but rather the constant readaptation of community sentiment to the available options. As Gerhard Ritter says about German Socialist culture, "Possibly the greatest achievement of the working class has been the creation of their own highly developed network of associations."[12] This was the case for their immigrant cousins in America as well. In some ways, at least, the social and cultural institutions founded by German-American radicals not only ensured the continuation of Socialist commitment into another generation but also colored the evolving popular culture.

When the Aurora Turnverein celebrated its twenty-fifth anniversary in Chicago in 1889, the *Fackel* could proudly record:

> Through the brilliant progress which this twenty-fifth anniversary celebration commemorates, the Aurora Turnverein has shown that it has remained not only within the circle of the Turner traditions, but also within German culture. "Freedom, progress, and justice for all!" That was the set of principles upon which the Verein was established, and to which it remains committed after twenty-five years.[13]

While dramatic and fundamental changes had swept across Chicago's labor and Socialist movements during this time, the Aurora Turnverein had remained, by its own definition, "a brave vanguard" struggling for emancipation. The Turnverein's survival was of signal importance. The steady retreat of the national Turner movement from the radicalism of the '48ers made inevitable the Socialists' effort to found their own Turner halls where community services could be successful only if broadly conceived.[14] Certain fundamentals—for example, the celebration of specific holidays and the maintenance of athletic facilities—had to remain stable despite political changes.

This applied to the press as well. The English-language Socialist newspapers floundered for decades around the problems of party or private ownership, whether to be ruled by the whim of a central committee or a potentially eccentric wealthy individual. The Germans, like most ethnic groups, established a more neutral device, the publishing committee, composed of more or less prominent comrades and sympathizers. This system also had its defects. The press might represent the views of a bygone era; or, as in New York, the publishing committee could actually come to rule the party rather than being ruled by it. The commercial requirements might promote an opportunistic attitude toward satisfying trade union supporters, patronizing business institutions, or withholding criticisms for fear of reprisals. Yet the market actually worked as a valuable corrective for some time, because the readership consisted of more than a frankly radical constituency who actively supported the paper through buying shares, attending periodic benefits, and patronizing advertisers. Given a broader audience, the popularity and commercial health of the publication required a genuine sensitivity not only to shifts of political mood but also to a wide range of interests, aspirations, and anxieties among the readership. The *Vorbote*, the *Arbeiter-Zeitung*, and the *Fackel* became real mirrors, not only for leftist politics but also for cultural trends. Like the English-language press at its best moments, they contained the kind of observations of daily life that made Chicago a center for Peter Finley Dunne and others. Something about the city restrained high literature but promoted Socialist commentators as forerunners of Nelson Algren and Studs Terkel.

The picnic offers a fascinating example. Friedrich A. Sorge argued that the German-American radicals had actually pioneered the political-cultural day in the country in order for community members to mix pleasure with education, while evading the Sunday blue laws and repressive attitudes. The beer, the sports, the good times at Ogden's Grove, the revolving stage with revolutionary tableaux, suggest more than a great fraternal bash. The conscious inclusion of ever more varied groups in the picnic—Bohemians, Swedes, English-speaking radicals—expressed implicitly a view of working-class culture in formation and did it better, perhaps, than could have been done anywhere else in contemporary society. Late in the day, the elaborate organization of such events showed a keen historical consciousness, as a journalist in Milwaukee noted: "These festivals have the goal of reminding the people of their great historical tasks, inspiring them to new goals and imparting the sense of solidarity, rallying the enslaved and oppressed to rise up and gain their freedom." The grand scale of success offers the best proof of cultural activism's viability.[15]

After the late 1880s, the Turnvereine and singing societies flourished in part *because* the larger purpose had faded and their function had been subtly altered; but nevertheless they preserved radical spirit, comradeship, the sense of purpose to live on and to plan for the next generation. German-American cultural life perfected other forms subsequently taken over by later radicals from other immigrant groups. Without the German example, the organization of the Jewish *Arbeter Ring* and the Slovene National Benefit Society (SNPJ) would have taken shape more slowly, as would the wider apparatus of ethnic-labor networks that allowed the Socialist party considerable influence in the new immigrant communities. Even as late as the 1920s the German-American radical press still played an important role in preserving an independent position for immigrant groups vis-à-vis party leadership and in furnishing an entry point for young revolutionary intellectuals.[16]

THERE is no escaping the fact that the mood became more steadily and self-consciously inward, the nostalgia and reverie pronounced. "American Deutschthum, that has brought along in its blood Lessing and Feuerbach and Börne, dies with us, we who have lost our homes and are strangers in our houses," Robert Reitzel wrote, not long before his death at the turn of the century. But its glowing evanescence shed more light than is commonly recognized. Apart from individual cases, one cannot prove the influence of immigrant radicalism upon popular culture. Yet signs of continuity have flourished, from Free Thought centers like Sauk City, Wisconsin, as publishing havens for the wildest insurrectionary horror fantasy in American literature to the work of aging German printing craftsmen coloring the children's comic books of the 1940s and 1950s, from the memories of Haymarket that haunted popular labor journalists like Louis Adamic into the 1930s to the fraternal labor groups and sports leagues which even today carry the stamp of German pioneering organization in blue-collar neighborhoods.[17]

In 1888 a tired and disillusioned Robert Reitzel wrote, "We told the people / to light the fuse / While the hangman / prepared the noose."[18] One could not evade the sense of failure. But if Marx and Engels persistently assigned this failure to some mental lapse, we have broader grounds to consider the fate of the radicals, their bold effort to revolutionize American society and their more subtle, enduring contribution to a pluralist culture. They did not manage the transformation they anticipated. But they built, in many ways, better than they knew.

Notes

1. This declaration by Itche Goldberg, a leader of the Jewish fraternal movement in the Communist-led International Workers Order convention of 1943, stands as a high-water mark in the cultural self-consciousness of the Left-linked fraternal groups ("Di Yiddishe Kultur un di Yiddishe Shule in Amerike," in *Dienst fun Folk: Almanakh fun Yiddish Folks Ordn* [New York: Farlag fun Yiddishn Folks Ordn, 1947]: 70). I have written about fraternal groups' importance and the cultural question within the general immigrant Left in "Jews and American Communism: The Cultural Question," *Radical History Review* 23 (Spring 1980). Tapes with veterans of radical movements, especially those close to the journalism of the immigrant groups, are on deposit at the Oral History of the American Left, Tamiment Library, New York University.

2. See José Miranda, *Communism in the Bible*, trans. Robert R. Barr (Maryknoll, N.Y.: Orbis Books, 1982). See also Paul Buhle and Thomas Fiehrer, "Holy Warriors: Latin America's Moral Majority," *Village Voice Literary Supplement* 10 (September 1982): 8, 10–11.

3. Thorstein Veblen, *Instinct of Workmanship* (New York: Macmillan, 1916).

4. Mary Nolan, New York University, "Social Democracy, Political Ed-

ucation and the Organization of Popular Culture in Imperial Germany," (unpublished ms.).

5. Cited by J. S. Hertz, *Di Yiddishe Sotsialistische Bevegung in Amerike* (New York: Farlag der Veker, 1954), 153.

6. Joseph Stipanovich, "Immigrant Workers and Immigrant Intellectuals in Progressive America: A History of the Yugoslav Socialist Federation" (Ph.D. diss., University of Minnesota, 1978), vii.

7. This point is made with special sharpness by the literary critic Sh. Niger in a polemic of the 1920s against doctrinaire Communist claims of pure proletarian character in Yiddish literature (*Geklibene Shriftn* 1 [New York, 1928], chap. 3).

8. *Arbeiter Stimme* (New York), April 22, 1877.

9. Stipanovich, "Immigrant Workers," vii.

10. Quoted from Carol Poore, "German-American Socialist Literature of the Late Nineteenth Century" (Ph.D. diss., University of Wisconsin, 1979), 121.

11. Robert Reitzel, *Mein Buch*, vol. 3 (Detroit: Der Reitzel Klub, 1910), 19.

12. Gerhard Ritter, "Workers' Culture in Imperial Germany," *Journal of Contemporary History* 13 (1978): 172. See also Carl Schorske, *German Social Democracy, 1905–17: The Development of the Great Schism* (Cambridge, Mass.: Harvard University Press, 1955).

13. *Die Fackel*, February 22, 1889.

14. H. Ueberhorst, "The Turnvereine and the Experience of German Immigrants in America" (Paper presented at the Annual Convention of the Organization of American Historians, Boston, 1975).

15. *Friedrich A. Sorge's The Labor Movement in America*, ed. P. S. Foner and B. Chamberlin, trans. B. Chamberlin (Westport, Conn.: Greenwood Press, 1977), 176. The quoted matter is from the *Milwaukee Vorwärts*, March 19, 1898.

16. The complex relations of German Jews (a small minority of whom played leading roles in the German-dominated American Socialist movement) and the new East European immigrants are discussed in A. Tcherikower, "Tsvy Vegan fun Yiddishn Gezelshaftlekhn Eufbeu in Amerika," in *Geshikhte fun der Yiddisher Arbeter-Bevegung in di Fareinikhte Shtaten*, ed. A. Therikover (New York: Yivo Institute, 1943), especially p. 332. Also see the general discussion of the German-American Socialists' influence in the labor background of the Workman's Circle founding in the 1890s, in A. S. Sachs, *Di Geshikhte fun Arbeter Ring*, vol. 1 (New York: Der Natsionaler Ekzekutiv Komitte fun Arbeter Ring, 1925), 3–63. See my interview with a *Volkszeitung* writer, Martin Birnbaum, in *Cultural Correspondence* 9 (Spring 1979): 38–40.

17. The Sauk City publishing firm, Arkham House, for decades the only publishers of the Lovecraft Circle of horror writers, was founded and long directed by August Derleth, who during his youth in the 1930s penned left-wing horror fiction. Such vital contemporary local movements as the Community Labor Coalition of Providence, Rhode Island, continue German traditions in important ways: theatrical events for community support and fund raising; special support for youth athletics; linking of Socialist aspirations through talks and pamphlets about local labor history; and the picnic as the apex of the year's social schedule.

18. Reitzel, *Mein Buch*, vol. 3, 421.

German Working-Class Culture in Chicago: Continuity and Change in the Decade from 1900 to 1910

Klaus Ensslen and Heinz Ickstadt

THE search for a functional and empirically useful definition of working-class culture has been pursued in recent times on the broadened basis of anthropological and political theory. We do not intend to add to this general debate on the definition of working-class culture but rather to provide some empirical material on German workers' culture in Chicago for a specific time span. As a working definition, we will apply a concept of culture broad enough to include modes of perception, interpretation, expression, and action of working-class people as subjects in history; the definition is, however, not so broad as to consider any condition of the working class as cultural. The world of work and general living conditions, for instance, will lie outside the realm of culture in this essay because culture as understood here requires some measure of creative activity, i.e., of self-directed coping by the working class with the conditions which define it.

German working-class culture in Chicago had its most visible and politically vital phase in the decades before 1890, and as a consequence existing studies have so far concentrated on this earlier period.[1] Nevertheless, the period from 1900 to 1910 can claim particular interest, since the findings on this decade touch on many crucial issues, such as the continuation of well-established forms of political and immigrant culture in the face of an ascendant second generation and the arrival of masses of new immigrants from southern and eastern Europe. Unfortunately, however, the sources for an investigation of German working-class culture in the first decade of the twentieth century decreased rather than increased, since quite a few of the German-language union papers were absorbed by national English-language publications. In addition, the most renowned German newspaper of Chicago, the *Illinois Staats-Zeitung*, can function only as a supplementary source, since its episodic reporting on the activities of the local German working class lacks sufficient detail and sense of context.

Thus the major source for our specific and detailed information on German workers in Chicago must be the *Chicagoer Arbeiter-Zeitung* and its Sunday and weekly editions, *Fackel* and *Vorbote*, despite their somewhat limiting focus on the culture of the labor movement and their consequent neglect of broader cultural phenomena. The *Arbeiter-Zeitung* tended to view ethnicity as closely tied to class consciousness, as shown in the slogan, "ethnic identity and progress."[2] It became intensely ethnic in its opposition to American culture as a force antithetical to working-class solidarity. On the one hand, the paper transcended ethnic issues when it propagated the formation of an American working-class movement; in reporting on labor affairs like strikes, assemblies, and demonstrations, it consistently was international in outlook. But on the other, it was fervently committed to the forms and traditions of the German and German-American labor movements, and particularly to the working-class culture that flowered in Chicago in the 1880s, in retrospect viewed as the heroic period of working-class Chicago history, when the labor movement had largely been composed of and led by Germans. The *Arbeiter-Zeitung* tried to draw German workers into this circle of a specifically ethnic and working-class political culture and showed little interest in those who chose to stay outside, except for complaining persistently throughout the first decade of the new century about the political passivity and indifference of the great mass of German workers. The paper rarely bothered to understand the underlying reasons for such apparent disaffection, however. What it observed and analyzed as a rule only inadvertently touched upon what actually happened to German workers, in the sense of how they lived and organized their lives under changing social and economic conditions. Awareness or registration of change was clearly subordinated in the pages of the *Arbeiter-Zeitung* to the need for cultural stability and continuity and to the reenactment of the forms and traditions of the political culture. And yet the symptoms of change are there: in the indirect evidence of social and geographical mobility, in the dispersal and relocation of neighborhoods, in the death of old labor organizations, in the discussion of new strategies and alliances, in the decline in the knowledge of German, and in the awareness among the old guard of movement leaders that they were becoming increasingly isolated and historical.[3]

During the first decade of the new century, Chicago experienced three major demonstrations of its working-class, ethnic, and radical organizations which gave ample evidence that it was indeed the center of American organized labor and, at the same time, one of the most ethnically diverse cities in the United States. There was clearly a vital ethnic and working-class culture in Chicago at the time, but the position of Germans in it and the relation of the classical movement culture to it are harder to define.

The *Arbeiter-Zeitung* called the first of these demonstrations—on Labor Day in 1902—the largest workers' parade ever witnessed in Chicago.[4] Almost 47,000 workers marched through downtown Chicago for more than five hours. Eighty-six local unions participated, most prominent among them the thirty-two local unions of the National Teamsters Union, whose marchers comprised 28,000 men alone. But the carpenters, cigar makers, shoemakers, bakers, hod carriers, and building laborers were also present in large numbers. On several floats the various unions enacted their particular grievances with capital; others, less politically minded, had white-clad girls wave to the spectators; and the bakers, from their float, threw cookies into the crowd. The famed brass band of the Aurora Turnverein, the drum corps of several other German Turnvereine, the Columbian Knight Band, and three black bands marched at the head of other unions or sections; it was especially noted that throughout the parade black workers marched shoulder to shoulder with their white brothers. Members of the carpenters union carried a large American flag on which they asked the huge crowd lining the streets to throw money, thus collecting $10,000 for striking miners in Indiana. Even the *Arbeiter-Zeitung*, though dead set against the idea of a legalized Labor Day, had to admit that it was a magnificent demonstration of the strength of organized labor in Chicago.

On March 26, 1906, some four years later, 80,000 Germans, Bohemians, Poles, Hungarians, Danes, and Norwegians—"all so-called foreigners no longer willing to have a minute minority meddle with their rights and life styles"—came together from all parts of Chicago to protest against prohibitionist legislation. Close to a hundred German Vereine—Turner, singing clubs, and veterans' organizations—all with their bands, flags, and banners—formed the core of the huge parade. Next came the Bohemians, with sixty-nine organizations, twenty-five of them Catholic; the Poles had come "on horses and had even brought out their militia," and the "Ancient Order of United Workmen" (mostly Irish) was also there with all its sections, protesting against genteel regimentation. All resolutions read at the Armory, where the parade ended, were in English, but with one exception the main speakers were leading German-Americans. Most prominent among them was Wilhelm Rapp, chief editor of the *Illinois Staats-Zeitung* and the honorary president of the day's assembly, who called the demonstrators "good and patriotic American citizens," joined in protest in "the holy name of personal freedom and human rights." The representative of the Bohemians pointed out that the legislation, because it aimed at abolishing saloons ("the working-men's clubs") and at curbing festivities, was, in fact, an attack on the very heart of working-class life; he ended his speech with a plea to vote Socialist, to the dismay of the leading citizens, who insisted that the event was strictly nonpolitical.[5]

The third public event was the largest of a series of demonstrations occasioned by the imprisonment and subsequent trial of Big Bill Haywood and two others early in 1907. It occurred on May 21 of that year and was organized by some of the more radical unions and the Socialist party. The Federation of Labor supported it only lamely.[6] The 15,000 who participated were, according to the *Arbeiter-Zeitung*, "the revolutionary core" of Chicago's working class—the unions of carpenters, brewers, painters, hod carriers, woodworkers, bakers, tailors, and metalworkers plus the various ethnic branches of the Socialist party. There were a great number of Russian and Polish Jews, Lithuanians, Hungarians, Italians, Swedes, and Norwegians; and the signs carried in the parade were written in English, German, Yiddish, Russian, Italian, and Lithuanian. Even though the *Arbeiter-Zeitung* called the parade a great success, it clearly wished there had been more participants. However, when Big Bill Haywood visited Chicago three months later, after his release from prison, he was welcomed by all representatives of Chicago's organized labor and celebrated by an enthusiastic crowd of more than 45,000 who stayed to see him and listen to him all afternoon and late into the night.[7]

These demonstrations give evidence of Chicago's large ethnic population and of its active and diverse labor movement, and even though each event was quite distinct in character and composition, workers and working-class organizations participated in all of them. Yet it is difficult to assess the proportion and the role of the German element on these different occasions. Germans clearly dominated the antiprohibitionist demonstration but, though also participating in the Labor Day and Haywood parades, were much less visible amidst the multi-ethnic labor parades. However, if we

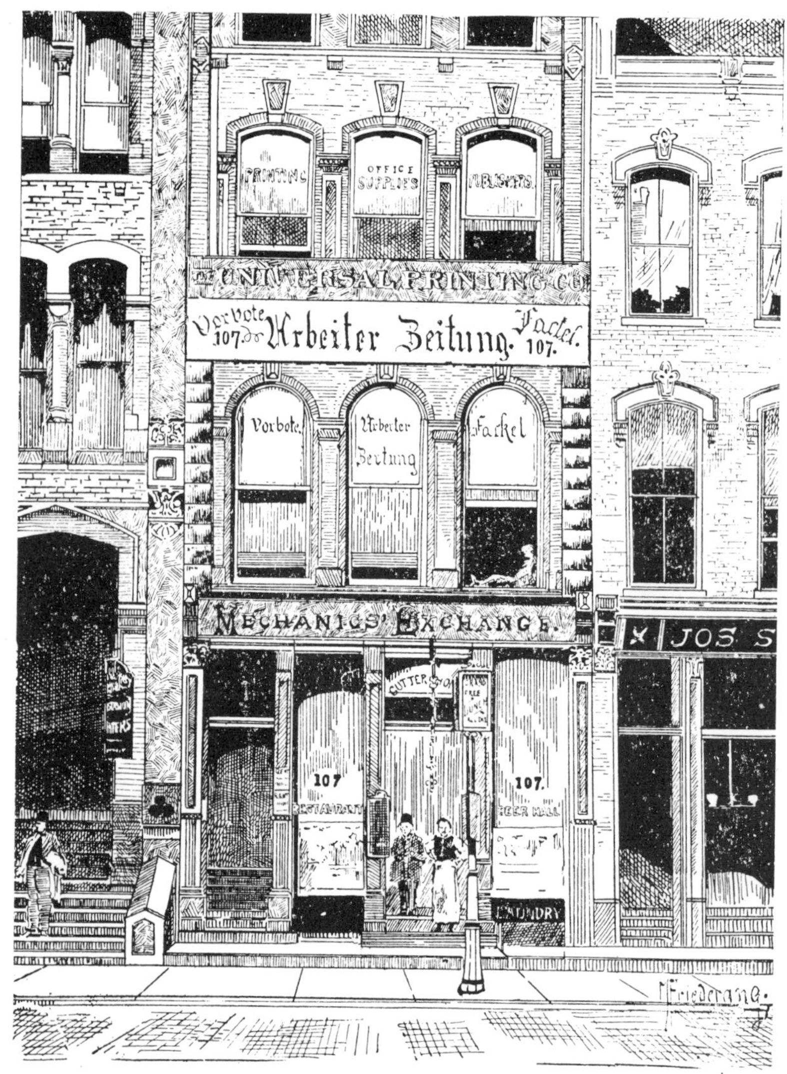

Office of the *Arbeiter-Zeitung*. From Michael J. Schaack, *Anarchy and Anarchists*, 1889.

look at the names of speakers or of secretaries and marshals of the various labor organizations as they crop up in the reports of the *Arbeiter-Zeitung*, they are, with very few exceptions, either English or German. When Bill Haywood, exhausted from his wild reception in Chicago, sought rest from the crowd, he retired to the home of Frank Schreck where "he received acquaintances and friends"—a great many of them, one may safely assume, also Germans.[8]

Was the lower visibility of the Germans in these demonstrations a matter of the paper's perception, or were Germans in fact not so important as they had been earlier in labor affairs and protest movements? Although the *Arbeiter-Zeitung* usually reported in glowing terms on the success of various meetings, picnics, and celebrations, there was also a persistent note of complaint. Commenting on the impressive ethnic demonstration in March 1906, the *Vorbote* remarked sourly that not one-fifth of those present would have gone to the streets to protest injustice and oppression.[9] And on May 24, 1908, the *Fackel* editorialized:

The number of pessimists within the working-class movement not only is larger than suspected, it is also steadily growing, among Germans to a horrendous degree. Where are they gone, the many who only a few years ago helped to build and to extend the organization of the new working-class movement? Many have turned completely bourgeois, and only a small number at least keep in touch with the organized workers by reading a radical paper of some kind. Looking back, it seems that this withdrawal is steadily growing in general favor. While it used to be that those active in the movement held on for at least ten years, some years later, one could count oneself fortunate if he saw the same faces for five years. But nowadays, they participate no longer than two years.

Pessimism, however, seems to have been a real temptation for the radicals around the *Arbeiter-Zeitung* themselves. Not even the many demonstrations of working-class solidarity during the period of the Haywood trial could convince Heinrich Bartel, then chief editor of the *Arbeiter-Zeitung*, that Chicago had a working-class movement that deserved the name. On the twentieth anniversary of the Haymarket executions—only three months after Haywood's tumultuous reception in Chicago—he bitterly attacked the growing materialism of the great majority of workers. America, a country of shops and dealers, was working the corruption of its laboring class. The strong and healthy revolutionary movement of twenty years ago had almost disappeared, its vision shrunk to the size of bread-and-butter issues and of dreams of owning "a little house." It is interesting that in his effort to reestablish the old vision, Bartel linked the rhetoric of working-class radicalism to a rhetoric of ethnic pride and cultural idealism. To work merely for the improvement of the workers' material conditions was not enough: "We may never forget the Ideal over the struggle for material things. To reveal Beauty, and Art and Science—this is also our duty. We want to change the world and to take possession of everything that makes life more magnificent and beautiful."[10]

Bartel's idealism, which may sound surprisingly genteel in the American context, in fact re-echoes official Social-Democratic attitudes toward high culture, especially as they were shaped by the writings of Franz Mehring in Germany.[11] This position was typical for the German working-class elite in charge of the *Arbeiter-Zeitung* who sought to counter the temptations of American materialism not only by educating workers in the true interests of their class but also by making available to them the benefits of high culture, including classic literature and general education. During the time of Bartel's editorship this antimaterialist stance became editorial policy. And throughout the period, the *Vorbote* and *Fackel*, especially the latter, impress one with the high quality of their political information, of their feuilleton, and of their own literary production. Even though, like all newspapers, they frequently used the lingua franca of nineteenth-century melodrama and sentimental fiction, they also serialized Maxim Gorki's *The Mother*, Charles Dickens's *A Tale of Two Cities*, Adolf Streckfuß's *Der Amerikaner*, and Frank Norris's *Octopus*. In addition, there are numerous articles on classical and contemporary European and American literature: on Corneille, Goethe, Freiligrath, Schiller, Tolstoi, Longfellow, Whitman, Upton Sinclair, H. G. Wells, and even on Chinese poetry and the paintings of Käthe Kollwitz. We also find poems and short stories by Hermann Hesse, Richard Dehmel, and others, as well as long and informative essays on Darwin, the most recent scientific discoveries, and the history of the French Revolution. Articles about John Brown and other heroes of the American radical past round off a wide spectrum of cultural and political interest.

Specific German working-class literary traditions—allegorical poems, dramatic and satiric sketches—which were central to the literary culture of the German working-class movement in Chicago in the 1870s and 1880s, though they had been somewhat neglected during the 1890s—were revived in the new century by people like Martin Drescher, Heinrich Bartel, and the Austrian-American Josef Schiller. The forms and conventions of this specifically ethnic working-class literature had remained remarkably stable. In Drescher's poetry there is some influence of contemporary German proletarian expressionism (Arno Holz, Richard Dehmel), but his allegorical nature poems and his Socialist reinterpretation of Christian sacred history continue traditions of early working-class poetry that had developed in Germany around the middle of the nineteenth century.[12] However, it is even more significant that the structure of the movement culture itself—the layout of its newspapers, the arrangement of its festivities, picnics and the like—changed so little over a period of more than thirty years. The effort to inform, to teach, and to entertain, to give everyday life and leisure a political focus, makes for the peculiarly staged quality of the political culture: its various productions—whether newspapers or the celebration of the Day of the Commune—are arranged or structured after a single pattern.

In his opening speech at the Arbeiter-Sängerfest which brought German workers' singing societies from the whole midwestern region to Chicago in June 1910, Bartel addressed himself to this double aspect of the German movement culture—that it was ethnic in tradition and sentiment yet political in awareness and purpose:

> The festivity today is not like other festivities that Germans usually celebrate in this country. . . . Even if our German singers deeply revere German culture, German language, German poetry, they know that the unity of Germans has its limits at the different size of their purses; they do not forget the unbridgeable gap among human beings, created by the present social conditions; they never forget the large issues of their time and that it is their mission to unite the Germans of this country so that they fight shoulder to shoulder with their American comrades and the comrades of other nations. . . . Of course, we touch the soul of the people when we sing our folk-songs, and we like to sing the "Loreley" when we are so moved. But we are not satisfied with that. Soon afterwards we sing the Marseillaise or the Socialist March.[13]

Working-class leaders made a clear distinction between German folklore and classical literature on the one hand and a certain kind of sham patriotism and chauvinistic "Deutschthum" on the other, the latter considered a derivation of pride in the German Reich and the desire to spread its imperial claims. The rejection of "Deutschthum" in this virulent nationalist sense comes through very clearly in an article describing the German policy and genocide in Southwest Africa against the Hereros; the article argues in no ambivalent terms that the concept of culture as a positive force in the view of the worker cannot be reconciled with the powers of state, church, and capital.[14] Thus the use of ethnic traditions for the politically active German workers was traditionally restricted to certain selected elements. The various texts (in the widest sense) of the German labor movement culture were ritualistically arranged: a political speech, song, or poem placed within a context of entertainment and of leisure transfigured the secular event and gave it a quasi-sacred significance. Indeed, *Weihe*, in the sense of "consecration" as well as "solemn mood," was a keyword of the culture. Such structured events symbolically created a people assembled in pleasure (or mourning) and united by common tradition, experience, consciousness, and purpose. Not surprisingly, the pattern of the celebration of the Day of the Commune was the same in 1908 as it had been twenty-five years earlier: the central political speech or play was framed by traditional forms of the community's expressive and performing abilities in music (orchestra, choir), recitation (poetry, song, instrument), acting (drama, comedy, tableau vivant, and gymnastics). Not all these contributions were of political content; in fact, a great number of them were not. Some of them—as well as some of the performers—can easily be imagined in other, nonpolitical contexts as part of the larger ethnic culture.

It would be wrong to interpret this structural continuity in itself as a sign of diminishing creativity. The stability of forms and traditions had rather a vital and creative function within the communicative processes of the group: it was a resource of personal dignity and cultural identity, it made for an easier integration of the newcomer, and for some it opened the possibility of continuing or beginning a career inside the group. Yet however much a generation of class-conscious immigrants might have restored its sense of purpose in the practice of old forms and habits, to those born in the United States the ritualistic aspects of the movement culture must have seemed outdated. Traditional German literary and political culture must be seen as having initially a stabilizing, but increasingly also a fossilizing, effect for Germans in Chicago, disconnecting the younger English-speaking age groups from a staunch and immutable immigrants' culture. Significantly, the *Arbeiter-Zeitung*, unlike the *Illinois Staats-Zeitung*, never reported on American popular culture; sports, especially baseball, were regarded as a means of distracting and controlling the masses.[15]

Therefore, if we want to know what ethnic culture meant for the majority of German workers or how they responded to the pressures and attractions of the American context, particularly of American popular culture, we have to go beyond the older movement culture, especially with its rigidly ethnic rejection of American values and life-styles. But since it is possible only in rare cases to move beyond the *Arbeiter-Zeitung*, we have to read the paper's various complaints and exhortations as evidence of ongoing change and of a constant but, in the long run, a losing battle to educate, motivate, and control German workers by appealing to their working-class as well as to their ethnic identity. One should begin by separating national cultural from grass roots or specifically lower-class ethnic traditions. The former become manifest in the upholding of a high standard of German, the esteem for classical Bildung and accepted forms of sociability like balls, concerts, and other social events of a public nature. Both language standards and classical traditions of art and literature would be equally upheld in the middle class and working-class German communities in Chicago. This can be seen most clearly in the case of the German theater, which in comments almost identical in style and substance, was propagated and reviewed extensively in both the *Illinois Staats-Zeitung* and the *Arbeiter-Zeitung*. Distrusting politically tendentious plays for aesthetic reasons, yet impatient at times with the silliness of folk theater, the *Arbeiter-Zeitung* was attracted to the model of the Freie Volksbühne in Berlin, which tried to combine popular and serious theater in the interest of the workers. And indeed by 1912 it had set up an arrangement with the Deutsches Theater by which German workers were offered reduced rates for a mixed bill of fare that alternated the classics with farce and operetta.[16]

In the forms of everyday social life we can distinguish between events such as New Year's, Mardi Gras, or summer dances—which became class specific only when tied to some beneficiary or fund-raising purpose—and more typically working-class occasions like picnics, gymnastics, boat excursions, and shooting contests. Often described in detail, these festivities provide important indicators for leisure activities of workers which embodied a cultural life far beyond the more politically conscious representation of movement culture. Similarly, the saloon, one such important area of everyday working-class culture which even drew the close attention of sociologists,[17] remained largely uncommented upon by the *Arbeiter-Zeitung*, probably because it was taken so much for granted as an essential part of everyday life that it seemed to deserve no special mention, except when serving some political purpose as a meeting place or newspaper depository. In his perceptive contemporary field study, the sociologist R. L. Melendy from the Chicago Commons settlement house described this institution of the workingman's everyday life as offering compensatory attractions outside of the job and home. He specifically mentioned substantial and low-priced food, toilet facilities equal to those of hotels, entertainment, and the exchange of information on job conditions and opportunities, the latter function reflected in such saloon names as "Mechanics'" and "Milkman's Exchange." Serving both material needs and the more intangible necessities of sociability and entertainment, the saloon was the "workingman's school" and the "social and intellectual center" of the neighborhood, or, in more general terms, "the clearing-house for the common intelligence" where "the masses receive their lessons in civil government, learning less of our ideals, but more of the practical workings than the public schools teach."[18]

While saloons had a working-class aura apparent even to outside observers like sociologists, the class character and function of ethnic associations, particularly those organized along regional lines, are harder to assess, as are the common but elusive phenomena of regional dialects and traditions which practically every German brought with him. Did German workers, regardless of (or even despite) their political affiliation, partake in regional associations like the Schwabenverein? Did a clear political affiliation, or at least some function in unions, Turnvereine, or the Socialist party, prevent them from joining regional associations? Most likely not, and one may safely assume that on the occasion of the large ethnic parade of 1906, a great number of participants had the choice of marching either with their regional association or their Turnverein, just as four years before on Labor Day of 1902 they might have paraded with their union.

We have some indication of how regional networks functioned in Chicago from the 1850s to the 1880s, even below the level of formal association. These networks of relatives, friends, or people from the same place of origin in Europe tended to reinforce patterns of settlement in the same neighborhood. They could thus lead to a close-knit infrastructure of personal relations based on regional characteristics which does not readily show on the level of political, union, or ethnic organization, particularly since associations like Turn-, Gesang-, and Schützenvereine apparently were less differentiated along regional lines in Chicago than they would naturally have been back in Germany.[19] However, the contours of a specifically working-class ethnic culture are clearest where it overlaps with and is pointedly activated by movement culture.

It is even more difficult to assess the extent of German workers' participation in the dominant culture. At least from the 1880s onward, working within the movement implied a life in two languages, as is evident not only from the inclusion of English speakers in the context of German festivities but also from the constant switching from one language to the other practiced by German labor or political leaders when addressing a multi-ethnic audience.

While the German working population insisted on having German teachers accredited by the city for teaching German in local schools, language assimilation must have been progressing rapidly. Favorable comments on a speaker's ability to still speak "pure German" increasingly appear toward the end of the 1890s, and in 1908 the emphatically ethnic German Turnervereine decided to admit "other languages beside the German" to their "cozily intellectual meetings," explicitly "for the sake of our dear young people most of whom can only claim a very insufficient command of the German language."[20]

At the same time German workers in some ways participated in American popular culture. Was this participation most pronounced in the one area where Germans undoubtedly contributed to American mass culture—the beer garden? Several of these were located at some of the popular excursion places at the end of streetcar lines or on the major roads leading out of the city.[21] As R. L. Melendy described the function of beer gardens in conjunction with vaudeville in 1900, there apparently was some intermixing of the indigenous vaudeville and the German beer garden tradition with its Schuhplattler dancers, zither players, and folk singers. Did American popular culture merely invade the beer gardens without broadening the leisure interest of the German clientele? Unfortunately, our observer was not interested in sorting out different groups in other places of popular amusement. Thus we can only conjecture how many of the 4,000 persons daily attending one of the big vaudeville theaters in the West Side industrial district would on the average be Germans.

What changed then, roughly between 1890 and 1910, was neither the form nor the content of German movement culture but its function within a changing social and communicative context. The labor press acknowledged these changes only indirectly in its vehement reactions to an ongoing process of Verspießerung, i.e., a falling away from ethnic working-class norms and loyalties as defined by the classical movement culture. The *Fackel* showed more discriminating insight, however, in its first issue of 1910, where it raised this interesting question: "What are the possibilities of the working-class child?" In doing so, *Fackel* indicated an element of choice in determining the economic status of the second generation:

There is indeed a segment of the working class which finds such a question appropriate: workers with higher wages in better and more secure positions. . . . It would be foolish and dogmatic to regard such parents, able and willing to provide their children with the chances for a better future, as traitors to the working class. Why should someone who has gained a better position in life inevitably lose his consciousness of class? Socialism is a matter of conviction, not of position.[22]

This is the only direct reference—beyond the usual complaints about German workers' growing smug, indifferent, and egoistic in times of relative prosperity—to an ongoing process of upward social mobility.[23]

Geographical mobility of the workers and adjustments in political strategy are further indicators of the changed context in which the movement culture operated. The school census of 1910 points out that the rate of physical mobility within the city was so high that it was difficult to locate the centers of settlement with any certainty.[24] Germans were no exception. By 1912 the Aurora Turnverein, one of the first of its kind to be founded in Chicago and still the center of the progressive German element of the Northwest Side, had moved further to the west as the whole German population in that part of the city was "inevitably moving westward."[25] The *Arbeiter-Zeitung* pointed out in 1907 that some of its financial difficulties were caused by subscribers who had resettled in the outlying districts of the city, thus causing delivery costs to rise considerably.[26] Neighborhoods were changed and torn down by urban expansion and urban renewal. Uhlich's Hall, Eugene V. Debs's headquarters during the Pullman Strike, was torn down in 1912.[27] The area between Randolph, West Lake, and Washington Street—once a run-down, dirty neighborhood of small stores, factories, shacks, pubs, and public houses but also the center of German radical activities throughout the turbulent 1880s and 1890s—had given way to a railroad station two years earlier. We find this piece of information in an article that is as much a nostalgic reminiscence of a neighborhood as an epitaph on the Central Labor Union which had been the backbone of the city's radical German unions but which had quietly expired in 1909.[28]

In 1906 the *Arbeiter-Zeitung* had still strongly opposed evolutionary concepts of social change and therefore attacked especially the unions gathered in the American Federation of Labor and the Socialist party.[29] Four years later the paper was able to insure its financial survival only by undergoing what it called a "change of principles."[30] On the condition that it back the Socialist party's struggle for political power and that its directors would consist of union men only, the German unions took control over, and accepted financial responsibility for, the *Arbeiter-Zeitung*. The anarchist tendencies of the earlier decades had given way to a broader integrational policy along the lines of the Socialist party.

The change was not quite unexpected. Voices had been wavering between nostalgia and a pragmatic adjustment to the inevitable. Speaking on the Day of the Commune in March 1909, Fred Bergman pointed out that "the times of radical fervor seem to be over. The great movement is now stuck in a union mire, and the only questions asked seem to be those of higher wages and shorter hours."[31] Eight months later, speaking once again in memory of the Haymarket martyrs, chief editor Heinrich Bartel had noticeably changed the rhetorical emphasis of his earlier speeches and cautiously indicated that Spies and his comrades might have committed an error of judgment in supposing that "The Change" was near and could be hastened. The American working class, since then, had gone into a different direction, and the German radicals, in ignoring the fact, had maneuvered themselves into a dead end. Clinging to the memory of Haymarket, they had locked themselves into the past:

> In the grave of time, the pain and fury about the misdeed of those ruling in 1887 have been corrupted to sweet nostalgia. . . . We cannot debate, over and again, about the great principles—we have to do the dirty work, we have to solve very many small problems if we want to solve the biggest of them all. . . . Even the largest battle comes down to individual fights, and whoever has his eyes on the whole must admit that, generally speaking, the cause of revolution has progressed beyond the stage it had reached when Spies and his friends were murdered.[32]

Two years later Bartel had moved on to Milwaukee; Julius Vahlteich, a veteran Socialist, had become chief editor of the *Arbeiter-Zeitung*; and the paper was now the German voice of the Socialist party in Chicago.

By way of summary, we can say that in the early decade of the twentieth century Chicago indeed had an active and visible new working-class movement but that its core was no longer German, even though Germans still participated in it. Thus the *Arbeiter-Zeitung*'s view of an ongoing mass defection among Germans from the ranks of labor and its organizations is certainly exaggerated, if not altogether wrong. The movement in the 1880s had been international in intention but firmly rooted in German radical tradition, and its centers were the Central Labor Union and the *Arbeiter-Zeitung*. After the dissolution of the Central Labor Union, the need for a new central organization was frequently voiced. Indeed, the *Arbeiter-Zeitung* hoped that its own alliance with the Socialist party would revitalize the "German labor movement in Chicago."[33] Yet by 1910 the movement had in fact two organizational centers—the Federation of Labor and the Socialist party. Both of them, however, were multi-ethnic and American, not German. Especially with the ascendance of the second generation, lines of ethnic, economic, and political organization became increasingly blurred. Second-generation Germans, active in the unions that their parents had helped organize, may have been unwilling to participate in the rituals and traditions of the old movement culture but might still have spent their leisure time in German ways. On the other hand, workers who had moved away from organized labor or the radical movement could still have participated in the culture of the labor movement through one of its ethnic institutions like carnivals, costume balls, picnics, or weekend excursions on Lake Michigan. Significantly, the *Arbeiter-Zeitung*, in commenting on the Haywood parade of 1907, noted the absence of the German Turner but then added that they had probably chosen to march with their respective unions; that is, they had chosen working-class over ethnic visibility.[34] Such switching of roles and choosing between several identities—that of the worker, the German, the Swabian, the Turner, the Socialist, the German-American—became characteristic for German working-class life in Chicago after the turn of the century.

Although the forms and organization of ethnic working-class culture still continued—and even thrived by the end of the period in question—we can definitely see the decline of a specifically German radical working-class movement and the concomitant rise of the Socialist party as a new radical political force. Its decline is dramatized in the dissolution of the Central Labor Union and the reorganization of the *Arbeiter-Zeitung*. Its culture was becoming part of Chicago's working-class ethnic heritage, just as its celebrations and memorials were becoming part of the history of Chicago's labor movement. In 1907 John Collins—member of the machinist union and once mayoral candidate of the Socialist party—tried to bridge his differences with the radicals of the *Arbeiter-Zeitung* by pointing out that it was the Germans who had made him a Socialist.[35] And in 1912 the English Socialist leader Keir Hardie, on return from a trip to the United States, acknowledged the great achievement of the Germans in shaping American socialism and the American Socialist party: "For years it seemed as if they had no influence whatsoever on the life of the nation. Now the good seed that they have sown has brought a rich harvest."[36] After the first decade of the new century, even the German radicals had found their place in the history of the American working class—and had themselves become Americans in the process.

Notes

1. Some examples are Hartmut Keil and Heinz Ickstadt, "Elemente einer deutschen Arbeiterkultur in Chicago zwischen 1880 und 1890," *Geschichte und Gesellschaft* 5 (1979): 103–24; Heinz Ickstadt and Hartmut Keil, "A Forgotten Piece of Working-Class Literature: Gustav Lyser's Satire of the Hewitt Hearing of 1878," *Labor History* 20 (Winter 1979): 127–40; Hartmut Keil, "Immigrant Workers in Chicago, 1870–1890: Workers, Leaders, and the Labor Movement," in press, in *American Labor and Immigration History: Recent European Research*, ed. Dirk Hoerder (Urbana: University of Illinois Press, 1983); Hartmut Keil and John Jentz, "German Working-Class Culture in Chicago: A Problem of Definition, Method, and Analysis," *Gulliver* 9 (1981): 128–47.

2. The phrase is taken from an article commenting on the twenty-fifth anniversary of the Soziale Turnerbund: "Auf zur Nordseite Turnhalle," *Chicagoer Arbeiter-Zeitung*, March 23, 1912 (hereafter cited as *ChAZ*).

3. "Seiner Märtyrer gedenkt Chicagos Arbeiterschaft," *ChAZ*, November 12, 1907; and "Ein Ehrentag," *ChAZ*, May 4, 1908.

4. "Massenaufgebot," *ChAZ*, September 2, 1902.

5. "Eine Volks-Demonstration," *ChAZ*, March 26, 1906.

6. "Trotzalledem," *ChAZ*, May 20, 1907.

7. "Ein Ehrentag," *ChAZ*, August 12, 1907.

8. Ibid.

9. "Editorielles," *Vorbote*, March 28, 1906. Complaints such as these were frequent. When Karl Liebknecht came to Chicago and spoke to a large crowd gathered in the Garrick Theater on November 6, 1910, it was noted that the German Socialists had not come together in such masses for a long time. In his opening remarks, Heinrich Bartel pointed out that German workers in general were content to confine their fight for freedom to a fight for beer ("Karl Liebknecht in Chicago," *ChAZ*, November 7, 1910).

10. "Seiner Märtyrer gedenkt Chicagos Arbeiterschaft," *ChAZ*, November 12, 1907.

11. In aesthetic matters, Franz Mehring was the leading theoretician for the German Social Democrats. Rejecting the notion of Tendenzkunst as alien to the true character of art and literature which were above narrowly political issues, he did not believe in the agitatorial function of art. Schiller, Goethe, and Lessing—i.e., the tradition of humanist idealism and enlightenment—were in this view models for the working class, representing a rather vague and general spirit of active struggle against repressive forces in their time. In some ways a pragmatic reaction to the suppression of any politically purposeful work within the various Arbeiterbildungsvereine (workers' educational clubs) under the Socialist Law, Mehring's position was reinforced by the Marxist esteem for knowledge in general, as represented in the slogan *Wissen ist Macht* (knowledge is power). See also Peter von Rüden et al., *Beiträge zur Kulturgeschichte der deutschen Arbeiterbewegung* (Frankfurt: Büchergilde Gutenberg, 1979), 29–36.

12. See Gerald Stieg and Bernd Witte, *Abriß einer Geschichte der deutschen Arbeiterliteratur* (Stuttgart: Klett, 1973); also *Deutsche Arbeiter-*

literatur von den Anfängen bis 1914, ed. Bernd Witte (Stuttgart: Reclam, 1977).

13. "Die Arbeiter-Sänger," *ChAZ*, June 25, 1910.

14. "Deutschthum und Kultur," *Vorbote*, August 22, 1906.

15. "Sport und Spiel," *Fackel*, June 12, 1910.

16. Compare the *ChAZ* reviews of the Deutsche Theater throughout 1912. Similar arrangements had been made with a number of German Vereine.

17. For two contemporary assessments, see E. C. Moore, "The Social Value of the Saloon," *American Journal of Sociology* 3 (July 1897): 1–12, and especially Royal L. Melendy, "The Saloon in Chicago," *American Journal of Sociology* 6 (1900–1901): 289–306, 433–64.

18. Melendy, "The Saloon in Chicago," pp. 293–94.

19. Hartmut Keil and John Jentz, "German Workers in Industrial Chicago: The Transformation of Industries and Neighborhoods in the Late Nineteenth Century" (Paper presented at the Annual Convention of the Organization of American Historians, Detroit, April 2, 1981).

20. "Bruderzwist," *ChAZ*, June 30, 1908.

21. Melendy, "The Saloon in Chicago," pp. 445–48.

22. "Was soll das Arbeiterkind werden?", *Fackel*, January 2, 1910.

23. See Hartmut Keil, "Chicago's German Working Class in 1900," in *German Workers in Industrial Chicago, 1850–1910: A Comparative Perspective* (DeKalb, Ill.: Northern Illinois University Press, 1983).

24. "Schul-Census," *ChAZ*, July 21, 1910.

25. "Festlichkeiten," *ChAZ*, April 13, 1912.

26. "Die Chicago Arbeiter-Zeitungs-Conferenz und die 'Arbeiter Zeitung,'" *ChAZ*, October 14, 1907.

27. "Die Uhlich's Halle wird abgerissen," *ChAZ*, April 29, 1912.

28. "Erinnerungsblatt an die Chicagoer Central Labor Union," *Fackel*, June 19, 1910.

29. "Reformistische oder revolutionäre Gewerkschaften," *ChAZ*, August 1, 1906.

30. "Prinzipienerklärung," *ChAZ*, July 10, 1910.

31. "Communefeier," *ChAZ*, March 15, 1909.

32. "Zur Erinnerung," *ChAZ*, November 12, 1909.

33. "In addition there was a feeling of great satisfaction soon to have a large, strong and united German workers' movement in Chicago" ("Sie waren da!", *ChAZ*, July 11, 1910).

34. "Trotzalledem," *ChAZ*, May 20, 1907.

35. "Unser Protest," *ChAZ*, February 18, 1907.

36. "Keir Hardie über Amerika," *ChAZ*, October 15, 1912.